The ABCs of Literacy

The ABCs of Literacy

A Guide for Parents and Educators

STEPHEN N. JUDY

New York   Oxford
OXFORD UNIVERSITY PRESS
1980

Copyright © 1980 by Oxford University Press, Inc.

Library of Congress Cataloging in Publication Data
Judy, Stephen N
The ABCs of literacy.
Bibliography: p.   Includes index.
1. English language—Study and teaching—United States.
2. Language arts—United States.
3. Community and school—United States.   I. Title.
LB1576.J82   428'.007'1073   79-4475   ISBN 0-19-502587-3

For Susan
Not only with love,
but with thanks

Contents

Introduction, xi

I The Teaching and Learning of English

1. Great Expectations: Schooling, Literacy, and Society, 3
2. Whatever Happened to English? 21
3. What's Basic and How Do You Learn It? 54
4. Setting Priorities: From Ideal to Real, 76
5. One Hundred Projects for Improving
   Literacy Instruction, 111
6. Testing and Measuring Growth in English, 138

   Interlude: English Teacher: 2001 A.D., 167

II Literacy in the Schools

   Introduction, 173

7. The Dimensions of English, 176
   1. English and the Curriculum, 176
   2. The Elementary Years, 181
   3. Junior Highs and Middle Schools, 190

4. Senior High Schools, 203
5. A Note on College English, 226

8. Literacy in the Humanities, 228
   1. The Humanities and English, 228
   2. Approaches to Humanities / English, 251

9. Science Reading and Writing, 271
   1. Integrating Science and English, 271
   2. Science and the Humanistic Classroom, 285

10. Language and Community, 308
   1. Reading and Writing "for Real," 308
   2. Community-Based Literacy Projects, 325
   3. Careers in Wordsmithing, 343

Bibliography, 347
Index, 357

Acknowledgments

I wish to extend thanks to a number of people whose assistance was invaluable in the preparation of this book: to John Brereton of Wayne State University for his comments on the early drafts of the manuscript; to Maggie Parish for reviewing the bibliographies of children's and young adult literature; to Rhoda Maxwell for collaboration on the work described in Chapter 7; to Caroline Sutton and Elaine Koss for editing the final copy; to Jean Shapiro for help at all phases of the project; and especially to John Wright of Oxford University Press for his interest and enthusiasm for the project from the beginning and for his support, criticism, and encouragement throughout.

For permission to reprint, appreciation for the following is acknowledged:

From *The English Journal:* Mark Springer, "Science in the English Classroom" 65(October 1976): 35–36; Eva Moore, "Choosing: How To, Not What" 64(November 1975): 40–45; Burton Cox, "The High School English Teacher, the Freshman Composition Instructor, and Walt Whitman" 62(December 1973): 1245–1247; William Cushman, "A Letter to Parents" 66(October 1977): 45–48. Copyright © 1977 by the National Council of

Teachers of English. Reprinted by permission of the publisher, the National Council of Teachers of English, Urbana, Illinois. "A Letter to Parents" appears with the permission of the author, William Cushman.

From *Loving and Beyond: Science Teaching for the Humanistic Classroom* by Joe Abruscato and Jack Hassard. Copyright 1976 by Goodyear Publishing Co. Reprinted by permission.

From *Topics in English* by Geoffrey Summerfield. Copyright 1965 by B. T. Batsford Limited, Publishers of Books, London. Reprinted by permission of the publisher.

From *Reality-Centered Learning* by Hy Ruchlis and Belle Sharefkin. Copyright © 1975 by Hy Ruchlis. Reprinted by permission of Citation Press, a Division of Scholastic Magazines, Inc.

Introduction

Americans have always been deeply involved in their schools and enjoy talking about them, as often as not, critically. In recent years public concern has reached an all-time high as reports of test score declines, coupled with complaints from colleges and universities, have led the media to describe a "crisis in literacy." *Newsweek* magazine may have spoken for a great many Americans when it stated: "Willy-nilly, the American educational system is spawning a generation of semiliterates" [1976],[1] Just about everyone knows or has heard about a straight-A student who went off to college and flunked freshman English or was placed in a remedial section. We have been told that textbook makers have had to lower the reading levels of their books because students can no longer handle the material. The odds are that your daily newspaper has reported that young people don't read as much as they used to and can't read the books that were required when you went to school. You have probably heard that grammar isn't taught any more, and you've read about law suits: of high school

---

1. Complete citations for all references will be found in the bibliography. The date of publication is placed within brackets.

graduates suing boards of education for failing to teach them to read, write, or speak English.

Like any crisis, the exact nature of the literacy issue is difficult to assess. Certainly, the problems have been greatly exaggerated by the press. For instance, descriptions of the decline of the English language at the hand (or in the mouths) of today's young people are based as much on suspicion and fear as they are on observable fact. Even so, the fact remains that Johnny and Jane —the anti-heroes of every newspaper or magazine article on literacy—can't, won't, and don't read, write, or speak the way anyone wants them to. Their parents aren't happy; their teachers are dissatisfied; the administrators of their schools are frustrated; and the newspapers delight in (or despair over) printing examples of their illiteracies for us to laugh at (and lament). The upshot is that parents, school administrators, and teachers are united on one point, at least: that something must be done to improve literacy education in America.

The problem invites many diverse answers, including this book. At one end of the spectrum we have the back-to-basics enthusiasts, who call for a return to fundamentals in both subject matter and child management. At the other extreme are the so-called romantic reformers who perceive the problem as inherent in schools as an institution, an institution they think needs to be abolished. The back-to-basics advocates frequently oversimplify discussion of "what's basic" and are romantics in their own right, glorifying schools of the past that probably were no better and no more satisfactory than today's schools. The radical critics often ignore the sentimental attachment Americans have to their schools and oversimplify the evils to which the present system is prey. Whether fundamentalist, radical, or moderate, the critics seem to have a common trait of looking for simple solutions—"Teach more grammar!" "Abolish the schools!"—or a single set of measures that will bring about a solution to the crisis (and right away, too).

Thus "back to basics" ignores the fact that heavy stress on skills instruction historically has *never* done a particularly good job of creating a literate society; nor is there any significant evidence to suggest that there has been a wholesale abandonment of skill work and drill in the schools. Similarly, it is naïve when the radicals counsel that we cannot reform the schools, for whatever schooling (or deschooled learning) emerges in the future will evolve from the present system; it won't spring, fully formed, from the head of a reformer.

Simple solutions just won't do for the literacy crisis. It is important for all concerned with reading and writing to recognize that minor tinkering with the curriculum—buying a new grammar book, instituting a new standardized test, writing a list of skill objectives—will accomplish little. To begin, then, I want to state a central, crucial premise of this book: *Literacy instruction cannot be improved without a major overhaul of both its aims and its methods and without a drastic alteration of teaching conditions.*

How is this to be accomplished? In an ideal world, it might be good for us to shut down the schools for a while—a year, or better, five years—and in relative peace and quiet, with no bells or classes or budget crises to intervene, to think through the basic aims and functions of literacy education and totally redesign the system. If teachers, administrators, and parents could talk to one another under those conditions, I suspect both basics advocates and romantics would agree that the current system does not educate children well, that the schools stifle the imagination, that they are disconnected from the real world, that they are inefficient, and that they frequently teach the opposite of what they are supposed to teach, including the skillful use of English. With the leisure to discuss issues, I think it might be possible to reopen a school system that would differ substantially from the old.

Unfortunately, we don't have the time or the money for such casual study. (Besides, who'd take care of the kids?) Further, education is massive and well established, possessing incredible inertia. It is difficult to see Americans discarding the basic structure of their schools, despite their dissatisfaction with results. In all probability, the public schools will retain their present form for the immediate future. It may only be to keep young people off the streets or to field a football team, but the nature of the school system is such that the schools as we know them will continue for at least the next several decades. Indeed, if for some reason the educational system were closed down tomorrow, I think it likely that prompt steps would be taken to re-create the schools just as they are. Thus "deschooling" society might just result in the creation of a new set of schools with all the faults of the old. This clinging to one's institutions is unfortunate, but it's a fact of life.

Thus I find myself in the apparently contradictory position of arguing for major reform of education while confessing that the nature of the system operates against it. I can solve that logical problem only by introducing a second major premise of the book: *The time is right for dramatic change in literacy instruction.* The schools are staffed by educators who are unhappy about the way they teach Johnny and Jane to read and write. Equally dissatisfied are millions of parents and school administrators. The will to change exists. So do the resources, for that matter, because teaching reading and writing is remarkably inexpensive, requiring only books, pens, and paper, not a massive infusion of funds for electronic hardware, laboratories, or elaborate programs.

I am convinced, then, that the potential for change exists, that whether or not the structure of the school system itself is altered, the ways in which we teach young people to read and write can be substantially improved in coming years. This, then, is a within-the-system book that argues in optimistic but realistic terms for the positive evolution of literacy instruction in the schools as they presently exist.

That conviction should also be amplified with another premise: *Change in literacy instruction must begin with individual teachers and local schools, spreading outward, rather than being imposed by external agencies.* Improving reading and writing skills is not like sending men to the moon or building a supersonic plane, where programs can be "crashed." There is already negative evidence about the impact of outside programs from the early 1970s, when state and national testing programs attracted a great deal of attention and consumed millions of dollars yet failed to bring about anything remotely resembling public satisfaction or positive growth in young people's learning to read and write. While government agencies *can* contribute positively to the process of change (chiefly, I think, by helping teachers re-educate themselves or by helping to reduce class loads in English), externally designed programs are not likely to produce the results that we want. When more literate children are educated, teachers, not federal or state officials, will educate them. That will happen only in schools and districts where teachers, parents, and administrators make a commitment to change and then act on it.

My final premise is central to the organization of the book: *The teaching of literacy must increasingly become an interdisciplinary effort.* The teaching of reading and writing is a school-wide concern, not just the responsibility of teachers of English. Without attempting to diminish the importance of any disciplines or areas of inquiry, I will show that the use of language is central to all of education. Further, English is much more than reading schoolbooks and writing exams; it is deeply tied up with thinking, feeling, and acting. In the fullest sense, literacy is bound up with the quality of life that we all experience. Thus, reading and writing instruction is too important to be left or consigned to the English teacher. I will even go a step beyond and say that it is too important to be left to the *schools*, that reading and writing are out-of-school concerns as well, that community members must lend a hand in the literacy education of their own children.

To whom, then, is this book addressed? First of all, it is written for the growing number of parents who have demonstrated deep interest in the teaching of reading and writing in the schools, for without considerable public support, no substantial amount of change in school instruction will be possible. Further, the book should be helpful to parents who feel they have been excluded from full participation in the schools by giving them an informed base from which to operate. Next, I hope the book will prove useful as a guide to school administrators and members of boards of education, those responsible for instituting programs on a system-wide basis, for it is only with their assistance that teachers can work together to solve the literacy problem. The third group I want to address is teachers in subjects or fields other than English—including the sciences, humanities, and the vocational fields. I am not going to be so presumptuous as to try to tell these teachers what they ought to be doing in their disciplines; nor am I going to tell them (as some have) that they'll just have to teach literacy on their own. Rather, the approaches suggested here will allow teachers in many fields to include reading and writing in their classes in ways that may actually enhance the interest level and depth of their courses without adding to their teaching burden.

Finally, I want to address the book directly to English teachers, who, after all, must play the central role in literacy instruction. Though I am calling for interdisciplinary, system-wide approaches to reading and writing, new programs must begin with English/language arts teachers and will remain in their principal responsibility. Further, it is English teachers who have the basic training in reading, writing, and literature—the expertise that is necessary to develop and organize new approaches. I propose that they assume the lead in designing and developing school-wide programs. This is a new and important role for English teachers, and one I think they ought to take up with enthusiasm.

Each of these groups will, no doubt, read the book for different purposes. In Part I, "The Teaching and Learning of English," I offer a review of the aims and principles of instruction in reading and writing, a discussion that sets out the framework of the book and ought to be of interest to parents, administrators, and teachers alike. Part II, "Literacy in the Schools," is somewhat more specialized. In consecutive chapters I describe teaching approaches in English, the sciences, the humanities, and the community. This section is addressed principally to teachers and describes practical teaching techniques and strategies. At the same time, I have not made the material so specialized as to exclude either parents or administrators, and I suspect these chapters can prove useful in supplying a series of benchmarks for community schools.

In the broadest sense, then, this book is addressed "to whom it may concern," and that means any parent, teacher, school leader, journalist, legislator, or even public school student who is worried about literacy education in America and wants to see something done about it.

S.N.J.

Okemos, Michigan
May 1978

I
The Teaching and Learning of English

1

Great Expectations:
Schooling, Literacy, and Society

> Between wars and other political economic crises, concern for literacy has become one of the pressing world problems for this century. One is tempted, initially, to say that like motherhood and the flag, literacy is an unequivocally accepted goal of the literate for the non-literate.
>
> ROBERT L. HILLERICH (1976)

> Reading has become a canonized activity. . . . We believe in clean underwear, milk and reading, in that order, starting at infancy.
>
> ELAINE L. KONIGSBURG (1970)

Improvement in the attainment of literacy is something everybody approves of and expects. Robert Hillerich, of Bowling Green University, and Elaine Konigsberg, an author of children's books, rightly recognize the motherhood-and-apple-pie status of the first two R's in this country. No one, it seems, is opposed to the teaching of reading and writing.

On the whole, Americans have shown more commitment to literacy than any other people. For example, Professor Hillerich observes that while UNESCO figures show world illiteracy at approximately 50 percent (a figure that has gradually been lowered over the years while the actual number of illiterates has increased), the United States Office of Education in 1970 launched a national Right-To-Read program aimed at reducing functional illiteracy to a mere *one* percent of the adult population by 1980. We expect our children to learn to read and write while they are very young, and we want our citizenry to be, a bit like Ivory soap, 99 and

44/100ths percent purely literate, a goal that is admirable though probably unreachable.

As a result of this intense interest in literacy, the teaching of reading and writing has undeniably become big business. Traditionally, some form of language instruction has been obligatory in each of the twelve grades of the public schools (thirteen if you count alphabet practice in kindergarten), English being the only school subject to receive this kind of emphasis. High school English requirements have been reduced in recent years, but taking into account skill labs and remedial centers, one can say that just about every child in school in the country meets on a regular basis with an English, language arts, or reading teacher each year from age five to eighteen.

This, in turn, means that each school district supplies at least one English textbook per year for every child in the system, a fact not lost on publishers, who have produced spellers, readers, skill workbooks, grammar texts, literature anthologies, and programmed instructional texts in profusion. These materials have increasingly been backed up with expensive electronic hardware and accompanying instructional software: overhead projectors and transparencies; filmstrip machines and filmstrips; speed reading machines and controlled readers; and packaged language laboratories complete with tape recorder, headset, language tapes, textbooks, and checklists (the box itself is converted into a "privacy screen").

At the college level, freshman English is required in one form or another for almost all students, a fact that can tempt even the most dedicated scholar out of his or her study to engage in writing a freshman English book which, if marketed successfully, can pay for a second home in the mountains or at the shore, where more serious scholarly writing can take place.

There are about a million and a half elementary school teachers employed at public expense in this country, all of whom teach literacy daily; a quarter-million or more English teachers in the high schools; at least 100,000 college English teachers, a majority of them employed at public institutions. We pay language arts consultants at state and local levels, hire reading specialists for almost every school building, and even bring in paid paraprofessionals and aides to do everything from tutoring Johnny and Jane in hard words to grading their compositions.

Clearly, Americans have been willing to put their money where their mouth is.

The Historical Functions of Literacy

In the earliest days of American schools, the commitment to literacy was clear and the aims apparently simple. No sooner had the colonists settled into New England and gotten a patch of corn growing than they began thinking about schools for their children. The Massachusetts School Laws of 1642 and 1647 required that schools be established in all townships of more than fifty households, and these laws provided, further, that the schools were expressly for the purposes of teaching literacy. The School Laws defined two purposes for instruction, which were concerned with religion and law: The children of Protestant New England were to grow up being able to read the English Bible for themselves and to read and understand the laws that they and their fellows were creating.

Literacy was endowed with almost magical qualities. For example, *The New England Primer*, a principal source of instruction in colonial New England, opened with this poem, "Good Boys at Their Books":

> He who ne'er learns his A, B, C,
> Forever will a Blockhead be;
> But he who to his Books inclin'd
> Will soon a golden Treasure find.

The "treasure," in this case, turned out to be religious doctrine printed at the back of the primer called, "The Assembly of Divines and Mr. Cotton's CATECHISM, Spiritual Wisdom Drawn from the

Breasts of Both Testaments." However, one can hardly blame the young scholar who was not metaphorically minded for expecting some sort of material reward for learning to read and make his letters. To this day literacy and wealth are seen by many adults and children as being connected, and though it is obvious that reading and writing are necessary skills in many job areas, a good many children of our own time have been misled by promises of wealth through linguistic success: "If you want to get a high paying job, you'd better do your grammar."

From the earliest days of instruction, literacy has also been said to instill wisdom. The perceived connections among literacy, knowledge, and civilization are made explicit in this passage from a nineteenth-century instructional book, *The Tales of Peter Parley in America,* by Samuel Griswold Goodrich:

> The Indians were very ignorant; they could not read or write; their houses were very small and inconvenient. They had no such fine rooms in them as our houses have, nor had they any chimneys or fireplaces. The Indians had no chairs to sit in, nor tables to eat from. They had no books to read, and had no churches or meeting houses.   [1827]

Particularly interesting here are the author's punctuation and syntax, which link literacy and culture. In the opening sentence, for example, two semicolons separate three grammatically equal statements: that Indians were ignorant (stated at the beginning of the sentence), that their houses were small and inconvenient (at the end), that they could not read or write (smack in the middle). Reading and writing thus provide a syntactic as well as logical link between the Indians' supposed ignorance and their lifestyle. Similarly, the closing sentence, a compound sentence with two coordinate clauses, provides a syntactic equation that links the Indians' illiteracy with a presumably inferior culture that "had no churches or meeting houses."

The moral values attributed to literacy were evident in the Massachusetts School Laws, but even after biblical instruction was removed from the schools, reading and writing were said to improve the morals of the young. Conrad Geller, an English teacher from Chappaqua, New York, has observed:

From the beginning, the American public has demanded that its schools teach morality along with academics. All kinds of propaganda functions, tricked out as "courses"—drug use, sex education, driver training—have become part of the curriculum. Social studies is expected to "foster" patriotism, and in at least one state, the biology teacher must give as much time to the Biblical story of the creation as he does to evolutionary theory. But nowhere has the onus of morality been more explicit than in English. The study of literature, for one thing, continually raises ethical questions, and above all, language behavior is persistently equated with moral choice: Good English is good, it is correct, refined, tasteful; in short, it is civilized. And the duty of the English teacher is to teach Good English. [1974]

One has only to look, for example, at this discussion of language and morality from a nineteenth-century composition textbook by a college professor, J. H. Blodgett, to see what its author took to be the relation between the two:

Purity of language expresses and aids clearness of thought: vulgarity, profanity, coarseness, carelessness in language, deepen the characteristics they express. [1870]

Teachers of "good English," then, were (and continue to be) on the side of right and moral order, cleaning up the minds of young people by cleaning up their speech and writing.

But perhaps the most consistent value applied to literacy instruction through the years is one that has little to do with the content of reading and writing: a concern for social polish and grace. John Locke, the seventeenth-century British philosopher, highly influential in supporting the growth of English in the secondary schools, saw achieving stylistic polish as a central value:

To write and speak correctly gives a grace, and gains a favorable attention to what one has to say: and, since it is English that an English gentleman will have constant use of, that is the language he should polish and cultivate.

Locke wanted less Latin and more English in the schools so that a growing aristocracy of mercantile men could master the same dialect as the landed gentry. In the United States his views became popular as the schools extended their base to working class and immigrant children, who naturally spoke something other than Standard English. The kind of polish of which Locke spoke has always seemed important to Americans, and a central task assigned to English has been to teach children a form of speech and writing that supposedly would allow them to operate in society independently of their class origins. Whether such an aim is practical or even desirable is subject to debate, but there is no question that it is part of the English teaching tradition.

We can see, then, that reading and writing instruction represents far more than mere decoding and encoding of print. Unlike any other subject in the curriculum, English historically has carried an enormous load of social, academic, cultural, and intellectual expectations. Learning English, it is said, will make you wise, get you a job, teach you etiquette, make you a virtuous person, fill you with culture. It will do nothing less than make you a full person, socially acceptable at that. These are, to put it mildly, great expectations.

How Much Literacy? For Whom?

Upon closer examination, however, one finds that, despite our expectations, literacy has been taught with conflicting aims and purposes that have often made instruction ineffectual. Many Americans are ambivalent about the literacy they want taught to their own children and to other people's children as well.

There is, for example, the perplexing matter of the censorship of school books. Censoring what children are allowed to read is a very old practice, yet it has taken surprising directions in the past twenty years. In the early 1960s, for example, high schoolers began reading and teachers began teaching J. D. Salinger's *Catcher in the Rye,* a novel in which teenaged Holden Caulfield and his friends use what we in English euphemistically call "street language" and in which "fuck," the most taboo of swearwords, appeared. In the protests that followed, it seemed to matter little to angry parents that Holden actually wants to *protect* his little sister Phoebe from seeing such language chalked on schoolroom walls (he himself actually serves as a censor). *Catcher* was attacked, and nation-wide several schoolteachers who taught the book were fired. Eventually, the times passed *Catcher* by, for the use of street language changed so in the late 1960s and early seventies that *Catcher* came to seem like mild stuff. Books for children and teenagers dealt directly with what formerly had been forbidden topics: drugs, divorce, premarital sex, pregnancy, birth control, and abortion. Four-letter words appeared on prime time TV and in PG movies, and the taboos largely disappeared.

What is surprising, however, is that although four-letter words and formerly taboo topics are common knowledge to today's young people, censorship cases in the 1970s were more rampant than ever, capped off by the well-publicized Kanawha County Charleston, West Virginia, episode where something like three hundred text and library books were removed from school shelves. In many cases, books have been censored for content that is a good deal milder than what is pumped into the home in TV's family viewing hour. As Ken Donelson of Arizona State University has remarked:

During the past couple of years I have witnessed censorship attacks on many books, periodicals, and films—everything from the "filth" of *Silas Marner* to the "controversial matter" of *I'm Really Dragged but Nothing Gets Me Down* to the "anti-Christianity" of *Slaughterhouse Five,* from the "subversive elements" of some early Charlie Chaplin short films to the "unAmericanism" of *High Noon* to . . . the "leftist propaganda" of *Scholastic Magazine* to the "right-wing trash" of *National Observer.* [1976]

The question of the kinds of control parents can and should exercise over the reading matter of their children (and their neighbors' children) is complex and is somewhat outside the range of my discussion here. While I am opposed to the censorship of schoolbooks, I adamantly support the right of parents to play an important role in helping to choose the material their children will be taught. What is disturbing in the censorship cases is not so much that some parents were denying other people's children a right to read, but that their desire to control often represents an underlying distrust of literacy. "Books," the censors are tacitly arguing, "can hurt you." Yet the censors are for the most part products of the American school system and its literacy education. They ought to know that as powerful as books may be, they do not have powers of mind control. Censorship, however, persists, and in a great many communities one finds two contrary movements curiously linked: one group of taxpayers complaining that kids can't read; another (with many of the same members) worrying that kids are being given objectionable material to read, which implies that the children read *too well* for their own good.

Suspicion about literacy is far deeper than censoring four-letter words, for despite the American interest in promoting literacy, there remains a good deal of suspicion of people who like to read. "Bookish" people, for example, are frequently portrayed on popular TV as ineffectual, weak, and helpless, the very opposite of the qualities that reading is generally said to enhance. It is an attitude typified by a "Happy Days" television program in which the Fonz, symbol of happy-go-lucky machismo, was able to draw laughs by announcing that he had actually once read a book and by being astonished by the fact that "They've got a card at the 'liberry' for every person!"

Inconsistencies in the commitment to literacy appear in other areas of the curriculum as well, most notably in the teaching of so-called Standard English. The term "standard" is misleading, since linguistics has shown that many legitimate variations of language exist in society, and a skillful speaker or writer will be a master of many of them. Nevertheless, the schools have traditionally taken on the task of teaching a *single* standard—the "Queen's English"—to all children, making the assumption, as did John Locke, that if you change the way people talk, you give them access to higher levels of society.

As a matter of fact, mastery of Standard English is not really as vital for success as has been supposed; millions of people who haven't learned the distinctions between *lay-lie, sit-set, like-as,* and *who-whom* are functioning quite happily without being the possessors of Standard English. Nor is there any reason to believe that changing one's dialect actually brings about considerable mobility. Even if the schools were to succeed in teaching every child to speak a single standard, it is predictable that social classes would continue to exist, that some children and adults would be excluded from "the good life." John Locke was wrong in what we might label his "veneer" theory of dialects.

Although the schools and society have expressed interest in teaching Standard English to all people, they have exhibited considerably more zeal in meting out penalties to speakers of nonstandard dialects and creating barriers for them to pass (or trip over). Almost from the day he or she enters school, the non-standard speaker has errors pointed out, "flaws" corrected, his or her "illiteracies" put on display. Since the non-standard speakers are frequently members of minority groups, the emphasis on Standard English is used, in effect, to ensure that the children of the class in power—the children of white, middle-class Americans—will be labeled as "successes," with higher test scores, higher grades, and better job opportunities. Thus, while the schools claim to teach Standard English as a way of "democratizing" education or "opening educational opportunities to all children," in fact, dialect differences are used, subtly to be sure, to just the opposite effect.

In the same vein, the schools and society *say* they offer reading instruction as a route to wisdom (and financial success). Yet they have been guilty of using the skill of reading to reinforce the division between the haves and the have-nots, between the literates and the non-literates, between the upper-middle-class children (most of whom come from print-oriented families) and the others (where oral English rather than print receives principal emphasis). Children from a non-print background are labeled "remedial" and given workbooks and drill, supposedly to correct reading deficiencies. But this kind of treatment has the effect of dooming them to spend the rest of their school lives in non-academic and lower achievement tracks, excluded from the courses where upper-middle-class children receive their schooling on the way to the university and the good jobs.

My purpose is not to argue that teaching reading is bad or that we should somehow democratize education by offering only that instruction which does not cause difficulties for some students. I want to emphasize, however, that while consistently pledging allegiance to the values of reading, the schools have in fact created a reading-based system which effectively *ex*cludes rather than *in*cludes.

It is important to show that sometimes language instruction fails to measure up to its expressed goals *with tacit approval from both teachers and parents.* For instance, the schools claim an interest in teaching such processes as "clear thinking" and "critical reading"; they purport to help students write strong, forceful prose and speak articulately on a wide range of issues and topics. Yet, as Jonathan Kozol, an author and critic of American education, has noted, literacy instruction in the schools has almost always bypassed crucial issues and moral questions, teaching, as often as not, a language of moderation, evasion, and compromise:

Serious issues which confront the nation, agonies and discontents which devastate the poor, are matters of considerable "interest" to a conscientious English teacher; yet the teacher is most often well-persuaded that such matters have no direct application to his classroom-labor. English is for the school—ethics for the weekend or late afternoon. Very few English teachers are prepared to understand the power which they hold in their hands to shape the minds, distort the views, imprison the imaginations—or else liberate the soul—of those who sit before them each day in the public schools.   [1975]

In a similar vein, Richard Ohmann of Wesleyan University has suggested that freshman college English, which generally aims at liberating minds and language, teaches a set form of problem solving that leads, not to better writing, but to doublespeak, gobbledygook, and even the language of Watergate (1975). One of my students, Bob Hazelton, recalls one such assignment:

I was to read one of the essays by a pilgrim to this country and from this write an essay on the relationship between God and Man. I detested the assignment, had little knowledge to go by, and wound up starting one of those arguments typical of an undergrad dorm in which the only thing everyone agreed on was that I was going to Hell.

This assignment generates language—five hundred words, a thousand words, whatever is required by the instructor—and engages a student in a pseudo-logical process. Yet it is so far removed from real-life concerns—*Is* there a God? Am I going to Hell?—that it merely provides training in being superficial and evasive.

There is no question that some of the inconsistencies and variations I have described in this section are either unintentional or well intentioned. Yet the effects are the same. The schools want to bring young people into the mainstream by teaching reading but wind up guaranteeing the isolation of minority children. English teachers genuinely want to offer correctness for all students and, in effect, merely stress the differences between races and classes. The colleges intend to give students a good basic course in "clear writing" and produce students who are adept at generating professor-pleasing gobbledygook. Intentional or not, these disparities reflect underlying inconsistencies in the educational system and profound uncertainty over the questions: "How much literacy? for whom?"

A Definition of "Literacy"

Part of the problem is that we have not really clarified what we mean by literacy. For example, a report by a prestigious College Entrance Examination Board panel (1977) blithely commented that "less thoughtful and critical reading is now being demanded and done in the schools" and that "careful writing has apparently gone out of style." Yet the panel didn't bother to say what it meant by "thoughtful and critical reading" or "careful writing." Nor did it present any samples of student work to show what these terms meant or what lack of their presence leads to in student writing. If one were to take that statement at face value, without seeking clarification of terms, one would suppose that the schools had actually launched a campaign against good language use. Yet anyone who spends any time at all in the schools knows that teachers are just as concerned as anyone about the misuse of language. Thus the sloppy use of terminology by the CEEB panel itself contributes to confusion over the nature of the so-called literacy crisis.

Of course, defining literacy is devilishly difficult. For instance, in the statistics I cited earlier, UNESCO bases its figure of 50 percent world illiteracy on achievement at a fourth grade reading level. The national Right-To-Read effort, with its aim of 99 percent literacy, was concerned only with "functional literacy," which is altogether different and could, in fact, mean that a near non-reader could be quite functional in pockets of this country where print is seldom used.

Talk of reading "grade level" is equally deceptive. A few years ago, many textbook publishers lamented that they were having to reduce their texts to the eighth grade reading level because of illiteracy among college students. Yet the college texts being produced would, because of their content, still be largely incomprehensible (and most certainly boring) to most twelve-year-old children. In this instance, the term "eighth grade reading level" is almost meaningless. Similarly, though teachers complain that some of their eighth grade students only read at a second grade level, those same kids would be embarrassed to death by the Dick-and-Jane prattle of a second grade reader yet are frequently capable of processing the fairly sophisticated prose of *Mad* magazine, *Spiderman* comics, or *Modern Screen*.

To complicate the matter further, "literacy" has, until recently, referred only to alphabet-related forms—reading and writing. But with the mass media explosion of this century, more and more educators have begun to speak of "media literacy," the ability to "read" (comprehend and evaluate) and to "write" (create in) media forms. There are many dangers in this kind of extension of the concept of literacy, for, clearly, one does not read a television screen or film in ways that one reads the daily paper. At the same time, it makes a point that any language use ought to be considered when we discuss school literacy programs. Critics have noted that because the bulk of language use is *oral,* the schools ought to be far less concerned with *literacy* (from the Latin, *littera,* or "letter"; meaning "learning," "grammar," "culture"; "instructed in letters"; "specifically, the ability to read and write") and focus on *oracy* (a coined term from the Latin *orare,* "to speak"). A more satisfactory coined term might condense "language competency," including oral, print, and non-print forms to create "languacy" (from the Old French, *la langue*—"tongue," "language," "the body of words and methods of combining words used and understood by a considerable community"). In any event, one can see that "literacy" can be defined only if one takes into account the broad functions of language in people's lives. Literacy has to do with speaking as well as writing, with theaters as well as libraries, with television as well as novels.

Robert Hillerich, whose epigraph opened this chapter, has assessed numerous definitions of literacy that have been used by educators and organizations like UNESCO. He proposes the following, which I shall adopt as a point of reference for this book:

Literacy is that demonstrated competence in communications skills which enables the individual to function, appropriate to his age, independently of his society and with a potential for movement in society.   [1976]

I am uncomfortable with the phrase "communications skills" and would prefer to substitute the more global word, "language," so the opening sentence refers to "demonstrated competence in *language.*" But as definitions go, this one seems to me to work well, first, as useful for discussion of schooling, and second, for its implications about the nature of language and learning. Its strong points include the following:

1. *It acknowledges the literacy of children.* Because of its refer-

ence to language use "appropriate . . . to age," Hillerich's definition credits the young with being literate. This is not to say that the schools should be content with keeping people at a "childish" level, but it spares teachers the awesome (and frequently destructive) responsibility of trying to turn every child into an adult literate every year. It implies that teachers should concentrate on extending the dimensions of literacy for children by building on existing language rather than worrying unduly about skills not yet mastered.

2. *It includes print and non-print forms.* Rather than restricting itself to print literacy, the definition refers to *all* language-based communication: film, video, books, conversation, magazines, newspapers, speeches, business letters, personal letters, and so on.

3. *It stresses independence.* Hillerich is suggesting that to be fully literate, one must be able not only to send and receive simple messages—e.g., to read written directions or write down a grocery list—but to use language flexibly, creatively, purposefully, and imaginatively. This is language use that moves far beyond the "survival level" being stressed in so many back-to-basics programs.

4. *It recognizes the social values placed on the language by society.* Hillerich recognizes that social and economic movement comes *within* society; one lives, thinks, and works within a culture that limits what he or she does in life or with language. While the notion that one can improve one's lot by changing the way he or she talks is simplistic, this part of the definition implies that the literate person will be aware of the nature of Standard English and be able to employ some variation of it for his or her own purposes. It also acknowledges the role language plays in making the individual aware of society and its political, moral, economic, and social customs.

5. *It focuses on language use.* The beauty of the statement is in centering attention on the individual and his or her use of language for specific purposes. One doesn't have to set up an elaborate test to determine if another is literate. Rather, answering a

very simple question will suffice: Is the person succeeding in doing what he or she wants to do through language? The task may be as simple as ordering a pizza on the telephone or as complex as writing a Ph.D. dissertation. But the test is fundamentally the same: Did it *work?* Did the message arrive? Was the job completed successfully? Often, no external assessment will be required at all: The language user will be able to assess success or failure on the spot, knowing whether the message was "heard."

Using the Hillerich definition as a measure, it is clear that the schools are not doing an excellent job of teaching literacy. The products of our schools do not function especially well as users of language at *any* age, and the charge that Johnny and Jane can't read and write well enough is valid. At the same time, as we search for solutions to the problem, this definition allows us to ask fundamental questions: What does one need to know about language to function well in society? What language competencies are appropriate for the young? for adults? How do young people and adults come to learn these skills? What kind of instruction do we need to offer to achieve the literacy we want? These and dozens of related questions will be taken up in succeeding chapters.

Dimensional Education and Literacy

If a literate person is one who can use the language independently and successfully in appropriate settings, then it follows that the more different situations in which a person—adult or child—can function, the more literate he or she will be. Thus the schools cannot afford to limit the dimensions of the literacy program. Teachers should focus on extending the range of literacy experiences open to every child. Young people should read and write in a rich variety of language forms, under a wide range of conditions, in as many different communication situations as possible. We should stop speaking of "ill"-literates and attempt to help students become more skilled at using language for a diversity of purposes.

But one additional element needs to be added to this discussion, that of the relationship between literacy education and what we call "the real world." Language instruction has always shown a tendency to divorce itself from reality. Joseph Rogers of Washington University has noted that early Greek education was "dimensionalized," with the learning of human values deeply intertwined with what he calls "dimensional reality." The Greek young person

. . . participated actively in a program that not only developed his sense of self-worth but deepened his awareness of the value of his fellows. As he pulled on his oar on the rowing bench, or struggled to get down sails in a squall, or wheeled in a phalanx, he registered not merely at ideational levels but in every fibre and sinew an awareness that his own meaning depended upon the meaning of others. Spared clouds of word vapor about Humanity, Brotherhood, the Great Society—dimensionalized education gave little heed to capitalized abstractions—he learned to support and to rely upon the man who stood on his left and upon his right in the battle line. His deep awareness of being an earthling among earthlings, his meagre sense of category and classification, saved him from being either patronizing or deferential.   [1975]

As Western civilization evolved, Rogers suggests, the dimensional quality of education gradually diminished. Scholars and educators increasingly came to rely upon abstract words and concepts to conduct their business, substituting books and talk for the experience-based language of Greek education. Most extreme, perhaps, was the scholasticism of the Middle Ages, where discussions and disputations (how many angels can dance on the head of a pin?) took place totally without reference to reality, the symbol systems and abstractions having assumed a life of their own.

This tradition led to the creation of what Rogers calls "decalang," an abstracted, non-dimensional form of the language, that was passed on to American schools through the Latin grammar schools. Rogers writes:

The distance between the dimensionalized training of Hellas and the verbalistic training of New England is shown by the fact that most of the youths who put to sea in the 1840s and 1850s, the great days of the American whalers and clipper ships, could not swim. In every year of these decades, hundreds of boys from New Salem, New Bedford, and

Gloucester who could carry the verb *nato, natare,* through all its forms fell overboard and drowned because they could not swim a half-dozen strokes.

Bob Hazelton's freshman writing project, cited earlier, shows how decalang has been carried on to our own time. Much school-based literacy instruction is conducted in decalang so that students have to negotiate a maze of terminology—*topic sentence, unity, coherence, emphasis, introduction, body, conclusion*—before they can write a paper; where they must show mastery of parts of speech and sentence functions—*noun, verb, indirect object, gerund, participle*—before they can write down sentences they have been speaking all their lives; where they write about personal dimensionalized experience—"My Summer Vacation"—but only to show whether or not they are skilled manipulators of Standard English.

Even the career education movement, which would seem to be an attempt to dimensionalize education, has itself become bound up in decalang, presenting children with an abstracted view of work. In career ed programs children learn abstract concepts about "Career Clusters" and try to master what someone has labeled "Entry-Level Job Skills." Even leisure time is categorized and compartmentalized as merely one subset within the "Career Education Matrix."

Making education dimensional does not, in the twentieth century, mean sending children to the trireme or assembly line for on-the-job training. Nor does it require discarding humanistic values to focus all instruction on the "relevant," the "practical," the "here-and-now." Rather, dimensional literacy instruction simply requires that language activities make connections with a real world. Students need to read and write on subjects that concern, move, and involve them, rather than spinning out their academic days studying abstractions about language or reading. The skills of language users must be measured, not against standards or norms, but in terms of success and failure at specific tasks as young people move independently through society. For education to become dimensional we must overcome our obsession with basics, minimums, standards, and norms, to concentrate on something much broader and, at the same time, much more fundamental: helping each child on an individual basis extend his or her use of language in as many directions as possible, so that he or she can participate fully, creatively, and independently as a literate member of society.

2

Whatever Happened to English?

This chapter will review the recent history of English teaching in this country, looking back as far as 1957 and the launching of Sputnik, but concentrating particularly on the crisis in literacy that erupted in the 1970s. The discussion seems necessary to help clear away some of the misconceptions and misstatements that have emerged in the past decade or so on the topic of teaching reading and writing. To begin, I want to offer a parable that I first wrote as an editorial for *The English Journal* (1977). I call it, "A Likely Story":

My cousin Herbie is a smart cookie. He's in the advertising business, working for a major company in New York. Although they keep him pretty well tied up with the dog food accounts, Herbie always knows what's going on in "The Industry" (as he calls it). Not too long ago he came through town for a visit on his way back from a "Noodler" (that's his term for a "meeting") in Chicago. In the course of the evening, during which Herbie put away incredible numbers of a fashionable new drink called a Connecticut Yankee (made with Tequila and clam juice), his tongue began to wag, somewhat slurrily, to be sure.

I had been telling him a little bit about my graduate course in composition for teachers when he interrupted me:

"Aw, bag it, Doc." (He always calls me "Doc" when he's about to tell me something I don't know anything about.) "Cut that academic crap. You ought to know by now that literacy is dead in this country. Dead. Kaput. Over and done with."

"Oh, no, Herbie," I replied, going to the bar to fix him another drink. "There is extraordinary concern for reading and writing in this country nowadays. The nation's press has alerted us to the crisis in literacy. Parents are eager to see their children master essential skills. At no time in our nation's history has there been more interest in literacy."

"You dumb academics!" he snorted. "It's a good thing *my* people are running the country, not yours. You'd screw it up in a month."

He looked at me with careful scrutiny, as if to see whether or not I could be trusted, then drew up his chair and said in a hoarse whisper, "Splot!"

"What?"

" 'Sa plot! A campaign. They gotta whole secret department over at BBG&M working on it night and day. Big time hush hush client."

"Who?" I asked.

"Can't tell you," he said. "Industry secret. But I can tell you their linguists make you academics look like kindergartners learning their ABCs."

"What are they doing?" I was frankly curious.

"That I can tell you," Herbie said, and he proceeded to unfold a rather astonishing tale for me.

It had all begun back in the 1960s, he told me, when the house linguist at BBG&M noted a peculiar public response to an ad campaign for Winston cigarettes. Everybody had worried that a new slogan, "Winston tastes good like a cigarette should," would be offensive to the public because it substituted the preposition "like" for the traditional adverb "as". (The admen considered "like" more casual and less stuffy than the adverbial form.) Sure enough, the public was mightily offended. Soon people in the street could cite the new ad as an example of "bad grammar" and make statements about the outrageous and flagrant misuse of language in public places.

The funny thing was, however, that Winston sales soared, and, further, the linguists noted, the language usage of the man on the street didn't change a whit. People kept on using "like" for "as" in everyday speech, just as they had for generations.

Well, the admen had a Noodler on this and reached the conclusion that there exists in the population what they call "Inverse Wordfear," which simply means that for the most part, people are *afraid* of words and language, and they sublimate their fear by talking noisily about "offensive" language and "affronts" to good taste and by worrying about whether the language used nowadays is worse than it used to be. The BBG&M people checked out Inverse Wordfear and traced its historical roots. They discovered with amusement that it has been around as long as people have been writing dictionaries and grammar books, and, in fact, those tomes are little more than a scholarly manifestation of Wordfear. ("That puts you and your cronies in their place, don't it, Doc?" asked Herbie with a leer.)

Like good scientists, having made this discovery, the adpeople asked a practical question, "How can we use this information to sell something?"

And as they asked this question in their weekly planning session, in the door walked a representative of a very important U.S. company, and that person was very upset. Angry and jealous, actually, for he had just paid over twenty-five dollars to fill the gas tank of his limousine.

"Goddam EXXON," this person was saying. "They've got us by the fuel tanks. We don't know how much oil they've got. We don't know how much oil there is in the ground. We don't know what they're carrying inside those supertankers. Those bastards can just raise prices whenever they please, and there's nothing we can do about it. Nothing. Soon they'll have us paying five dollars a gallon and tell us to be thankful for it."

And then this person uttered a sentence that struck an important spark: "Why don't you guys come up with a campaign that will do for my company what the oil shortage has done for EXXON?"

And they did. The adpeople took the concept of Inverse Wordfear and made it the keystone of Operation DL (for Destroy Literacy). The boys at BBG&M launched it by floating some phoney statistics about what they called "adult illiteracy." These were picked up with exclamations of horror by the nation's press, and pretty soon all over the country, people were saying things like "Did you know that ninety percent of New Yorkers can't read timetables well enough to take the subway to the Bronx Zoo?" (These statements also substantiated a new corollary of Inverse Wordfear called the "Verbal Preposterousness Quotient," which held that the more outlandish a statement about language, the more likely the public is to believe it.)

Next they located a former TV newscaster who happened to have a collection of obsolete dictionaries and an extraordinary fear, left over from grammar school, of making usage errors in public. They encouraged Ed Newspeak to write up his fears, and his two books, *Grammar on the Q. T.* and *Watch Your Tongue!* zoomed to the heights of the best-seller lists and convinced people that the English language was in danger of disappearing altogether.

Then, manna from Heaven, Educational Testing Service announced that scores on the Scholastic Aptitude Test (Herbie calls it the Satirical Applesauce Test) had declined during the decade. The admen went wild. Drawing on the Verbal Preposterousness Quotient again, they wrote statements like: "Clearly the scores on this multiple choice aptitude test, used by colleges to accept, reject, and pigeon-hole students, show that the schools are failing and literacy is dying." ("And people actually believed it!" Herbie chortled into his drink and almost choked on an ice cube.)

"So that's about it," Herbie said. "It's working like a charm!"

"I don't understand," I said. "People are *upset* about literacy. They want *more* reading and writing taught in the schools, not less!"

"Ah, you dummy," said Herbie, "Don't you even know about Bull's Eye Overkill?"

"I'm afraid not," I confessed.

"Well, they do at BBG&M. The first thing they did was to tell all their publishing accounts to get ready. 'Grammar and phonics will be big next year,' they said. So the publishers got out all their obsolete language texts, put flashy new covers on them, and the suckers come flocking, saying, 'Let's hit the nail on the head; let's shoot the bull in eye; let's get back to basics.' "

"I still don't quite understand," I said. "Surely a little work on language fundamentals never hurt anyone."

"Maybe so, maybe not," replied Herbie, "but you've already forgotten about Inverse Wordfear. You can talk about reading and writing all you want in your lah-dee-dah seminar, but out there in the schools, folks are gonna be teaching nothing but basics. They're gonna do spelling and grammar and phonics and diagrams until kids go nearly crazy, and in the process, they're gonna raise verbal insecurities to an all time high."

He continued: "BBG&M predicts that before long SAT scores will begin to rise, while actual *use* of language for reading and writing will decline. If Operation DL works as planned, reading and writing will have virtually disappeared by 1990. People will be too uptight over basics to dare risk their egos on writing or reading!"

"Preposterous!" I said. "Besides, who would gain? Reading and writing are as American as apple pie and motherhood. Who could profit from destroying literacy? Who is this 'secret client' anyway?"

Herbie stared at me through the ice cubes of his nearly-empty glass, appraising me carefully with a preternaturally large eye.

"Well, Doc," he said, "I'm gonna tell you, because it will eventually cost you your job and I want you to be able to start looking for a new one now."

"It's Ma Bell," he said softly. "They've already begun advertising that it's easier to phone than to write. They're spending a fortune trying to brainwash you into believing that long distance is cheap, even though it's far more expensive than writing a letter. Their campaign will become more intense as verbal fears increase, and as literacy dies, the phone company will become more aggressive in pursuing your business."

"Astonishing," I said, a bit frightened by the tone in Herbie's voice.

"In ten years," he continued, "when total illiteracy sets in, they'll have you by your Trimline Extension. You'll be paying a dollar a call ten dollars a call!—and you'll be thanking Ma Bell for the privilege."

"Herbie," I said, "you've had too much to drink."

I took him by the arm and led him toward the stairs.

"Besides," I continued, "it's a ridiculous story. Something like that could never happen here."

But I'll tell you, that night he slept better than I did.

"A Likely Story" is fiction, of course, but like any parable, it is intended to point toward the truth. The two pseudo-linguistic concepts—"Inverse Wordfear" and "The Verbal Preposterousness Quotient"—are satirical descriptions of real phenomena that underlie a crisis in literacy. Americans are particularly sensitive about the "proper" use of language and even more afraid of possible misuse. As a result, they are susceptible to any threatening statement, accurate or not, about the state of the English language or its teaching. With that understanding of our linguistic insecurities, one can better appreciate the impact of a single event: a report of declining college aptitude scores.

English in Distress

In December, 1973, representatives of the College Entrance Examination Board, an organization that has been concerned with examining students for college entrance since the turn of the century, and Educational Testing Service, a non-profit corporation that prepares the Scholastic Aptitude Test, held a press conference to announce an interesting fact: Since 1964 average scores on the SAT verbal and mathematical tests had been declining; the total decline in English was something like 40 points (on a test scale that runs from 200 to 800), and the drop in mathematics was somewhat less. The ETS/CEEB officials cautioned that such information was easily misinterpreted, and they stated that the decline should not be equated with a decay in the quality of schooling. There were, no doubt, a number of contributing factors, and the people at ETS and CEEB confessed that even they were perplexed. William Angoff, Executive Director of College Board Programs for Educational Testing Service, writing a follow-up discussion, emphasized:

To attribute the score decline to a deterioration of the educational system is to neglect the other highly pervasive educational influences outside the formal educational environment and more generally to ignore the broad complexity of the human learning process and the interaction of the myriad factors that affect it.   [1975]

Such warnings from ETS/CEEB had little effect, however. In 1973 the nation was in the midst of Watergate and still in a state of shock from the anti-war protests of the late 1960s. Viet Nam was winding down and the United States was getting out. Americans had to acknowledge that for the first time ever, their country had lost a war. The economy was in recession and unemployment was high. And churned in with all this unhappiness was growing suspicion of the schools.

Parents had heard of teaching the "New Math," where, it was joked, nobody cared if kids got the answers right, just as long as they *understood* what they were doing. They had also heard of a "New English," where, it was rumored, teachers ignored grammar and correctness and were concerned solely with *creativity*. Traditional courses in English seemed to have disappeared, and high school students were bringing home long lists of elective course descriptions for English, including courses like "Science Fiction" and "Death," and excluding "The History of British Literature" or "Chaucer."

The traditions in schooling that parents recalled seemed to have been abolished. The older students on college campuses were rebelling against everything their parents had stood and worked for.

And now the SAT scores were in decline. Clearly, it seemed to most people, the school system was at the bottom of the whole thing. Despite warnings by ETS and CEEB, parents responded: "Whatever happened to English, math, morals, values, the schools?"

Although one has to credit ETS and CEEB for issuing their warnings and cautionary statements, one also has to question their wisdom in releasing the test score data without having a comprehensive explanation of the phenomenon. To put it baldly, ETS/CEEB didn't really understand what was happening to the data of its own tests. Instead of holding press conferences to release easily misinterpreted data, one would have thought that the testers would have quietly re-examined their own methods, procedures, and findings.

The response of the nation's press was an interesting one. Fresh from the successes of Watergate, reporters were in an investigative mood; if there was scandal afoot, the press wanted to know what was happening. Predictably, following the announcement of the score decline, magazine and newspaper reporters began looking into literacy. But the research the reporters did was anything but comprehensive.

To the best of my knowledge, only one reporter for a major publication, Steven Brill writing for *New York* magazine (1974), looked in the direction of Princeton, New Jersey, to Educational Testing Service itself, inquiring into the Scholastic Aptitude Test and its makers. What he found was deeply disturbing. Brill's review of "The Secrecy Behind the College Boards" was sharply critical, finding ETS to be sheltered, isolated, unresponsive, and above all, secretive about its tests. He observed that ETS exerts extraordinary control over the lives of millions of students who take the College Boards and has a strong hand in testing programs that range from achievement tests to graduate and law school aptitude tests. Despite its obviously influential role in testing, Brill found that ETS was largely unregulated and was accountable only to itself:

For years E.T.S. has ignored or brushed off criticism of its tests and its near-monopoly status. The issues that critics have raised relate to the reliability of the tests, their possible racial bias, the effect of coaching on "aptitude" scores, cheating, the quality of service given to students, overemphasis on test scores by admissions officers, the way E.T.S. spends its money, and E.T.S.'s possible violation of antitrust laws.

Of particular interest to persons concerned about literacy in America was Brill's discussion of the accuracy and reliability of the Scholastic Aptitude Test itself:

Even E.T.S. admits that aptitude and achievement cannot be measured in terms nearly as specific as the score that is recorded. If, for example, among possible scores ranging from 200 to 800, you get a 600 on your S.A.T., this only means that there is a two-in-three chance that your "true score"—the score you'd receive if all external factors like luck in guessing, could be eliminated—would fall somewhere between 570 and 630.

If one recalls that the test score decline that originated the brouhaha was in the neighborhood of 40 points, it is clear that day-to-day fluctuations in the test scores are larger than the decline itself. Further, Brill continued, when one gets to the point of interpreting test scores, the inaccuracies are even greater:

An E.T.S. Booklet reveals that a 72-point difference between two students' scores on the S.A.T. math section (and 66 points on the verbal) is so statistically insignificant that "it cannot be taken seriously."

How "seriously," then, should one take the 40-point decline in English?

Brill also reported equally disturbing statistics about the biases of ETS-created exams, which almost invariably led to lower scores for members of certain ethnic and racial minorities. While such bias did not affect the predictive values of the exams, it nevertheless made one wonder about both the intrinsic merit of the SAT and the effect that minority recruitment campaigns of the sixties and seventies were having on average scores. ETS/CEEB had little to say about either.

Brill ended his article on a note of deep suspicion. He reinforced a call that Ralph Nader had issued for an investigation of test makers and concluded that it is "clear that we've got to get some kind of control over the gatekeepers. Testing is just too important to be taken completely on trust."

A majority of reporters, however, did not spend a great deal of time considering the validity of the tests themselves. Rather, despite the disclaimers of ETS/CEEB, the press generally assumed that the score decline was somehow directly related to an overall drop in the quality of literacy education. To find out whether this was correct, reporters went to another source: the directors of freshman English at any number of the nation's colleges. Freshman English directors from Yale to Berkeley, from Bowdoin to Pomona, found themselves being interviewed. Now, freshman English directors have one of the most challenging jobs in the academic world. Each autumn, they are faced with new faces—a few hundred at the small colleges, ten to fifteen thousand at the multiversities —all of whom need help with reading and writing. Freshman English directors have to deal with as much bad writing and have to suffer over as many poor readers as anybody in the world. They run programs all too often staffed by graduate teaching assistants who are underpaid (three to four thousand dollars to teach three to five sections of freshman English per year) and who, for the most part, would rather be pursuing their degrees than teaching writing anyway. Nobody ever seems satisfied with the results of freshman English programs, and if a student misspells or writes a barbarism on a history examination or on an economics paper, sooner or later the director hears about it.

Further, in 1973 freshman English directors were attempting to cope with the results of massive university expansion and affirmative action programs. College enrollments increased tremendously in the 1960s and early seventies, and admissions officers actively sought minority students who had previously been excluded from higher education. In casting the net wider, the colleges naturally attracted students from less and less literate backgrounds. Literate parents (who also tend to be the affluent) are always the first on their block to send students to college, while minority students, whose literacy backgrounds and schooling are less strong, have traditionally had a harder time getting into and staying in college. I have no doubt, then, that in 1973 freshman English people were seeing an increased number of students who needed help—lots of it—with reading and writing. Enrollments in remedial sections went up, and increasingly colleges felt it necessary to institute skill development laboratories. The freshman English directors reported all this to the press.

But it appears that the reporters made a very simple oversight in talking about the problem: They confused increased instances of a phenomenon with average change. That is, discovering new students who could not read and write well, the press seems to have lumped all students together—the good and the bad—and taken some sort of "average." And out came the headlines: "State U. Students Illiterate," "Whatever Happened to the First Two R's?" "Reading and Writing Ain't Important No More."

The College Entrance Examination Board and Educational Testing Service did little to clear up matters. CEEB set up what it called a "blue ribbon" panel to review the test score decline. The panel, twenty-six members in all, included some very distinguished people. It was headed by Willard Wirtz, former Secretary of Labor, then Chairman of the National Manpower Institute of Washington. Although some equally distinguished educators were on the panel, including Ralph Tyler of the Center for Advanced Study in the Behavioral Sciences; Robert Thorndike, Teachers College, Columbia University; Wilbur Schramm, the East-West Center, Honolulu; and Benjamin Bloom, University of Chicago, the panel included not one linguist, not one reading specialist, not one composition expert, not one freshman English director. It did include a lone English teacher, Sandra A. Clark, English Department Head, Sammamish High School, Bellevue, Washington. The report of the panel, *On Further Examination: Report of the Advisory Panel on the Scholastic Aptitude Test Score Decline* (CEEB, 1977), disappointed because of both what it said and what it failed to say.

The first two sections of the report dealt with the Scholastic Aptitude Test itself and "the particular interest of the College Board and ETS . . . in determining whether anything about the test itself has contributed to the decline in scores." The answer, which required only ten pages of the 80-page booklet, proved to be "no": "The SAT score decline does not result from changes in the test or in the methods of scoring it."

Absent from the report was any detailed discussion of what the verbal test—which includes antonyms, analogies, sentence completion, and reading comprehension—is, in fact, testing. While a young person's answering these multiple choice items correctly may show some correlation with probable success in college, the Scholastic Aptitude Test is hardly a comprehensive measure of literacy and certainly no indicator of the performance of the public schools. In other words, if antonyms, analogies, sentence completion, and multiple choice reading questions predict success in college, they are useful in that predictive value only. They are at best a minor measure of a student's ability to use and comprehend language and they cannot be transferred to serve as a measure of the quality of literacy instruction in America.

The panel's own data revealed that most, "probably two thirds to three fourths," of the decline between 1964 and 1970 could be traced to the changing college going population, so that much of the literacy problem in the colleges can be seen as a reflection of a new era in college education, not a withering away of language at all.

But the panel did not limit its appraisal to the data at hand, and, unfortunately, it proceeded to engage in precisely the kind of speculation that CEEB itself had long deplored: It treated the score decline as a direct measure of literacy achievement of American young people. The rationale for this speculation was weak: "Although the SAT score figures are too small a window for surveying this broad condition [literacy education in the schools] they provide special insight into it." In other words, the panel claimed that even though the SAT scores provided inadequate information to make sound judgments, the panel would nevertheless offer what it labeled "informed conjecture" about the state of literacy education in America. The remainder of the headline-making report was devoted to weakly supported hypotheses about social and societal matters for which, in fact, the SAT scores provided no data at all. The panel wrote accusingly of such matters as "proliferation of elective courses, particularly in the area of English and verbal skills; a diminished seriousness of purpose in the learning process as it proceeds in the schools, the home, and the society generally," "the impact of television," changes "in the role of the family in the educational process," "disruption in the life of the country" between 1972 and 1975 (meaning, one supposes, Viet Nam and Watergate), and "an apparent marked diminution in young people's learning motivation." While such social phenomena may possibly have affected literacy skills (we'll probably never know for certain), the panel's speculations were done without adequate research, and the tone of the report made it sound as if the panel members had caught a case of Inverse Wordfear.

Note, for example, the alarmist tone of the first paragraph of this conclusion from the report:

While we ask why the scores on college entrance examinations have gone down, T. S. Eliot's probing goes much deeper: "Where is the learning we have lost in information? Where is the understanding we have lost in knowledge? Where is the life we have lost in living?"

In the panel's view of it all, the fact of hard asking—of both kinds of questions—offers new promise of new answers. We find nothing in the record we have reviewed to discourage the conviction that learning in America can be made all that it is hoped for. What is clearest is the reflection, in the reactions to these test scores and to the poet's lament alike, of renewed purpose to implement these hopes. The future continues to seem like a good idea.

The second paragraph is ringing and rhetorical, yet vacuous and simplistic, clouding as many issues as it clarifies and attempting to create a false consensus with its empty optimism.

Since the panel invited "hard asking" of questions, critics of the report might raise one: Why did the College Entrance Examination Board and Educational Testing Service concern themselves with the quality of schooling in America at all? Despite the implications of "Board" and "Service" in their titles, CEEB and ETS are business organizations. For the test maker to attempt to influence the institutions whose students it tests is both a conflict of interest and a breach of trust.

On to the Future,
Looking Backward All the Way

Few would disagree with the platitudes that ended *On Further Examination*. Of course we're all interested in the future and have a degree of confidence in realizing "the conviction that learning in America can be made all that it is hoped for." But the brouhaha to which the report contributed was anything but future-oriented. Rather, it resulted in little more than a set of reminiscences about schools as they used to be, a lamenting of things supposedly lost. In virtually all of the discussions of today's literacy problems, there is a hint of nostalgia, a longing for the good old days, a "Golden Age of Literacy" when students presumably wrote and read to everyone's satisfaction. When was that era? To help put some myths to rest, I present the following comments on the state of literacy instruction in America dating from 1840:

> For a long time I have noticed with regret the almost entire neglect of the art of original composition in our common schools, and the want of a proper textbook upon this essential branch of education. Hundreds graduate from our common schools with no well-defined ideas of the construction of our language.
>
> A county superintendent of schools,
quoted by George Pyn Quackenbos
(1841)

The need of some requisition which should secure on the part of young men preparing for college proper attention to their own language has long been felt. Bad spelling, incorrectness as well as inelegance of expression in writing, ignorance of the simplest rules of punctuation, and almost entire

want of familiarity with English literature, are far from rare among young
men of eighteen otherwise well prepared for college studies.

> Charles William Eliot
> President of Harvard College
> (1871)

From every college in the country goes up the cry, "Our freshmen can't
spell, can't punctuate." Every high school is in despair because its pupils
are so ignorant of the merest rudiments. A reformation everywhere is
demanded. It is being brought about, and so rapidly that most textbooks
are stranded in the idealism of a decade ago, and many teachers are floundering badly in the new conditions. It is hard to keep pace with swift
change, hard to know what it is all about, or why our duties are preached
to us in such contradictory terms. "Inspire" is still the watchcry; "drills in
rudiments" is soon to be the fact.

> C. H. Ward
> Teacher, Taft School,
> Watertown, Connecticut (1917)

The effects of this breakdown in the public schools, this abandonment of
training for intellectual heights, this ignoring of college requirements—are
clearly evident at the college freshman level. There, except where rigid entrance requirements eliminate the unfit, college teachers are suffering increasing frustrations from the astonishing ignorance of entering classes,
whose members often know little or nothing of the fundamentals of all
education—"readin', writin', and 'rithmetic." Many do not know the
alphabet or multiplication table, cannot write grammatically, and seem to
have been trained to hate mental exercise. One way to handle them is to
force them to take "remedial" courses (often they cannot read intelligently, and dislike any reading), a slow process of remedying the ills
of a slothful public school life. Another is to test them, fail them, and
send them home—rather heartless, but perhaps less so than to encourage
morons to go on. A third, too often done, is to accept them and work
with their mediocrities; the inevitable result is a lowering of standards.

> Philip Marsh
> Professor of English,
> Adrian College (1956)

I really worry about the great unwashed mass of students sloshing around
out there. Diagramming sentences is out, and there are all those kids talking and rapping with each other, not knowing how to examine what they
think in one discursive sentence.

> James Knapton
> Former Supervisor of English
> at Berkeley (1975)

Although these quotations concentrate on college preparation, they represent literally hundreds of similar statements that have been issued over the past 150 years. They are remarkable both for their similarity of tone (with minor stylistic revisions, any of these could be printed in tomorrow's newspaper) and for their common content.

Although most of today's back-to-basics advocates seem to feel they discovered the "deplorable" state of literacy, the fact is that dissatisfaction has existed as long as schools have taught English. *Every* generation seems convinced that it is in the midst of a decline in literacy, that standards have fallen, that the schools have been allowed to abolish all concern for the English language.

This worry about literacy is related to apparently universal concerns about the decay of language itself. A linguist, Harvey Daniels, at Rosary College of Chicago, writes:

Looking back into the history of English, it is easy to find some prominent figure announcing the collapse of the language at virtually any time one selects. In 1710, Jonathan Swift announced in the *Tattler* that the degeneration of the English language was quickly proceeding, and that only drastic measures could prevent its becoming unintelligible to its own speakers inside of twenty years. . . . Swift's crusade was later taken up by Lord Orrey, who slightly adjusted his predecessor's view of the problem. Orrey felt that Swift had saved the tongue from corruption during his age, but that since Swift's death the language had precipitously declined. . . . Some twenty years later, James Beattie reassessed the situation: English had moved with its customary glory through Orrey's time but was (around 1773) suddenly losing ground and threatened with corruption.   [1976]

The concern over "corruption" can be traced directly to our own time; we see the popularity of Edwin Newman's *Strictly Speaking* (1974) and *A Civil Tongue* (1976), books that provide interesting collections of euphemisms and gobbledygook, but confuse misuse with decay and fail to examine the problem with any real degree of linguistic sophistication. Like Swift, Newman seems to think that language is on the brink of destruction. Both failed to recognize that language is a matter of convention and custom and is not either fixed or "pure" in one form or another.

When the Conference on College Composition and Communication explained in a document entitled "The Students' Right to Their Own Language" (1974) that change in language is normal, that change does not necessarily represent decay, columnist Don Oakley (1975) flew into a panic. "Whatever happened to English?" he asked, and then he sarcastically waved, "Bye-bye, Shakespeare. Bye-bye Declaration of Independence and Gettysburg Address."

Are the fears of the Newmans and the Oakleys justified? If their laments focused simply on attacking the misuse of language, one could sympathize with them. But their worries over decay and dissolution are ill-founded. If the complaints about the decline of English over the years were even half true, literacy would have hit rock bottom generations ago, and we would be communicating with grunts and hand signals.

Those who have publicly worried about the decline of English have often failed to do their linguistic homework. They have also failed to review the relationship between the historical tendency toward expanding the public educational system and the language skills of the children and young adults who are being educated. In fact, every outcry of "back to basics" has followed on the heels of major expansion of the educational system.

In the 1860s and seventies, for example, the free public high schools were eroding the dominance of the private preparatory schools and producing large numbers of students seeking a college education. This new college-bound group included a number of young people who were *not* the children of wealthy, literacy-oriented professionals. And it is likely that their skills were not as sophisticated as those of the young people the colleges had traditionally trained. In the midst of the expansion we suddenly find the colleges (represented in the quotation by Charles William Eliot of Harvard) complaining about the preparation of students.

By the turn of the century the public schools roughly tripled in size, absorbing, in the process, huge numbers of immigrant children, and we find Ward (1917) worried about students "ignorant of the merest rudiments." In the post-World War II period when colleges grew in astonishing ways (my own institution went from an agricultural college of 5000 students in 1950 to a multiversity of 43,000 by 1966), Philip Marsh (1956) spoke of the "abandonment of training for intellectual heights." And in our own time, following two decades in which the colleges and universities successfully attracted large numbers of minority students and a generation of women who previously would have gotten married and stayed at home, we have Knapton, Newman, Oakley, and hundreds of others claiming to have found a serious deterioration in language skills.

Historically, the American education has always attempted to expand its base, and this is a form of growth which I believe to be healthy. As a society we have announced that we are willing to educate all comers, and we have actively worked to offer quality education to everybody. Obviously, each time the base of education has been extended, new students, frequently coming from less literacy-oriented backgrounds, have been drawn into the system. Thus it is undeniable that the college recruitment campaigns of the 1970s and the expansion of high school education one hundred years earlier brought in students with less skill in reading and writing—though not necessarily with less linguistic ability—than previous groups. However, this should in no way be confused with a decline in language or a lowering of standards. Indeed, instead of the cries of outrage, it seems to me that the colleges and the public might have done well to engage in self-congratulation on educating new students, rather than complaining about side effects.

But there is something quite disturbing about the tone of the statements I have cited, for they reveal an attitude of contempt—even repugnance—toward those who lack literacy skills. There are suggestions of an unwillingness to deal with the problem and of pure and simple elitism. Thus Knapton speaks of "the unwashed masses," Marsh of "morons," Eliot of the "ignorance" of young people. All too often, having attracted new students, teachers at all levels have refused to teach them. Academic liberalism seems to wear thin when it comes to teaching the "unwashed," to offering solid instruction in reading and writing to young people who need and want it.

Coupled with dislike of students with underdeveloped skills one frequently finds exaggerated descriptions of their problems. A writer for *The Chronicle of Higher Education* talks of clichés about reading and writing:

> It has become an academic and, indeed, a societal cliché that higher education is facing a serious crisis. The same Johnnies and Janes who could not read 10 or 15 years ago are now in college—and they still can't read. They also can't spell, write clear prose, or think logically and critically.
>   [1977]

Yet, instead of investigating these clichés, the writer continues to explain that "this literacy is clearly terrifying." Why "terrifying," one has to ask? Are things really as bad as all that? More to the point, is it true that students "can't read . . . can't spell, write clear prose, or think logically and critically"? Can they not read at all or is it possible that they *can* read, but not well enough? Are we to believe that students are literally incapable of logical thought, or is it safe to assume that their thinking merely fails to measure up to their instructors' expectations? Was Philip Marsh correct when he claimed that students in 1956 were showing up knowing "little or nothing" of the fundamentals or that "many do not know the alphabet"? Was Ward describing things accurately when he claimed students were "ignorant of the merest rudiments" in 1917?

The fact is that as badly as Johnny and Jane read and write, their deficiencies hardly measure up to those extravagant claims. Any person who has ever listened carefully to the babbling of two-year-olds, the dramatic play of pre-schoolers, the hubbub of an elementary classroom, the tête-à-tête's of high schoolers, the exchanges of college classrooms, and the talk, gossip, and conversation of shop lines, supermarkets, pubs, public vehicles, and sporting events, knows full well that human beings have vast knowledge of English, with or without any formal schooling. Much of that knowledge extends to reading and writing as well. Direct observation of virtually any schoolroom reveals that the claim that students "can't spell, write clear prose, or think logically and critically" is patently absurd. Even the least qualified of our high school graduates is able to spell thousands of words, write quite a few sentences, and display a degree of logic.

Here, for example, is a paper from a student who, on the basis of his test scores, was enrolled in a remedial college freshman English class. Just how badly does he write?

First off my reason for being in this writing course is to better my writing habits, to break old habits and begin to use the new ones that I acquire from this writing course In hopes of writing a perfectly constructed paper. I like to write sometimes but it depends on what I am writing. If I can write stories that I makeup then I enjoy writing but if it is on topics that don't interest me I have a hard time getting involved in writing, I love to write stories that are fun to create and make others enjoy reading what I have wrote. The changes I'll have to make in this course are to break habits such as incorrect sentence structure, improper placement of commas and periods. In the past the writing I did was very limited from letters to my family and while I was away from home to writing an essay on why I would like to go to the Super Bowl football game. In the future I plan on doing a lot more writing than I did in the past! Writing is used by mostly everyone in their daily lives. I think writing is used from the first time you learn your abc's to the end of our existing lives. I believe I have good and bad qualities in writing different kinds of papers. My creativity and spelling are my strongest points of writing while sentence structure and proper punctuation are a few of my weakest points. And I'm sure you will get acquainted with some of my others!

The grade I get in this course is the grade I earn! A writing course I think is designed to help you not hurt you. You should try to learn from your mistakes and use what you have learned to write a better paper. I think if you do all your assignments, come to class and participate in class discussions, and keep up on your portfolio there is no reason I can't get a B for a grade and if I really buckle down maybe I can earn an A for a grade. The time I think is required for this course is 1 to 2 hours daily not saying this will always be done but this is the only way to survive in a writing course. The people that can help me are my fellow classmates by catching my mistakes and the person that can help the most is our in-structor. Books that will aid me in this course are the dictionary for proper spelling, and the one called "The Little English Handbook" by Corbett and I would imagine there are other books in the library that will help in writing a good paper.

There are many problems with this paper, but "illiteracy" isn't one of them. This student, like a considerable majority of college students, does, in fact, have reasonably good control of the basics, even though he has doubts about his own competence in "improper placement of commas and periods." What's wrong with this paper is not so much its use of language as its content and coherence. It rambles and wanders; it indulges in cliché ("The grade I get in this course is the grade I earn!"); and it attempts to "snow" the instructor ("I plan on doing a lot more writing than I did in the past! Writing is used by mostly everyone in their daily lives"). In fact, much of what's wrong with the paper reflects, not an unwillingness on the part of the schools to prepare this student, but rather, over-instructing him in the formalities of essay writing, so that his writing is generally strained, stuffy, and unnatural. Perhaps the most telling phrase in the paper, one which speaks volumes about his past experiences, is "A writing course *I think* is designed *to help you not hurt you*" [italics added]. He is not quite certain, and the evidence of "teaching" in his writing shows that his suspicions are correct.

My point in presenting this essay is not to defend it as adequate or to ignore its obvious problems. Nor do I offer it as representative of all freshman writing. (There is much worse and much better writing available.) But I want to note that this so-called remedial student has a great deal more language power at his disposal than most people give him credit for. Further, this kind of paper reveals that much talk of student illiteracy is based on impressions that no one has bothered to investigate. Having accepted the widely publicized idea that literacy is in decay, most critics have never bothered to look for anything but confirming evidence.

Those Were the Good Old Days?

I have spent a considerable amount of space discussing perceptions of a decline in literacy, attempting to show the oversimplifications in the widely held belief that reading and writing are on the wane. The doom-and-gloom mentality of decline, of being "terrified" by lack of basic skills in young people, has been destructive, and, in fact, has been a red herring in the debate over literacy instruction: People have been so busy worrying about the decline and attempting to remedy it that they have lost focus on the basic issues at hand. In looking backward to a Golden Age of Literacy, both teachers and the general public have trapped themselves in retrospective thinking.

Just for the record, then, I want to supply some documentation of "the good old days" to show precisely how good (or bad) literacy instruction was, borrowing some reminiscences collected by Leon Renfroe Meadows in a doctoral dissertation written at Columbia Teachers College (1928). These statements are representative of teaching practices in the second half of the nineteenth century, when composition was first established as a school subject:

My teacher was more particular about the form than the thought. We wrote with a goose quill pen and used homemade ink. Often the paper was poor and the ink would spread as on a blotter; this necessitated a recopying of the composition.

We were required to outline essays that we read. Later, we wrote original essays from outlines which we had prepared. The subjects were usually very uninteresting and the papers that we wrote were vague and meaningless.

We had what the catalogue called rhetoric instead of composition. We memorized selections and "declaimed" before the entire school. As students advanced, they wrote orations, and these were later delivered before the class and on public occasions.

We were required to memorize the rules of the textbook and illustrate these rules in writing.

We paid little or no attention to the actual practice of writing in the true sense. Most of our time was spent in the study of the parts of speech and their relationship to each other.

I do not recall any of the subjects we were required to write on. Most of the compositions were dry and insipid. We dealt with the formalities of composition, such as the proper use of semi-colons, question marks, etc.

While a handful of contemporary critics would say that this kind of instruction is precisely the sort to which we should return, the fact is that the nineteenth century was anything but a Golden Age of reading and writing. Not much actual composition was done in the schools, and when students wrote, they had to choose from pseudo-philosophical or abstract topics. The teachers' corrections stressed formal English and penmanship at the expense of content. Students spent an exorbitant amount of time memorizing the grammar book, a book of rhetoric (the "laws" of discourse), and biographical facts about the lives of authors. Most brutal of the nineteenth-century practices was *parsing,* in which students wrote detailed grammatical analyses of the functions of every single word in a passage of prose. (One of Meadows' informants recalled having to parse the entire first book of Milton's *Paradise Lost.*)

We know, too, that few were satisfied with training in reading and writing. Parents were concerned, and the colleges were up in arms over what they took to be the poor preparation of entering freshmen. My own research into the history of English teaching (1967) turned up dozens and dozens of articles, both in professional journals and in the popular press, decrying the inability of young people to read and write.

Did things improve later? Dr. Lou LaBrant, Professor Emeritus of English at Dillard University, reminisces about her own school education at the turn of the century:

While we had nothing labeled "English," we had reading and grammar. Readers were fairly solid affairs, designed to do more than develop skills. They included chapters from novels by Dickens, selections from *Walden* and *Gulliver's Travels,* and poems by various English and American poets. Four Americans always appeared: Longfellow, Lowell, Poe, and Whittier. Pictures of these worthies (all but Poe fully bearded) hung on the walls of most grammar schools. *The Psalm of Life, Barefoot Boy,* parts of *Thanatopsis,* and Lowell's stanza on June were usually memorized. . . .

Our chief emphasis, however, was on grammar. We learned definitions, diagrammed sentences, classified clauses, phrases, and single modifiers, and then we parsed. We also wrote out full conjugations, active and passive, in indicative, subjunctive, potential, and imperative moods, along with all the infinitives and participles and the active and passive periphrastic. We learned about the dative as the case in the indirect object, and to distinguish the *me* in *He gave the book to me* and the *me* in *He gave me the book.*

Usage was taught by the simple device of stopping anyone who made a mistake and correcting him right there. Chief targets were *It is me* or *him,* and confusion in using the parts of irregular verbs as in *I seen, I done,* or *I have went.* I recall that during the morning Bible reading, one teacher paused to remark: "Notice, children. The Lord said, 'It is I; be not afraid,' and not 'It is me'." [1977]

Did this kind of education work? Was it better than what we have today? Should we return to the memorizing of *The Psalm of Life* and teaching the periphrastic? Professor LaBrant, who began teaching English in Kansas in 1911, spent her entire professional life searching for better methods. She offers this interesting comment on the state of affairs, then and now:

Through the years I have read letters to the public mind; articles submitted to a national magazine I once edited; themes submitted by grade, high school, and college students. I have not been impressed by statements that we once had a national population of good writers. Many are now attempting to write who would have given up in years gone by. . . .

Certainly most of the problems we struggle with today were with American education in the early years of the century; the great difference is that they are more obvious today. We then had unassimilated groups, students who learned with difficulty, unruly youngsters. Most of these were ignored because the curriculum was an inflexible standard. Many did not even enroll, others stayed only briefly. [1977]

Clearly, from this report and others like it, we can be reasonably certain that the first quarter of this century offered no panacea for the teaching of reading and writing.

Was there dramatic improvement in the 1920s and thirties? J. N. Hook, former Executive Secretary of the National Council of Teachers of English, describes his high school experiences:

My English courses in high school were linguistically barren except they taught me to say "If I were" and "between you and me." I had come from a "me-and-him-was" background. No doubt the purism of my high school English teachers prepared me for purism I would encounter later in college. . . . Language had no history, no life; it was just lying there, inert. It existed in two forms—correct and incorrect—and my classmates and I persisted in our penchant for the wrong choice. Language was intended mainly to be subjected to intense analysis: picking out all the adverbs, underlining this and that, constructing linear diagrams much more elaborate than anything we drew for geometry.   [1977]

Did it work? Professor Hook continues, "The linguistic gain was only slightly above zero. . . ."

Of course by no means all memories of schooling are negative, and some people recall their school days from the middle third of the century with fondness. Jane Schmidt, presently of Phoenix, writes:

My memories go back 55 years so most of them are very dim and I expect a lot idealized. I can remember learning "Deedle Deedle Dumpling, My Son John" in kindergarten. One thing I'm very sure of—we were not catapulted into the adult world but were allowed to enjoy fantasy and adventure during most of our grade school years. . . .

I had an overwhelming hunger to learn to read. I think I liked spelling because I learned new words and how to use them. I also found orthography, which was taught during 7th and 8th grades, fascinating.[1977]

Of grammar, she notes:

We were so thoroughly drilled in grammar during grade school that I just coasted through high school English. I suppose I liked it because it was easy for me.

But unlike Mr. Hook, Mrs. Schmidt came to school already speaking the standard dialect: "Mother's grammar was so nearly perfect that what I learned at home was the same thing we were taught in school. There was no feeling of awkwardness, no unlearning or relearning." As she notes, the exercises of English were easy for her because they rehearsed what she already knew.

In fact, whether the kind of traditional instruction described here changed very many students seems doubtful. Complaints over the illiteracy of young people were as loud as ever in the 1930s and forties.

Now it's my turn to reminisce about a public school career that stretched from 1945 to 1959. My own literacy education reached a high point in fourth grade, when Miss Celia Reynolds allowed us to write on our choice of topics every week throughout the school year. Most of us loved this "story day," and as I recall, we wrote comfortably. Miss Reynolds also established a contest to see which student read the greatest number of books outside of class. We had an in-class library of reading books as well, and I can recall reading and rereading biographies of Kit Carson, John Paul Jones, and Davy Crockett. After this relatively pleasurable year, my schools settled into the real "business" of English: grammar and usage. ("The goats have [drunk, drank] their milk," ran one exercise. I always wondered if goats drank milk!) In high school, we advanced to sentence diagramming. Except for examinations and book reports, writing almost disappeared from the curriculum after grade seven, and I can recall only three writing assignments in four years of high school: a poem for English 1 which I began, "Trees come in many a kind," a sophomore composition "explaining a process," and a senior year exercise translating Robert Browning's "My Last Duchess" into a one-act play to prove that it was a dramatic monologue. Literary study was equally limited: one Shakesperean play each year through high school, American literature junior year, British lit for the seniors.

Did it work? Were things better then? When the Russians launched Sputnik in 1957, my college-bound classmates and I cursed our teachers for their failure to educate us properly in English and physics, and in English class I debated in favor of homogeneous grouping for increased efficiency of instruction. Though my SAT test scores were satisfactory, my feelings of inadequacy about writing were so great that I spent the summer before college giving myself impromptu themes to write as practice. That self-educating strategy didn't work, and for the first half of the college year I was in serious danger of flunking freshman English. I can tell you, *those* weren't the good old days.

Perhaps, then, the 1960s can be identified as the high point of literacy instruction in the United States. In terms of standardized test scores, they were, for in 1962–63 SAT verbal scores peaked at a national high mean of 478 points. The reasons for this peak are not altogether clear, though some attribute it to the "seriousness" of sixties students, coupled with the fact that the baby boom and minority recruitment campaigns had not yet begun to swell college enrollments. Certainly no one has claimed that the scores were a direct result of quality instruction. A survey conducted by James Squire and Roger Applebee on behalf of the National Council of Teachers of English (1968) found that the high school curriculum was overloaded with history-oriented literature courses. Writing was largely ignored, and Squire and Applebee regretted that only 15.7 percent of English teachers' time was given over to composition, with the bulk of that being spent after the fact of composition in the marking of errors. It does not seem as if English teachers can claim credit for the higher SAT scores. Nor, if you look past the test scores, do the sixties seem to be that elusive Golden Age of Literacy.

A Recent History of English Teaching

Since the sixties fail to produce an ideal model for literacy instruction, I want to review the changes in teaching English since then, roughly the period of the SAT score decline. Many "new methods" of teaching English have been connected with the score decline, just as the "new math" has been blamed for the drop-off in SAT mathematical scores. But it is important not to make spurious connections.

Although my eager-beaver high school friends and I didn't know it, we were not the only people upset by the Russian victory with Sputnik in 1957. Even though it seems unfair that the educational system was somehow blamed when American technology failed to orbit Vanguard ahead of Sputnik, the Russian success led to a prompt and angry attack on the schools. First to receive criticism were science and math, and they were the first to receive support for curriculum revision. Within three years of Sputnik the federal government was offering extensive summer institutes for teachers through the National Science Foundation. In 1958 Congress passed a National Defense Education Act, which linked schooling directly to the defense effort.

At about the same time a widely publicized conference of academics—mostly scientists—and educators at Woods Hole, Massachusetts, enunciated some basic principles that were to form the center of reform in math and science education (Bruner, 1960). The Woods Hole conferees argued that school subjects needed to have a valid intellectual center, that university scholars must work closely with teachers to find that center, that any subject should be teachable to any child in some form at any age, and that key concepts should be repeated in the curriculum in a "spiral" fashion. Following the Woods Hole conference new curricula emerged: chemistry programs that focused on understanding quantum theory rather than memorizing the characteristics of elements and compounds, biology courses that emphasized the organic concepts of growth and evolution rather than the mere mastery of taxonomy, and, of course, the new math with its concern for understanding mathematical principles—numeral, set subset, base systems—rather than memorization of math facts. The Woods Hole concepts were later to influence English as well.

Initially, literacy studies were left out of the picture; Congress was worried about ICBMs, not words. In 1960, however, the National Council of Teachers of English passed a resolution urging Congress to extend the National Defense Education Act to English and the humanities and shortly after published a book, *The National Interest in the Teaching of English* (1961), which linked English to the sciences and national defense with such arguments as these:

1. The teaching of English plays a vital role in preserving human values in our technological society. . . .
2. Our democratic institutions depend upon intelligent, informed communication, which in turn depends upon the training of all persons to think critically and imaginatively, to express themselves clearly, and to read with understanding. . . .
3. Competence in using English is essential in every subject. Unless English is taught well, every subject suffers.

Congress responded by extending the NDEA to establish "Project English," a series of research, curriculum development, and demonstration centers around the country. Each center (most were housed in universities) investigated a different area of the curriculum—the University of Minnesota examined language study, Northwestern University looked into writing, Nebraska studied the literature curriculum. Scholars and teachers at the centers were agreed on one item: that the tradition in English teaching, with its emphasis on the historical study of literature, memorization of grammar terminology, and error correction in composition, was inadequate. Research studies as far back as the turn of the century were examined, and it was obvious that the tradition in English teaching hadn't worked.

It was time for something new, then. The centers experimented with a variety of new curriculum models, most attempting to discover and elucidate the kind of central structure for English that Woods Hole had advocated for science. "Project English" threw English teaching into critical self-examination that was to last a good fifteen years, though funding for the centers themselves came to an end after six.

In the 1960s other forces were reshaping English as well. In the mid-sixties a group of "romantic" critics of education—John Holt, Jonathan Kozol, Herbert Kohl, George Leonard, and James Herndon—attacked the structure of the schools and called for giving students increased freedom. In a related movement, concern for inequality of education led to new interest in teaching the so-called disadvantaged, and English teachers began developing reading and writing programs for use in inner-city teaching situations. Until 1960, book publishers, for the most part, had limited paperback books to low-level literature; then they began bringing out a range of good literature in paper covers, which helped English teachers individualize learning for a wide range of students. A conference of British and American teachers at Dartmouth College in 1966 placed great emphasis on naturalistic language learning, on the development of the student himself or herself (Dixon, 1967, 1975).

In the classroom, these various forces operated to produce some obvious changes in English instruction. Perhaps the most successful innovation was the use of paperback books in the schools. Previously regarded as "pornographic" because of their association with the near-naked female bodies on drugstore paperbacks, soft-cover books came into their own in the 1960s and were brought into the classroom as a valid way of individualizing reading programs. Paperbacks seemed successful with non-readers and readers alike, and although the common, hardbound anthology still persisted, paperbacks gave a new look to English classrooms and allowed teachers to do a substantially better job of reaching larger numbers of young people (see Fader, 1976).

In composition, teachers focused on the ideas of the student rather than exclusively on grammatical correctness. Students were encouraged to write imaginatively and to write about personal experiences as well as about academic topics. Teachers also discovered that students could "compose" in electronic and visual media, which, in turn, created great interest in the making of films, slide tapes, sound tapes, and the like.

Language study flirted for a while with "new grammars," which were based on scientific linguistics, but neither structural grammar (which teaches how words function within sentences based on the speaker's intuitive knowledge of language) nor transformational grammar (which shows how basic "kernel" sentences are "transformed" linguistically into longer ones) satisfied very many teachers in their search for a better way to teach sentence sense. Perhaps most significant is that teachers realized the conventional approach to grammar was not producing the results that were desired. The "old" grammar instruction could not even claim success in raising college board scores, because grammar questions had been eliminated from the SAT in 1948 (Barth, 1965).

Toward the end of the 1960s, the English profession discovered an old-but-new curriculum idea—elective courses—and the late sixties saw traditional high school offerings—English I, II, III, IV—being replaced by elective courses with catchy titles: "The American Dream," "Sports Literature," "Man vs. Woman." In many schools, elective courses were the catalyst that brought all of the components of the new English together by encouraging teacher selection of paperback materials, individualized reading/writing assignments, and student selection of courses of interest.

The Impact of the New English

Undeniably there were abuses, excesses, and unsuccessful experiments associated with the new directions. For instance, in their zeal to free students to write, some teachers told young people, mistakenly, that "correctness doesn't matter." While trying to locate "relevant" literature, some teachers let students read just about anything, including literature of questionable value. Teachers were acting on the well-intentioned but somewhat misguided notion that *any* kind of reading was better than none, and that arousing a student's interest in reading *anything* was preferable to possibly boring him or her with the standard texts. Elective courses proliferated without rhyme or reason; some popular courses had virtually no substance and could not be justified even in the name of meeting individual needs. The term "freedom" was misinterpreted, and some teachers confused it with license.

But these abuses should not be confused with the aims and intentions of the new English nor allowed to negate its successes. After all, there were abuses in the old English as well, including the marching of millions of children, lock-step, through aimless grammar drills and the reading of nearly incomprehensible adult literature.

The public, however, has an altogether negative impression of the revolution in English teaching. Parents and school board members typically perceive the new English class as undisciplined, chaotic, permissive in the extreme, with students successfully avoiding hard work while their teachers stand idly by speaking of "creativity" and the "rights of the individual." When asked what's wrong with English, the public points to a course called "The Literature of the Supernatural" and asks, "Whatever happened to English?"

Yet these concerns of the public are based more on isolated episodes and press reports than actual fact. In 1977 my colleague at Michigan State, Candida Gillis, conducted a survey of English programs on behalf of The English Journal. She disproved the popular stereotype of the typical English class as a place where "a raggedy bunch of undisciplined students mill around doing only what they 'wanna' do." To the contrary, the survey found that the swing of the pendulum had not been nearly so great as most had expected. Summarizing the results, Professor Gillis wrote:

If you are a student in an English class taught by a mythical "average" respondent, you are in a senior high school class with students with above average or mixed abilities. Your class stresses literature and writing. You study subjects such as how writers use language, themes in literature, spelling and vocabulary, "standard" usage, and how to organize paragraphs. You write exposition, narratives of personal experiences, and interpretations and analyses of literature. You read many short stories and novels and your text is an anthology. You spend time in class talking freely about the literature, discussing study guide questions, and writing. If you enrolled in the course wanting to make movies, write scripts or advertisements, read off-beat, technical, or minority literature, take field trips, or study transformational grammar or features of dialects, you are out of luck.

The survey was not a random sample of the nation's teachers; nor did it attempt to make comparisons with previous periods. Thus we don't know whether the survey reflected a static situation, a drift away from tradition, or a return to it. But the English classrooms of 1977 represented in the survey were anything but radically innovative or out of control. There was nothing in the survey to indicate that English teachers were pursuing a revolutionary course independent of the wishes of parents. In fact, many of us in the field of English education were disappointed that the survey revealed so little change from the 1950s and sixties. The "revolution" seemed to have passed many English teachers by, leaving them still teaching with methods that had been thoroughly discredited by the research of the previous two decades.

Looking into the history of the teaching of English is useful as a way of understanding the origins of the present English curriculum and assessing past attempts at reform. I hope, then, that this brief review points out the need for synthesis of ideas, rather than blanket acceptance or rejection of either old or new. Many of the principles of the new English were, in fact, quite old, having been part of the repertoire of good, experienced teachers for generations. Nor have the effects of the old curriculum been altogether harmful; a great many children have graduated from the public schools reading, writing, speaking successfully for their own purposes and to the satisfaction of their elders, despite some practices that obviously didn't work.

The opportunity of the 1980s, it seems to me, is for teachers and administrators, with the support of the public, to seek the best, most workable, proven ideas of both the new and old English and to search for a model of language instruction that will realize the promise and potential of today's teachers and today's children. I shall present such a synthesis in the next chapter. For the moment, it is important to reemphasize that the search for the Golden Age of Literacy is not an historical quest; rather, it is something that must begin in contemporary classrooms the first thing each Monday morning.

3
What's Basic and How Do You Learn It?

This chapter is about the basics of language: what one has to know or do to use English successfully, what teachers have to teach if youngsters are to become skilled in reading, writing, and other language uses. But this discussion can be extraordinarily complex. Seymour Yesner, English consultant for the Minneapolis Public Schools, writes:

In referring to the deplorable state of language basic skills, I hear such things as: students can't spell, punctuate, identify parts of speech, do "grammar," express ideas, detect ideas and facts, comprehend what they read and hear, use dictionaries, grasp syntactical order, manage agreement of subject and verb, use proper form, generalize, take tests, fill out application blanks, compose a business letter (or any kind of letter), specify, solve problems, handle logical relations, find words to express themselves, make semantic distinctions, understand usage forms and proprieties, cope with dialects, manipulate sound-symbol relationships, encode, decode, remember spelling rules, read fast enough, write a sentence (preferably two), write a paragraph (preferably several with some logical connections), infer, deduce, induce, interpret, and god knows what else.
[1973]

Yesner suggests that we must carefully distinguish *general skills*— which are the global, complex activities of reading, writing, speaking, listening—from *basic* skills, which are numerous subskills—penmanship to verb agreement—which go to make up general skills. Such a distinction would, for example, put an end to gross statements like, "Kids nowadays lack the basics of reading and writing," which confuses basic and general skills and implies total illiteracy when criticism of subskill mastery is probably intended.

But even separating general from basic language skills is not enough, because most of us will agree that some basic skills (e.g., making a coherent point) are vastly more complex than others (e.g., spelling a word correctly). In fact, one can create an entire hierarchy of basic skills, beginning with simple encoding and decoding activities (spelling and word-calling), leading up through higher-order basic skills (composing or reading an entire sentence) and a wide range of substratum or supportive skills (like organizing and comprehending), which are themselves made up of other skills or processes. This would produce what might be called a Taxonomic Model of English Skills, a complete listing or naming of all the basic skills and processes required to execute a general skill successfully. The Taxonomic Model would show that the general skills consist of skill levels of varying importance and specificity. Close to the top would be social or community skills—the ability to use language in a variety of real situations—directly supported by the second order processes (complex as they are) of thinking, organizing, and comprehending. At a third level we might find the skills that go into the making of sentences, and at the fourth would be very specific subskills such as recognizing and making letters. These levels are sketched in Figure 1.

Actually, the number of skills that could be listed at each level is *infinite*, since there is no practical limit to the number of language processes a person can and, in fact, *must* master. (Consider the number of perceptual and thinking skills that go into so simple an act as recognizing a letter of the alphabet. How do you know that each of these is the same letter? A a *a* A a a A A 𝔄 α a A a *ꓮ* A *ɑ* a) Preparing an exhaustive taxonomic representation of all the skills of English would be a monumental task

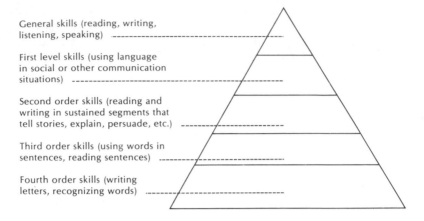

General skills (reading, writing, listening, speaking)

First level skills (using language in social or other communication situations)

Second order skills (reading and writing in sustained segments that tell stories, explain, persuade, etc.)

Third order skills (using words in sentences, reading sentences)

Fourth order skills (writing letters, recognizing words)

Figure 1. A Taxonomic Model of English Skills

and would engage the minds of many graduate students for dozens of years, producing a stack of unpublished Ph.D. dissertations.

The taxonomy would, in fact, be a very interesting one to examine, and it would certainly be more useful than many of the ragtag skill lists that have been produced by educators and textbook writers over the years based on hunch, intuition, and moral imperative rather than linguistic research. But it would not be particularly helpful to teachers and might be quite misleading. What would the teacher do with such a list of the basics? What would he or she begin teaching? If the teacher began at the lower level and worked up, the task would never be completed. Anyway, it seems apparent that the language skills are learned in global fashion, from the top of the triangle down, rather than from the bottom up. It is within the context of practicing general skills (reading, writing, listening, speaking) that people learn the requisite basic skills (spelling, comprehending, punctuating, etc.). To teach all the substratum skills first is a futile effort.

Visualizing this model helps to explain why the teaching of formal terminology—e.g., grammar—has never shown itself to be a satisfactory approach to literacy instruction. It is an attempt to teach a whole by presenting the names of innumerable parts. Linguists estimate that the native speaker of English has mastered in the neighborhood of *four thousand* language operations called "transformations" that allow him or her to string words into sentences. The native speaker recognizes, for example, that "How do you do?" is English, that "Do how you do" is not, all without recourse to grammar instruction. In addition, a question like "How do you do?" is an idiom, which goes beyond the formal laws of syntax, and it relies on knowledge of numerous sociolinguistic skills. Each of us has learned (after initial confusion, perhaps) that one does not supply a literal answer to such a ritualistic greeting. The proper answer to "How do you do?" is "Pleased to meet you," or a similar phrase, not a catalog of the *hows* that one *does*.

Other areas of human communication are equally complex. In "framing an argument" or "making a point," one pulls together such a vast array of skills and subskills that detailed analysis is impossible. Paul Simon sings, "When I think of all the crap I learned in high school/It's a wonder that I can think at all." Verse two might well comment, "When I think of all the basic skills I've mastered/It's a wonder I can talk at all." Molière's *bourgeois gentilhomme* was astonished to learn that he had been speaking "prose" all his life. We might well express amazement that we've been speaking and writing basic skills all our lives.

Interesting though it might be, then, the Taxonomic Model of English Skills is not an especially useful one in theory or practice. Its principal value is in exposing the fallacy of solving the reading/writing crisis by calling for more basics. But in order to deal with the teaching of literacy in the schools realistically, it is necessary to examine language use in more than superficial ways, by looking at the ways in which it functions not only for purposes of communication but in perceiving and thinking.

Language and Perception

We are from our waking moments plunged into the world of experiences. The alarm goes off, the radio comes on; someone talks, we listen. Although people are conscious of much of what is happening around them, they also become quite adept at filtering experiences to retain and recall only those that affect them directly and personally. Unlike computers, which remember everything fed to them, human beings are selective at the "input stage." And it's a good thing, too, for if we remembered all but a small fraction of what happened to us day by day, our brains would quickly become so clogged with trivial information that we couldn't think. (If you doubt this, try an experiment: For one hour simply try to write down *everything* you perceive. I suspect you will fail at the task [I did] because you can't write down things as fast as they happen. Even in the span of a few minutes you can produce a long list of sights, sounds, smells, conversations, happenings that will prove the point.) Further, this selection process is language based. The language system is used to help us categorize, abstract, define, and store experiences. Human beings use language and symbols to represent experiences for themselves, to store away experience.

How this happens can best be seen through a simple example from early childhood language learning. Babies Johnny and Jane are lying in the crib and gradually become aware of a fuzzy face peering over the edge. A voice in the distance shouts, "Fido, get down off there!" Since Fido is curious, persistent, and puzzled by the human beings in the crib, this episode is repeated several times. As time passes, Johnny and Jane grow and sit up and pet the fuzzy head, and they begin to sound out the symbol that their parents have chosen to represent the dog: [Ph-eye-dough]. The children eventually learn another word that is frequently associated with Fido, and that is "dog."

So at age two they go for a walk, taking "Fido," "the dog," with them. Their experience is expanded considerably when a huge German Shepherd (they don't call it that) comes across the park at a dead run and attacks poor Fido. "Bad dog!" shouts mother or father, beating off the intruder and rescuing "the dog." At this point, the kids' language categories expand. "Dog" takes on new meaning. Eventually the children abstract from experience and come to realize that "dog" is a symbol for something more than Fido (or the German Shepherd). Johnny and Jane come to form a language concept of "dogness," so that every time they perceive a particular kind of four-legged animal they are quickly able to supply labels for the experience: "Oh, look at the dog!" In part because of their mastery of language, they don't have to start from zero each time they see an animal. It is this kind of labeling that makes perception a linguistic process.

It follows, then, that the language system influences the process of perception. As writers in the field of general semantics have pointed out, a symbol is at best a *representation* of reality: "The word is not the thing itself; the symbol is not the same as the thing symbolized; the map is not the territory" (Hayakawa, 1972). In other words, as a person abstracts from reality, creating labels that simplify classifying, he or she also loses a degree of touch with that reality. Generally speaking, the more abstract a symbol becomes, the fewer direct correspondences it has with reality.

There is danger in a human tendency to let symbols do too much work, becoming substitutes for firsthand experience. A charge commonly leveled at education professors, for example, is that they are so far removed from actual classroom experiences that their abstractions—"child management," "discipline," "goal-setting"—are disconnected from reality; they use the decalang referred to in Chapter 1.

The symbolizing function of language can also make discussion (and thinking) difficult. For example, while I was drafting this chapter an age-old question came up in one of my classes: "Are English teachers professionals?" The question is guaranteed to produce debate not only because of its content but because it is a semantic trap. The word "professional," for instance, is abstract and fairly vague, yet the question invites us to treat it as a simple, well-defined concept, one which can be examined in yes-no, two-value terms. But "professional" can mean vastly different things, just as "dog" means different things depending on whether the referent is Fido or a ferocious German Shepherd. Are English teachers "professionals"? Not if you compare their "professional" organizations to those of doctors or attorneys or truck drivers or coal miners. But if you take "professional" simply to mean "paid for services," then English teachers are pros, just like doctors and the Los Angeles Lakers. On the other hand, if you take "professional" in its connotative sense of "being good at what you do," then you have to look very carefully before applying the term to specific teachers (just as you would have to exercise caution in applying it to your neighborhood physician or the Lakers). As Carl Jung has suggested, an abstract word like "professional" is not a static symbol, but a "psychic event." It is different for every speaker and hearer, and it depends very much for its meaning on the individual's past experiences. Language does not place limits on experience or thinking. Human beings develop the symbol system required to let them categorize and describe their experiences. At the same time, once the symbol system is formed, it strongly affects the way we view the world. Language both shapes our experiences and is shaped by it.

Language and Thinking

For generations the schools have included as a standard curriculum goal: "To teach the student to think." But the verb "to think" is one of those abstractions that can get us into serious trouble if we allow it to rule our perceptions and do not examine its multiple meanings carefully.

As behavioral scientists have long argued, thinking is a "black box" function. That is, thinking takes place in the inner world of the mind and cannot be directly observed. About all one can do is observe what goes into the black box (perceptions) and what comes out (responses). The behaviorists generally refuse to speculate about what goes on inside the box and concentrate on the input and output—the stimulus and response. Of course, one *can* approximate what happens inside the black box of the brain, and this is an area of investigation that intrigues brain surgeons, neurologists, biologists, philosophers, psychiatrists, rhetoricians, linguists, and logicians, each of whom sets up a model or paradigm of the thinking process based on study of input, output, and on educated guesses about what must go on in between.

Obviously, this is not the place for presenting a theory of thinking or a cognitive/behavioral debate about the validity of such speculations. I simply want to make two points about this mysterious process that we simplistically label, "thinking":

1. *Thinking is vastly more complex and less rational than is often suggested.* Traditionally we portray "the thinker" as a supremely orderly person, processing experience and premise to reach sound and valid conclusions. But as a matter of fact, thinking is anything but orderly, and the conclusions that we draw in day-to-day living grow from many sources: from past experiences, intuition and insight, "common sense" (whatever that is), blind luck, and so on. While some decisions may come out looking supremely logical, the chances are that considerable illogical mulling and wheel spinning took place inside the black box before the decision was reached. Of course thinking follows some recogniz able patterns; we learn through experience and example that certain ways of problem solving and responding to experience work better than others. Such patterns can be mapped or modeled by psychologists, logicians, rhetoricians, and so on to create rules or laws, which most people naturally follow. But when one charts patterns, one automatically excludes individual and idiosyncratic distinctions. Thus in talking about patterns of thinking, too often psychologists and teachers tend to ignore individual traits and to miss the intuitive side of thinking.

In terms of current popular psychology, Robert Ornstein (1972) and others have described a physiological/psychological split between right-brained thinking, the intuitive, insightful side, and

left-brained, tending toward more conventional, patterned thinking. It is their contention that the schools have focused attention
on the left-brain functions, teaching mastery of knowledge and
understanding of static concepts at the expense of helping students
develop the powers of the right brain. Such a discussion has important implications for language instruction as well, for literacy
instruction has suffered from the same imbalance, emphasizing
cognition over intuition, grammar over ideas and metaphor.

It is important, too, to cut through the semantic blurring that
takes place in the widely circulated statement that "Kids nowadays can't think!" Of course they *can*. As often as not, a statement
that "kids can't think" actually should be translated, "Students do
not, cannot, or will not put their 'thoughts' into a form (and language) that is recognizable to me." While the effects may be the
same to the listener (incomprehension), the implications for instruction differ greatly.

2. *Thinking is inextricably bound up with language and experience.* "Perceiving" and "thinking" are not, of course, separate
processes. Perceptions flow directly into thoughts, just as individual words flow into sentences. Though firsthand experiences with
the world are the "basic stuff" of thinking, that stuff is processed
through the abstracting process of symbolization. Much (if not all)
thinking, then, is language based. We think by manipulating symbols rather than by struggling directly with experience.

How language performs this function and the degree of formality of the symbol-using process in thinking are, again, information
trapped in the black box, but it seems clear that human beings
have a range of languages they use in thinking. For example, when
I am engaged in writing, I am compelled to pace the floor, getting
up from the typewriter perhaps two or three times per manuscript
page to stroll around the house, and as I walk I talk—"pre-writ-
ing" orally what I will put down on paper. In this case, thinking
and using language are quite close to the surface, and the language
I (and most people) use when talking aloud to themselves is reasonably standard English.

Below that level, however, I recognize in myself a non-spoken talking to myself. Here I use full sentences or fairly coherent sentence fragments. If I wrote down my internal talks, you would be able to read and understand much of them.

Below *that* level, however, I am dimly aware of words flashing by from time to time, a kind of deeper talking where words (and probably phrases and clauses) send telegraphic messages ("Late!" "Get to class!" "Dull!"). Most of these, if written down, would not make much sense to you; they serve as a kind of mental shorthand.

I cannot carry my own conscious recognition any deeper than that level, but linguists speculate on pretty sound evidence that the symbol-making process churns away in our subconscious and semiconscious at all times. Some have even postulated that each of us has a kind of "pre-verbal" symbol system where we use symbols other than words to represent chunks of experience to ourselves, but it is difficult to prove the existence of such a function.

It has often been said that "Language makes us human," that possession of the language facility allows human beings to do things beyond the skills of so-called "dumb" animals. If, to return to an earlier example, Johnny, Jane, and Fido encounter yet another dog on the way home from the park, the human and animal responses differ. Depending on how badly he was beaten up, Fido either runs away, cowers behind the kids, or does a routine dog-to-dog sniffing inspection to determine whether or not the new animal is hostile. Johnny and Jane use symbols and language to assess the process. They know that "dog" can mean something friendly like Fido or something mean like the Shepherd. They check for other signs: The wagging tail "reminds" them of Fido, not the Shepherd. By "thinking"—comparing concepts and symbols, playing hunches—they reach a conclusion: "Looks friendly to me," says Johnny. "Yes," says Jane, "let's find out."

The Uses of Language

As Johnny and Jane approach the strange dog to discover whether or not they are good critical thinkers, they switch into the last phase of the language/experience model: *languaging*. Creating language is sometimes represented somewhat simplistically as the sending of "messages." In fact, the public functions of language are vastly more complex than mere "communication."

Much writing, for instance, serves a function not so much of communicating with another person as allowing one to clarify his or her beliefs, thoughts, and ideas. Eldridge Cleaver writes:

That is why I started to write. To save myself. I realized that no one would save me but myself. The prison authorities were both uninterested and unable to help me. I had to seek out the truth and unravel the snarled web of my motivations. I had to find out who I am and what I want to be, what type of man I should be, and what I could do to become the best of which I was capable.   [1968]

Not all writing serves so dramatic a function, but getting something down on paper is frequently as important to the writer as to the readers. Many fiction writers, for example, have stated that in spinning narratives they are not merely providing entertainment or an aesthetic experience; they are, in fact, retelling variations of their own personal experiences—even if fictionalized—to gain a reaction or response. Oral language often provides a similar service. For instance, "idle" chat is anything but idle; it is a low-key exchange of ideas, problems, and information that allows both speaker and listener to explore and verify their perceptions and ideas.

Human beings use language to control experience as well. We produce language to become more than passive consumers of perceptions in the real world. We want and intend to shape it, control it, and much of the language we produce is designed to present our own perceptions of "what's happening" and to guide other people into sharing that perception.

The intriguing thing about the process of making language— talking or writing—is that it involves exploration and discovery of language itself. That is, as we speak and write, creating language to fit our particular statement or message, we learn about how language functions. In fact, the content of a message and the form of language in which it is cast cannot be separated. "You don't know a thing until you've said it" is one way of expressing this relationship. Another way is the exclamation, "How do I know what I'm going to say until I've said it?"

Briefly, here is how the language as a process of discovery works: Every human being, from age two on has developed some understanding of the language system, based not on grammar and spelling books but on imitation, synthesis, and generalization. The baby is immersed in a language environment and figures out how it works. This is precisely the way in which Johnny and Jane learned that "Fido" was a two-phoneme sound which applied to the dog, and in this way they moved toward longer and longer utterances. They listened to language, generalized their understanding, and tested out new possibilities for its use.

Psycholinguists have done some fascinating research with children as language learners to create a model of the process. They spend a day with a child who is at the early stages of language acquisition—putting together two- and three-word sentences: "Fido dog." "Mommy come." "Bye-bye Daddy." After recording the child's utterances, they construct a "baby grammar" and lexicon—a description of the child's sentence patterns and his or her working vocabulary. On the basis of this elementary grammar they make predictions about the kinds of utterances that are possible and unlikely for the child. Following up with additional visits with the child, the linguists have found three interesting things. First, children do, indeed, produce predictable utterances; they intuit the structural relationships of English well enough to understand how the language works, and once it is done, they follow the rules, no matter how elementary. Second, many predictable but previously unheard utterances actually turn up in the child's conversation. That is, even the youngest child creates language structures, new for him or her, that follow the rules of English. Thus, language learning can be shown to be more than imitation of the utterances of adults; it is a creative process right from the start. Third, the child also makes mistakes, but uses those "errors" to learn more about the language. For the child errors are anything but fatal; they prove to be highly productive in discovering the limits of English.

Baby grammars do not remain fixed. Children learn language structures so rapidly at the two-year-old stage that one would literally have to construct grammars on a weekly basis to explain how the child is learning. But by age four or five, the syntactic growth levels off; Johnny and Jane will have mastered most of the syntax known by an adult. Not that they will speak like adults; they obviously will have the thoughts and vocabulary of five-year-olds. Nevertheless their mastery of sentence structures is largely complete. Language growth does not cease at this point, however. Language learning also involves such complex matters as rhetoric, style, and logic. Throughout their lives people are constantly engaged in inventing new ways of saying things, through success or failure, imitation and intuition.

Let's age Johnny and Jane up to fourth grade, age nine or ten, to see this process at work. The kids, watching TV ads, learn that a new kiddie thriller is playing at the Bijou and decide that tonight's the night to go. They then turn on the ten-year-old Language and Logic Machine and start working on Mom and Dad. "Why can't we go?" says Jane. (Do you remember your composition teacher who always said, "You must give me *reasons* for your opinions?") "Everybody else is going to go," says Johnny, attempting to apply group pressure. "Besides, we need to have seen it for our social studies project," adds Jane, not-too-subtly trying to link this film with a better cause ("coat-tailing it," in political jargon). "And we can stop by the store to pick up the milk," throws in Johnny (a variation on coat-tailing with a little bit of red herring thrown in). In desperation, Mother or Father shouts, "Stop all this *argument!* We'll hear no more about it!" This almost shuts off the Language and Logic Machine, but Jane sniffles twice and adds, "You're mean" (*argumentum ad hominem*).

Argument!? Who taught those kids that stuff? Not the public schools, to be certain; the schools are much too busy with spelling and vocabulary drills. Where did Johnny and Jane learn this incredible display of languaging and reasoning strategies? In fact, they learned by the same process through which they learned "Fido dog," but on a larger scale. They learned by seeing and hearing language, by perceiving experience and observing behavior, by exploring language and testing it out. You can predict fairly certainly that before they go to bed tonight, Johnny and Jane will try one last ploy, having learned from their failures: "Mommy, Daddy, if we're good tomorrow, can we go see the movie?"

Implications for Schooling

Language and thinking are hopelessly (and happily) intertwined. Language provides a major basis for our perception, our cognition, our contacts with the world. We use it to know ourselves and others, to explore and understand the world. We even use language as a tool in discovering itself, which is to say that we learn to use language by using it, testing it out in a variety of situations, and keeping "what works" in our language repertoire. The fully literate person uses language in every part of his or her life, not just as a tool for communication, but as a medium for *knowing*.

It is on the concept of literacy as a process of discovering and knowing that this book is based. I want to suggest that English studies are truly and naturally interdisciplinary, for the process of knowing, based on language, makes literacy central to *every* human activity. Whether students are doing science, history, shop, or the dishes, they are engaged in languaging processes—perceiving, thinking, communicating—and learning even more about language.

For a long time, English teachers have had a motto, "Every teacher a teacher of English." They would like history teachers to take over part of the instruction of how to write history papers, for science teachers to explain how to read in their field. Subject matter teachers have understandably balked at this idea, no doubt having seen English teachers struggling out the door of the high school on Friday at three o'clock with a briefcase full of themes for weekend grading.

But at the same time, the call for "every teacher a teacher of English" is a bit after the fact, since *every* teacher is already deeply immersed in teaching literacy. When the science teacher begins by saying, "This, class, is a test tube," he is, of course, dealing in literacy; so is the biology teacher when she starts talking about classification systems; so is the mathematician when he presents the idea of set theory; so is the history teacher when she asks, "What are the three causes of the Civil War?"; so is the shop teacher when he says, "Before we build anything, you've got to know and understand how to use tools"; so is the driver's ed. teacher when she tells the class there will be a test on the rules of the road tomorrow.

Central to every subject is teaching the processes of knowing and understanding that subject. The chemist teaches the ways of chemistry; the driver's ed. teacher teaches the ways of the road; the historian tries to show students how history is created and understood. These are learning processes and they are all based in the manipulation of language. And because literacy is a process of knowing, English teachers are equally involved in the teaching of other disciplines, simply by the fact of their teaching young people to use language more successfully.

In Part II of this book I will present teaching ideas and strategies for interdisciplinary programs. I won't presume to tell science teachers what they "ought" to be doing; nor will I step into the domain of the historian or business education teacher. Nor will I ask English teachers to abandon literature and teach science. I will, however, show how the concept of literacy as a process of knowing can make interdisciplinary teaching natural and the teaching of reading and writing a good deal richer than it has been.

Johnny and Jane Go to School

In this chapter I have attempted to supply what amounts to a mini-lecture on the nature of language learning and language acquisition. To do the topic justice would involve reviewing volumes of material. Readers who want to learn more are referred to the bibliography at the end of this book. To be more concrete, however, I want to illustrate the implications of the discussion for teaching by presenting the school careers of the hypothetical Johnny and Jane. I will contrast the current state of literacy instruction, as represented by a series of "typical" schools, with some of the better alternatives that may be available to them.

If Johnny and Jane were to enroll in what I will label Typical Elementary School, characteristic of the many elementary schools I have visited in all parts of the country, they will find themselves immersed in basic skills instruction with contemporary expertise and technological vengeance. Before being allowed to read or write, they will be sent through a maze of tests: state-wide examinations, district-wide tests, IQ tests, and individualized skill tests. On the basis of this diagnosis, they will be programmed into highly structured activities in workbooks, basal readers, skillbooks, labs, and modules. (People who don't believe that basics are being taught nowadays ought to have a close look at Typical Elementary.) Such real language activities as story hour, show and tell, and library will be frills or rewards, and most of the reading and writing the children do will center on instructions and workbooks. Johnny and Jane, like so many elementary school children in this country, will spend six, seven, or eight years in pursuing the skill maze, doing well on tests, but growing up with astonishingly little experience with language use.

By contrast, I would hope they might wind up at a school I will name the Dewey School (after the father of learn-by-doing education)—a school that represents the potential of English studies in the 1980s. At Dewey they would find themselves immersed in an environment that promotes literacy. Instead of being phonicked half to death, they would find themselves being read to, coming to recognize words that crop up in their everyday lives, learning to shape letters and words in books and stories of their own creation, and engaging ceaselessly in actual contact with language: reading real books (not just readers); writing stories, plays, poems, notes, and letters; playacting through mime, charade, improvisation, and skits; and having their talk channeled in productive ways into show and tell, tête-à-tête's, conversations, group talks, and so on.

At the junior high school level Johnny and Jane may enroll in Typical JHS, and if that happens, the fun and language play of the elementary years will be over. "It's time to get down to business," somebody will tell them. "High school is just around the corner." If that happens, all the language exploration of Dewey will go out the window, and students will begin language study "in earnest." Out will come grammar books with materials on parts of speech, the structure of sentences, and above all an overwhelming concern for "saying things right." Creative and imaginative writing will disappear almost entirely, and work will begin on "exposition," with instruction on the paragraph, the topic sentence, the clincher sentence, and so on. The only time they will put pencil to paper will be in multiple choice or fill-in-the-blank tests of "sentence sense," or the writing of "model" paragraphs with prescribed topic sentences. They will also get another creation of their teachers designed to take the fun out of reading—the book report.

With luck, though, Johnny and Jane might enroll at Piaget Junior High, named after an influential Swiss psychologist who speculated about the stages of cognitive growth in youngsters. The PJHS teachers would have read Piaget and other developmental psychologists and would know that the children were entering a crucial stage in life—adolescence—during which they would grow from "babies" to being fully conscious, "self" conscious young adults. The teachers would know, too, that this growth is deeply tied up with language, so the literacy program at Piaget would involve having the students write and talk from the emerging self, about that self, gradually widening the circle of discourse to include friends and family. Although this writing could degenerate into undisciplined "self-expression," the teachers would also recognize that Johnny and Jane were growing more conscious of others in the world around them, and so the literacy program would also introduce the idea of writing for audiences. The youngsters' reading interests would expand with their writing and thinking, and they would move in their guided, self-selected reading away from "kiddie lit" into books that deal more and more with young adult and adult concerns. The natural voraciousness of their reading that led them, in sixth grade, to read the entire Nancy Drew and Hardy Boys series cover to cover, would not be dammed up, but channeled, so that their literacy interests would continue to expand.

Then it is on to high school. With luck, they'll avoid Typical High School, for if they wind up at THS, they will be told, "OK, the junior high fun and games are over. You can't get away with that stuff up here. After all, college is just around the corner." At THS they will be plunged directly into something called "Communications Skills I," where the English language is really broken down into fundamental, basic, rock-bottom nuts and bolts. Six weeks are spent on grammar (since nobody can remember whether it was taught in junior high or not, and the high school teachers don't respect the jhs people anyway), six weeks on the paragraph, six more weeks on the three-paragraph theme, followed by a wrap-up unit on oral communications, which will culminate in a five-minute speech to the class. After the ritual of Comm. I they will be free to enter into the elective system, where courses look a lot more interesting, with names like "Science Fiction," "Radio and TV Language," "American Heroes." They will find, however, that the so-called smart kids steer away from those attractive courses and pick ones that sound as if they came from a college catalog: "The Theme of the Hero in Western Literature" or "Introduction to the Humanities." In either case, Johnny and Jane will find that individual reading has pretty much disappeared while the class concentrates on certain novels, read by everyone and explicated by the teacher in lecture discussions, and that the writing of themes has disappeared altogether, the teachers assuming that writing was mastered in Comm I. Across the hall, the history and science teachers will complain that Johnny and Jane can't write, then assign multiple choice and short answer tests that don't even require the writing of a full sentence.

Alternatively, the kids might get to go to William Toorey Harris High School (named after a nineteenth-century Commissioner of Education whose interdisciplinary interests ranged from the evolution of the American "high" school to the feeding of starving elk in Alaska). At Harris High the teachers would also have read Piaget (and, to top it off, they would actually have looked at their students to see if Piaget was right). They would know that Johnny and Jane are getting to be pretty sophisticated human beings, with exploring, inquiring minds, ready to soak up experiences, ideas, concepts at an incredible rate. Instead of giving the kids predigested thoughts about literature, mankind, and pseudo-philosophy, the English teachers would set up a series of literacy based explorations into issues and ideas. The English class would send the young people running off to historical archives, science laboratories, politicians' offices, businesses, and industries to learn and report. In history class, Johnny might find himself involved in writing a cultural history of the community, and in the physics class, Jane's teacher would be quite willing to accept a well-drafted piece of science fiction instead of a term report. Perhaps Johnny and Jane would even be able to enroll in a new experimental wing at Harris, where traditional course divisions have been abolished and the curriculum would simply be split into two units—one in the sciences, the other in humanities—where their individualized work would be guided by a resource team consisting of a humanities person, a scientist, and a good counselor.

Then Johnny and Jane might go on to a university. Of course they have the option of not going on for more education, and if they had been to Harris High, they would enter the community with a good sense of themselves and their language; they would be fully literate, in short. But for purposes of discussing schooling, I want to continue their story for another four years.

If they enroll at Typical U., one of the first characters they will encounter is their freshman English prof who will tell them: "Forget all the crap you learned at high school. That juvenile stuff is over for good." The textbooks for the course will be the 18th edition of the *Hall-Random Handbook,* by Smock and Pequod, and *Selected Modern Essays,* by Wiggins and Turmot. Weekly themes will be rigorously corrected by the prof or his/her teaching assistant, and Johnny and Jane will be told regularly that their writing is muddled, awkward, incoherent, insubstantial, and non-academic. They will believe it, too. But fortunately, outside of freshman English, nobody will ask them to write much anyhow; like the teachers at THS, the TU profs would rather complain about their writing than actually assign any. Their reading will be pretty much limited to fat textbooks, but if they are not totally exhausted, Johnny and Jane might read a novel over Christmas break.

On the other hand, they might be able to enroll in Morrill University (after Justin Morrill, sponsor of the Land Grant Act of 1872, which opened up college education to rural students as well as the children of urban professionals). At Morrill, they would enroll in a freshman English course taught by a prof who had given some thought to their stage in life. He would know that getting away from home and coming to college were some of the most traumatic things that will ever happen to Johnny and Jane. He would know that they were frightened by Morrill U., that they were wondering how they compared with the other 40,000 students enrolled there. So he or she would begin the course by letting them read and write and then read each others' writing about the natural human concerns of adulthood and being out on one's own. When the prof was certain that their natural voices hadn't been extinguished by the institution, he or she would go on to deal with "practical" matters. "Look," the prof might say, "there's no way in the world that in high school you could have anticipated the reading and writing problems you'll face here. You're all competent people, and you've been using the English language successfully since you were two. Let's look at the language maze that you're now in and learn to solve it." So the class would examine the language demanded in academia and learn how to adopt writing for this new audience. Johnny and Jane would also enroll in other English courses that would invite them to read and write on a variety of issues and topics, this time, however, pausing to consider aesthetic and critical concerns and the nature of language and literature as well. They might sign up for a science course where the professor would have them read popular science books along with the chemistry text, and a history course that would open with a succession of historical novels ("So you can sense how people felt, not just know what they did," the prof would say). In the junior year they might elect an interdisciplinary program and find themselves in tutorial sessions with dozens of different professors, following programs that had so dissolved interdisciplinary boundaries that nobody seemed to know (or care) what anybody's "home department" and "field of specialization" happened to be.

If Johnny and Jane pursue the traditional track through the schools (and college), their story will pretty much end there. After their last diploma, their bout with literacy will be over: No more grammar, no more books, no more teachers' linguistic hooks. They will settle into suburbia, and watch a lot of TV. They will never touch a pencil except to write a grocery list and never pick up a book unless it has already been on TV. They will raise kids, and sooner or later, somebody will say of those kids, "What's the matter with them? They can't even read and write!"

On the other hand, this hypothetical narrative concludes, if Johnny and Jane were to be schooled at Dewey Elementary, Piaget JHS, and Harris High, and if they were to continue their training at Morrill U., it might just be that they would emerge from the schools as fully literate adults—comfortable with the language, able to use it flexibly and creatively in a range of situations. They would raise kids, and those kids would watch some TV, but Johnny and Jane would also talk with their children and read to them. Without much luck at all, those kids would turn out to be just as smart and literate—masters of just as many basic skills—as their Mom and Dad.

4

Setting Priorities:
From Ideal to Real

Without attempting to evoke a "crisis" atmosphere, I think it is safe to say that the future of both public education and literacy education in this country are very much in question at the moment. Public dissatisfaction with both is great. School enrollments are in decline; the "white flight" to the suburbs continues; and inflation makes maintaining the *status quo* increasingly expensive. Taxpayers are rightly in revolt, and many of the tax limitation measures being passed by the voters are having first impact on the schools by drastically curtailing funds. Although we acknowledge the need to make major changes in the way literacy is taught in the schools, it becomes increasingly difficult to think of evolution and improvement at all: "Survival" is the word of the moment.

The danger in this atmosphere is the tendency to seek short- rather than long-range solutions to the problems that are perceived. Americans want a pill that will offer "symptomatic relief" rather than seeking the more complicated (and conceivably more expensive) cures that may heal the ailment permanently. Thus, in one major city, when an area superintendent of schools learned that a high percentage of eighth grade students could not read or write up to grade level, he announced that the failing children would be held back until their basic skills were up to par. This action received wide press coverage and considerable editorial praise; someone was at last taking a "tough" stand on literacy education, doing away with unearned promotions. Yet few people paused to consider the long-range implications of this action. In the first place, a thoughtful critic might have pointed out, it is unlikely that a single year of remedial work would bring even a small percentage of those students up to grade level. Literacy problems stretch over all the elementary years and also reflect family experiences. One simply cannot remediate eight or more years of unsuccessful work with a single year of schooling. What then? Did the superintendent intend to hold back those failing again (presumably along with a new crop of failures)? The long-range implication of his short-range scheme is a set of eighth grade classrooms packed to the ceilings with high-school-age non-readers. Can anyone seriously propose that as desirable? Even more important, while flunking students may be dramatic and attract front page headlines, it does absolutely nothing to change the school system that obviously helped to create its own failures. Holding students back, in short, creates an apparently simple solution, one that gives taxpayers a sense that "something is being done," yet does not solve fundamental problems.

Many of the solutions to the literacy crisis are stopgap. Students can't read, so the administration, local or state, institutes a new round of standardized tests (instead of buying new books for students to read). Writing skills are said to be in decline, so teachers double their efforts to teach grammar and spelling (and assign fewer compositions than ever). While these approaches appear as taking direct action and may seem to solve a problem, in fact they deal only with the tip of the iceberg. It is predictable that if we seek quick and easy solutions to the literacy crisis now, we will merely see the same problems re-emerging, magnified a dozen times or so, a decade or two later. Reading and writing instruction are time consuming; they require the concerted efforts of educators and parents working over a long period of time. They are expensive. But in spite of the time and energy required, working on long-range solutions will, I predict, prove much less costly and far more satisfactory than the quick and superficial actions many recommend.

As we begin to think of educational reform, of shaping the schools of the future, we are faced with a problem described in an old gag about a sculptor. When asked about how he created a magnificent statue of a horse out of a chunk of granite, he replied, "It's easy; you look at the rock and chip away the parts that don't look like a horse."

The metaphor is a useful one for education: To create a better educational system, we need to visualize what we want, then set about chipping away the parts that don't fit. But like most metaphors, this one also raises puzzles. For instance, in contrast to the sculptor, many educators and parents don't really know what the horse should look like; that is, we don't have a clear vision of what we want the end product of education to resemble. Thus in educational reform we often start madly chipping away without a master plan, or, perhaps more aptly, we start hacking away on an ear or a hoof without much regard for the rest of the animal. The school system that has been created by this process looks like part horse and part kangaroo or, perhaps, a multi-headed horse facing several directions at once.

Further, in education the stone that we chip away also has significance, for the chips are people and programs. Indiscriminate "retrenchment" has not, in the past decade, solved anything and is, at best, a crude and often inhuman way of bringing about reform. A clean sweep is hopelessly ineffectual and, at the same time, wasteful of human resources. Writing in *The People and Their Schools* (1975), Mario Fantini suggests that educational reform must take as its aim "to keep the best of what we now have and to expand the framework of public institutions through increased diversity, options, and choice." The model is an appealing one. It states that it is not necessary to clean out all the old and bad before proceeding to create something new and more positive.

The schools need to have a vision of what they want to be and what they can become. In order to do that, the schools should begin to practice what I call Plan A/Plan B thinking. *Plan A* is an idealized, best-of-all-possible-worlds vision of what the school unit—be it district, township, city, school building, or department—sees as its shape ten, twenty, or more years into the future. *Plan B* describes what is possible, a program based on Plan A that will allow the unit to approach its ideal as closely, yet realistically, as possible.

Most of the school systems that I have observed don't have anything remotely resembling a Plan A. "We don't need that kind of pie-in-the-sky thinking," the argument runs. "We can hardly pay the fuel bills now; how can we think about an ideal plan for the future?" But without a Plan A school evolution is obviously piecemeal, with random growth and decay.

Further, Plan A is important because without it, one can't write a sensible Plan B, the plan that compromises with reality, yet forms a basis of action for what the department or school or district ultimately aims to do. Plan B recognizes that we're not all perfect sculptors, but that one can make a pretty passable horse out of less than ideal materials and with less than Praxitelean hands. Plan B aims at making the best-of-all-possible schools in the real world of today.

To illustrate Plan A/Plan B thinking I want to introduce a mythical community, Everytown, U.S.A. Everytown is typically American: It has heavy and light industry in its inner city and thus has attracted urban problems of housing, financing, and race relations; it is in a farm belt, and rural kids are bused into its schools; the executives have their own enclave of expensive homes near the city limits that creates a kind of suburbia. In short, Everytown faces many of the problems of communities everywhere. The school board of Everytown has created a Literacy Planning Committee representing parents and students, administrators and teachers, and that group has met to hash out Plan A for language instruction. Their ideal, best-of-all-possible-worlds vision for Everytown might run something like this:

"In the future, literacy education in Everytown should become interdisciplinary and system-wide. The word—written and spoken—should be at the heart of all subjects as students explore new knowledge and their own experiences through language. We envision that by the year 2000 the outmoded school buildings of Everytown will be replaced by a new kind of school called Community Learning Centers, each designed for manageable numbers of students—five hundred or less—of all ages, including adults. These learning centers will be staffed by interdisciplinary tutors, who will work carefully with each learner to plot out a course of instruction appropriate to his or her needs. The full resources of the community—including business and industry, the universities, and the library systems—will be available to tutors and learners at these Community Centers. Adjunct to these centers, in effect, replacing the old obsolete school buildings, will be a central resources core housing microfilm and microfiche collections, computer services, word processing services, etc. that are available to each learner."

That, of course, is *my* own vision for Everytown. Each group should come up with its own vision, but it should be every bit as pie-in-the-sky, as unashamedly optimistic, as my own. Plan A sketches out the best horse, the best school system that the community can envision.

Next, however, the Literacy Planning Committee must acknowledge reality. It would prove too expensive to discard the present, serviceable school buildings and replace them with brand new learning centers. Further, cross-age teaching doesn't seem to the Committee to be especially practical, so the traditional system of splitting students into elementary, junior, and senior high school will have to be preserved for the immediate future. Pleasant though it would be, creating a totally individualized system is too expensive, so Everytown might need to maintain some divisions into classes and courses. Given the nature of the teachers' training, some disciplinary divisions are necessary.

So the Committee begins work on its Plan B, which consists of taking the key conceptual elements of Plan A and plugging them into a real setting. Thus, even though a complete network of community learning centers is impractical, the Committee recognizes that a number of educational alternatives exist in the community already—arts workshops, learning exchanges, and public libraries. Why not include in Plan B provisions to draw these into the schooling process more completely? Why not give credits for appropriate out-of-school experiences? Even though abolishing grade level distinctions altogether may be impractical, the Committee might call for grade level clustering—(k–1–2) (3–5)—in the elementary years and ungraded upper-level courses for students of all levels at the high school. Since interdisciplinary studies are at the heart of Plan A (as outlined above), the Committee might propose abolishing the concept of "departments" at the secondary level, to be replaced by two major divisions—science and humanities—with subsequent reordering of courses. Plan B, then, talks about the future vision in terms of present possibilities.

Of course, even Plan B is not without its impracticalities. When the faculty at Everytown High School hears about the abolition of departments, it goes into orbit. Everybody knows that Mr. Acid, head of Chemistry, cannot possibly get along with Miss Chromosome, the dynamic chair of Biology; that old Scrooge of Economics will never work hand-in-hand with Ms. Hindsight of History. And everybody thinks that Mr. Webster of the English Department is greedy and ambitious, trying to use the concept of interdisciplinary literacy to create his own little verbal empire and to shore up a dying discipline.

At this point Plan B must evolve further, into a series of schemes and plans developed by groups and individuals. For example, even though Webster alienates his colleagues, members of the English Department sponsor a series of seminars on science/English and history/English courses with their colleagues. Chromosome discovers that she can assign writing in her biology classes without having to become a proofreader, and in exchange for English Department help, she produces a list of recommended biology paperback titles for addition to English libraries.

Plan B can evolve within the classes of individual teachers. Frustrated by the unwillingness of colleagues in other departments to cooperate, an English teacher (or science teacher or history teacher) begins offering interdisciplinary reading/writing work with his or her own class. With the school system unable to provide significant numbers of alternative community learning centers, a teacher decides to offer guided independent study and community-based assignments in her senior class. The strength and purpose of having Plan B is to remain conscious of where you are in relationship to your ideal, Plan A.

Perhaps the most important principle is that communities, school districts, buildings, and individual teachers must recognize their own needs and seek solutions to their own problems. Change cannot be mandated by external agencies: state departments of education, Federal programs. Everytown will solve its literacy problems only when teachers, parents, and administrators are willing to discuss their problems, visualize their own future, and design a plan to realize the best of what they can become.

At the same time, there are concerns and needs that cut across all schools and districts, from small mountain schools in Tennessee and Maine to urban schools in Houston or Baltimore or Boise. In this chapter I will offer ten global priorities for literacy education. I present these not as a series of *fiats,* but as a starting point for school and community discussion, the development of plans A and B.

I. Literacy as a Learn-by-Doing Skill

Literacy programs should be based on reading and writing experiences, not principally on the study of literacy-related skills. To say that young people learn to read by reading and learn to write by writing seems, at first glance, to be another simplistic solution. Yet teaching reading and writing this way is difficult and requires skilled teachers. For instance, as soon as students are allowed to write regularly, teachers find themselves faced with mountains of papers to correct, mark, grade, or comment upon.

Given typical high school class loads of 150 or more students, it is not surprising that English teachers tend to retreat into a more manageable, short-range approach—teaching "skills." Other subject teachers, seeing the number of papers to be corrected, naturally shy away from assigning writing, or suggest that mechanical matters be learned in English classes or somehow handled by the English staff.

Similarly, though teachers know (or sense) that their students ought to do much more guided independent reading than they do, a great many school classrooms do not have the appropriate materials. In the typical schoolroom one *doesn't* see a healthy supply of books. Instead, one will discover the standard issue anthology or text, or students reading a single novel under the direction of the teacher. In addition, teachers argue that a good individualized reading program is too complex to administer, and that school budgets are such that the materials are not available.

However, underlying these rationales—which admittedly have some basis in fact—lies another, more dangerous premise, one seldom spoken: "Children won't learn if I don't 'teach' them." Teachers (and parents) have a sneaking suspicion that children do not learn without adult intervention. But as I have shown in Chapter 3, the learning of language is largely a naturalistic process, and both parents and teachers have ample evidence of the natural learning skills of young people in other areas of their lives. Yet, uneasy at the concept of letting kids learn on their own, teachers intervene at regular intervals. The net effect is that the teachers *do* become too busy to let students read and write. The machinery of literacy instruction swallows up the practice.

If the schools were to cut out much of the workbook study and drill that passes for "teaching," there would be plenty of time to concentrate on letting students use skills in reading, writing, speaking, and listening projects. Similarly, if all the money currently being invested in expensive hardbound anthologies, paperback workbooks, skill labs, and kits were reinvested in inexpensive materials of literacy—paperback books, magazines, and newspapers—the schools could very quickly increase the amount of "hands-on" literacy materials.

To show the possibilities, here are four illustrations of productive programs:

1. Daniel Fader's *Hooked on Books* (1976) illustrates both the wisdom and the practicality of a program that puts literacy materials in every classroom. Fader has shown how, working with community paperback distributors, schools can get a supply of paperbacks, magazines, and newspapers for each teacher in the building. As many schools have discovered, *not* buying a single set of conventional anthologies frees funds for the purchase of hundreds of paperbacks. In schools that try Fader's free reading program, actual book use by young people has risen extraordinarily.

2. At Gardner Junior High School in Lansing, Michigan, the English faculty, working closely with the librarian, established one book a week as a reading quota for each student. Reading time and guidance are provided, and although not all students reach the goal, the students at Gardner read vastly more than their peers at other, more traditional schools.

3. Teachers of English in a Vancouver, British Columbia, high school attacked the writing problem by simply determining that every student in the school would write a full composition at least ten times each twenty-week semester. While that number does seem excessive, the teachers found that this quota left them with an acceptable theme-correcting burden of approximately seventy-five papers each week (assuming a class load of 150 students), yet resulted in a six-fold increase in the amount of writing actually assigned. (The teachers confessed that most of them had only been assigning writing once or twice a term anyway.) Across six years of secondary-level education, this program would mean that students would write carefully supervised compositions 120 times during their careers. One can predict that these students would emerge confident writers, skilled in composition. While other subject teachers obviously cannot assign ten themes a term,

is it unrealistic to expect that a child might write, say, two to three formal pieces each term, plus notes and reports?

4. Peter Elbow has written an exciting book called *Writing Without Teachers* (1974), which describes classes where students learn to write simply by writing and then discussing their own writing with one another. While Elbow describes this as a "teacherless" class, in fact the teacher involves himself or herself both by serving as an editor and by helping students learn to respond to each other's writing more effectively. The program cuts down on the paper-correcting burden and allows the teacher to serve in the role of editor/adviser. In addition, the approach has the very sound pedagogical effect of helping writers learn to take responsibility for learning to revise their own work.

II. Sequence and Articulation

Literacy programs must lead to continuous growth rather than offering isolated experiences or training. Having "sequence" (connection between grade levels) and "articulation" (connection between units of the school system) are two long-standing ideals for education, the assigned task of generations of curriculum committees and task forces. Yet in the area of literacy instruction, neither sequence nor articulation has ever been achieved to any real degree of satisfaction. Students go from grade to grade experiencing isolated language instruction without much of a master plan in evidence. If a teacher likes writing, the students write often; but they may easily wind up in a class the following year where no writing is done. Students may stick to the basal text one year but find themselves turned loose in a free-reading library the next.

Achieving sequence and articulation has been complicated by a tradition of having the direction of school systems determined by higher levels rather than by the personal growth patterns of children. For example, when I was a first-year teacher, my principal told me that I had been selected to represent the school at an articulation conference to be held at the state university. I thought it was an honor, but as it turned out, everybody else on the faculty had made the trip and refused to go again. A week or two before the conference I was to collect a set of student papers and mail them to the English department at the university. There, a member of the freshman writing staff graded the writing according to university standards, and at the conference he met with me to tell me how my students measured up. They didn't, of course. According to the instructor, only two of my thirty-two students could pass a "simple" freshman writing task. He gave me a booklet showing how instructors graded themes (four misspellings constituted an automatic F) and suggested that I apply it in my teaching (which, he implied, didn't measure up any better than the writing of my students).

Aside from the absurdity of grading high school students by college freshman standards and the questionable wisdom of teaching high school courses by college techniques, this experience was typical of the kind of articulation that has grown up. Students are expected to measure up to whatever standard the next higher level tries to enforce. The word gets passed down: The colleges tell high schools that the preparation of entering students is abominable. The high school teachers tell the junior high teachers that their students don't measure up to high school standards. The jhs people then lament the lack of attention paid to essentials in the grades and apply the pressure there. An extreme result of this pressure was reflected in a talk I heard a few years ago by a former elementary teacher who had moved into college teaching. Speaking to her former colleagues, she said she regretted her shortness of vision as an elementary teacher. Back then, she reported, she had always concentrated on getting her fourth grade pupils ready for the fifth grade. In fact, she said, she should have been thinking of preparing them for college all along. Why, one asks, should anyone concentrate the entire fourth grade year on preparation for anything other than the *present?* Wouldn't it be more satisfactory to work hard on fourth grade reading and writing activities than to worry about unknown tasks in the future, be they in fifth grade or thirteenth?

The top-heavy nature of the system creates the related phenomena of *skills lists* and *checkpoint examinations,* both of which prove to be generally ineffectual. Any teacher who has served on a curriculum committee can testify to the arbitrariness of the typical division of skills and materials among the grades. Frequently skills or goals wind up in one grade level simply because there is "no room" any place else. Reading material is selected, not because it is appropriate, but because it fits the symmetry of a curriculum guide. In one school I visited, the skills list was developed by going through the index of a college-level usage handbook. In another, individual skills were written on index cards and taped to the walls of the board of education meeting room; curriculum planning consisted of moving index cards around under grade-level headings until everyone was satisfied that the list "looked right" and all lists were the same length. In yet another school district, sequence was nothing more than a grade-level index of forbidden books: Teachers were forbidden to use certain literature, not because it was too difficult or inappropriate, but because the senior-level teachers liked to teach it and wanted it saved for their college prep and advance placement courses.

Checkpoint examinations, ranging from a simple eighth grade grammar test to the complexity of the New York State Regents or a California high school graduation examination provide barriers to which instructors are supposed to direct their teaching, and thus are aimed at securing a degree of uniformity and consistency in teaching. But once again, imposing levels from the top fails. Most checkpoint exams deal with a handful of superficial basics rather than substance, and tend to drag all teaching down to a common level. Instead of ensuring quality, they guarantee mediocrity.

There seem to me two broad solutions to the problem of sequence and articulation:

First, teachers at all levels need to learn to talk to each other with a high degree of respect and professionalism. The academic totem pole which perceives college teachers as above secondary, secondary above elementary, must be toppled. Further, discussions among levels must center on students and their needs, not the professed or perceived needs of institutions higher up.

Second, sequential programs should center on the developmental stages, both linguistic and psychological, of young people, rather than on discrete language skills or activities. In the 1960s there was considerable discussion of sequence but the programs of the sixties were mostly centered on the *content* of various disciplines—chemistry, math, rhetoric, grammar—and, in fact, bore little relationship to the students and their abilities or needs. As we speak of sequence in the eighties, we are considering a less rigid approach to curriculum, one in which students' experiences flow naturally and logically from one to another. In Chapter 7, I will offer a model of one such curriculum based loosely on G. Robert Carlsen's stages of growth in literacy appreciation. The work of James Britton and his colleagues at the London Institute (1975), which is centered on the ways students use writing at various times in their school careers, offers another possibility. For such a curriculum to be developed locally, teachers will need to learn a great deal more about their students, not through formal research studies or standardized tests, but through actual study of young people and the language that they use.

III. Knowing Students

We need literacy programs based on an understanding of how students use language and how they learn to use it better, not on assumptions about what students "should," "ought to," or "must" learn. This is another way of saying that teachers should deal with the language skills of students as those students arrive in their classes, recognizing and building on existing competencies, rather than striving to reach pre-established goals. To take students "where they are" and take them "as far as you can" is an old maxim—a good one, I think—but it implies learning about the interests and language of students in more detail than the schools have traditionally. Further, it requires eschewing reliance on standardized tests and being willing to look directly at the language students produce and consume.

English teachers are often quite naïve and thoughtless in the comments they make and the assumptions they adopt when they discuss students' language. Here are three direct quotes from teachers meetings I have attended recently: "Most of the students in my class cannot even write a complete sentence." "What my students need is work on adjectives, because they don't write clearly." "Isn't it terrible the Chicano can spend twelve years in this country and never learn a word of English?" As a matter of fact, almost all students can write at least one, and probably many "complete sentences"; the problems with unclear student writing are quite unrelated to knowledge of adjectives; and Mexican-Americans generally have knowledge of a great many words of English (learned with or without the help of English teachers). Too often teachers approach students' language with a set of adult, college-educated expectations. They perceive students' language through grammatical and rhetorical categories that they themselves only came to master late in their academic careers. Thus a statement that seventh graders "need" work in "the topic sentence" is little more than imposition of an adult rhetorical concept—the topic sentence—on children who often have no need to write such sentences.

One English teacher who has done precisely the kind of close observation of children's language I suggest is Daniel Dyer, a middle school teacher in Aurora, Ohio. Dyer conducted what he called "free writing Friday" for two years (1976). On Fridays, his students wrote on any topic of their choice. Over that two-year span, the students produced thousands of pieces of writing, which Dyer then collected and categorized into: *Personal Experience, Letter to Teacher, Fiction, Poetry, Exposition,* and *Miscellaneous.* He found a number of interesting things. For instance, his seventh grade girls were much more willing to write their personal experiences in the form of a letter to the teacher than were the boys, who tended to treat their own experiences in fictional form through narratives (something that tells us a good deal about how society trains young men and young women to handle their emotions).

Most intriguing, however, is that whether writing letters or fiction, Dyer's students did a predominant amount of their composition in narrative (storytelling) modes. Only 2 percent of the writing was in the area of expository writing. Seventh graders—many for the first time in their lives—are learning to express their emotional experiences and problems. Writing narratives is a perfect medium for their level of exploration.

Yet in the typical school "scope and sequence" chart, seventh grade is precisely the point where curriculum makers, quite arbitrarily, have decided it is time for students to learn to write expository paragraphs and essays. In far too many schools, narrative writing from seventh graders is discouraged. Students begin writing dishwatery expository paragraphs, "In my opinion, there are three reasons why. . . ." The "badness" of much junior high expository writing is a result, in part, of the fact that the students are simply not "there," linguistically or emotionally. An articulation program based on the personal growth of students (and following the pattern of Dyer's research) would suggest that we not force children out of a natural mode of expression into one with which they are not comfortable, but that we teach narrative, setting up a writing program where students become the most competent, versatile storytellers they possibly can.

On the reading side of the curriculum, two teachers in Wayland, Massachusetts, conducted informal research to explore the differences between readers and non-readers. Kathleen Lampert and Edna Saunders (1976) used a series of "homemade" attitude surveys to discover how the students felt about reading and about themselves as readers. They found one group of students who were "readers": They scored well on the school's standardized tests and indicated through the surveys that they enjoyed reading and employed it regularly in their lives outside school. Lampert and Saunders also found, predictably, a group of "unskilled non-readers," students who scored less well on the tests and who stayed away from print outside of school, perceiving themselves as poor readers. But a third group emerged: students whom Lampert and Saunders labeled "skilled non-readers." These students scored well on standardized tests (almost as well as the readers), and their school grades indicated that they were achieving satisfactorily in school. Yet, on the attitude scale the skilled non-readers

do not perceive themselves as readers or as coming from a reading background. Like the other non-readers, they express low interest in activities which are passive or represent a mediated interpretation of reality, such as reading news magazines or viewing documentaries on television. They also feel they learn best from explanation rather than from reading.

It is highly significant that almost any English program based on standardized tests and almost any traditionally articulated skills program would bypass this sizable portion of the school population. Having determined through a standardized test that the students had mastered basics, the school system would ignore them, missing altogether the fact that these "literate" students were non-users of their literacy skills.

Neither Dyer's research nor that done by Lampert and Saunders passes traditional criteria for formal educational research. The teachers did not collect data from random samples; they did not have control and experimental groups, closely matched. The results cannot be generalized beyond the town limits of Aurora, Ohio, or Wayland, Massachusetts. Nor, for that matter, should we be interested in pressing those results further. The importance of this research is that it provides models of what teachers can do inside the classroom to assess student interests, needs, and growth. Dyer, Lampert, and Saunders are the kinds of teachers you want to send your own children to, for instead of looking to the university or a standardized test for guidance, they are willing to look at students now, to assess who they are, what they can do, where they are going, and then to contribute to that growth in a sequential, articulated manner.

IV. Planning Time / Planning Autonomy

Literacy programs must be developed by the people who will conduct them—the teachers. As important as community planning and support may be, in the final analysis, teachers themselves must make the decisions as to what will be taught and how it will be taught. The kind of research I have described in the previous sections has important implications, because creating a systematic program, solidly based on an understanding of students' needs requires considerably more planning time than has traditionally been provided by the schools. In the Introduction to this book I suggested—only half facetiously—that it might be good for us to close the schools for a period to permit careful planning of the future of education. That being a Plan A-type goal, I'd be happy to settle for Plan B: simply guaranteeing that teachers have enough unscheduled time during the school year (and, ideally, both before and after) to consider carefully what they are doing. In *Crisis in the Classroom* (1970), Charles Silberman speaks of the "mindlessness" of education. In no small measure that lack of thoughtfulness simply mirrors the lack of thinking time that the schools provide for their employees.

By way of contrast, one of the most successful in-service programs I have seen has been conducted by Northwestern University at an English Curriculum Study Center directed by Professor Wallace Douglas. Through federal funds he was able to "buy time" away from the classroom for a number of elementary and secondary teachers. He brought them to the Center, and when they asked what they were supposed to do or accomplish, he simply told them, "Read what you want for a while. Read the books about teaching that you've wanted to read. Find a problem that troubles you in your teaching and read and think about that." Though they chafed at this lack of direction, some of the best teachers I have known are those who went through that experience of drifting, finding a direction, then pursuing certain goals in a kind of depth and detail that they never could have achieved while in the routine of teaching five classes a day, five days a week.

But external funding is not necessary to provide planning time. At least one school system has experimented with condensing class meetings into a four-day week by lengthening class periods by one fifth and doing away with study halls and unassigned or "empty" periods. This, in turn, created an open day at the end of the week to be used by teachers for planning and individualized conferences with students. Although the program had aroused some concern by its non-traditional nature, the teachers and students and parents in the community where it was tried found it to be more relaxing and at least as productive as a traditional five-day week (Stokes, 1975).

The traditional school planning time—in-service days, summer planning weeks, professional development days—can be used much more productively and positively than it has in the past. In-service days, for example, are often consumed by faculty meetings dealing with administrative matters that could just as easily be covered by a memo. Or, instead of listening to lectures conducted by outsiders, teachers could use scheduled time to write and implement Plans A and B.

Along with planning time, however, must come a revised conception of teacher autonomy, giving teachers responsibility and acknowledging their competence to develop the programs they must teach. Although the schools have long paid a kind of lip service to the notion of academic freedom—"the classroom is your castle"—administrators and the public have increasingly treated teachers as if they were irresponsible and incompetent. Nowhere has this been more evident than in the movement toward state-wide programs of accountability and assessment.

In its simplest form, "accountability" calls on teachers, first, to describe what they propose to do and, second, to assess whether or not it has been accomplished. Few teachers disagree with the general principle, and most are willing to be held accountable for their work. Yet most external accountability programs have been based on the suspicion that teachers have been "getting away with something," and the process has been used not so much to ensure quality of education as to call teachers to account. Accountability programs have been imposed upon teachers from the outside. State departments of education have created massive testing programs of skills they deem "essential." Politicians pledge their support to testing programs ostensibly designed to measure growth but secretly aimed at ferreting out slackers among the teaching staff. Along with the tests are state-mandated lists of minimal objectives or competencies proposed for every child in the state. In many areas, selected teachers have been involved ritualistically as consultants on planning committees, yet it is clear that accountability programs are developed by people other than teachers. Tests are given, scores are announced, and the clear-cut aim (though seldom the effect) of such programs is to drive out or penalize the "bad" teachers whose students don't measure up. Accountability programs have managed to intimidate many good teachers while reinforcing many of the practices that make some teachers bad.

Like many simplistic solutions, the accountability movement has considerable superficial appeal. It seems to demonstrate that somebody cares; it claims to pay attention to the basics of education; it implies that the state is serving a watchdog function, protecting the taxpayer's dollar. But, in fact, accountability programs are an extraordinary waste of taxpayer dollars. The test scores usually reveal the obvious: that the children who live and are educated in the inner city score less well than those who grow up in more affluent surroundings, a finding with both sociological and linguistic implications that range far beyond the basics and the question of whether or not teachers are teaching well.

Most important, accountability fails because instead of encouraging teachers to look at their own students—one by one—and to plan programs to meet student needs, it imposes blanket definitions of what's important and relies on mass measures of skill development. Imagine the presumptuousness of a teacher who says,

"I can tell you what's good for every child in the state!" Yet accountability programs have claimed to do just that.

Obviously teachers are not consummate professionals. There is a great deal of teacher incompetence around, at all levels of the school system. But mass testing, objectives, and accountability programs are not a solution to changing teacher behavior. What is required is giving teachers both the autonomy to make their own decisions and the help and support to make them as wisely as possible.

V. The Commitment to Teach

As one alternative to accountability, I suggest: *Teachers must be willing to offer instruction in reading and writing skills whenever and wherever those skills are needed.* The accountability people are correct on at least one point: Teachers have often passed the buck when it comes to reading and writing. Teaching literacy is difficult, time consuming, frustrating work. A great many teachers came into English to teach literature and literary appreciation, not principally to offer instruction in reading and writing. Thus in both schools and colleges, English teachers have almost invariably tried to shift the burden of instruction to someone else.

The story starts at the "top"—at the colleges. Professors have long felt that students are poorly prepared for college writing tasks and have made those concerns known vociferously. And in at least one sense, their objections are legitimate. There is no question that the schools have not done nearly enough teaching of reading and writing. But responding to the college outcry is not simple. Often there is an ulterior motive in operation, for, to put it quite simply, the colleges do not want and have never wanted to include freshman English in the curriculum. It has not been deemed worthy of university credit, and except for the fact that it provides pay for graduate students and generates inexpensive credit hours, most colleges would be absolutely delighted to be rid of English 101. The complaints, then, involve some buck passing.

Further, the college complaints have frequently created false impressions in the schools. "Give us more basics," says a professor, widely quoted in the newspapers. "Our freshmen perform abominably." So the schools resurrect grammar books and teach usage patterns. But at least three studies (Gere, 1977; Agee, 1977; Behrens, 1978) have shown that what most college professors seem to be upset about is not so much mechanics and usage (though most of them see red at misspellings) as matters of organization and structure. "They can't get out their ideas!" moans a professor. "Their 'basics' are adequate," says another, "but they simply can't organize." When the schools simply teach mechanics as a way of responding to complaints, they fail to get to the heart of the matter. They continue to teach superficial correctness, when what is needed is hard work on structure and organization.

The most articulate statement I have read on the whole question of college preparation was written by Burton Cox, Chairman of the English Department at Jackson Community College in Michigan. Addressing secondary teachers, he said:

What kind of freshman comp instruction *should* you prepare your college bound students for? I'm afraid that after having taught comp for the past ten years, I *still* can't make any comprehensive generalizations about what will happen in the classes your students sign up for (unless they come to me).

It might help if I could list all the types and sub-types of composition teachers that colleges have hired in the past half-century. Instead, just assume that if you have thirty-five students in your senior English class, those students will have fifty-seven varieties of teachers in their two semesters of freshman composition. Some of their profs will have chosen not to read anything more contemporary than Arnold Bennett; others will insist that Alice Cooper is writing the American Epic. One will stand behind lecterns expounding the virtues of pop culture to neat rows of students busily taking notes; another will sit crosslegged under a tree defending Matthew Arnold. Some will tell your seniors that their writing is inexcusably, shamefully below college level (in the trade that's known as "making the student aware of his limitations"); others will ignore pretty serious faults looking for anything good. Some will teach rhetoric or psycho-linguistics or traditional grammar; others will skip all that to discuss current issues. Some will make papers bleed, others won't even hand papers back. Some want to be called by their first names, others insist on the full formal title. ("Sir" is also acceptable.) If there were just one standard brand of comp prof, the high school teacher's job of "preparation" would be simplified.

Cox's solution to the problem draws on Walt Whitman, "I am only he who places over you no master, owner, better, God, beyond what waits intrinsically in yourself":

I interpret that for the English teacher as not so much doing your own thing as doing what you want because you feel it is important for the needs and interests of your students (or my doing what I want for the same reasons). I have quit the game of getting students ready for somebody's class next year. If Mr. ————— or Ms. ————— wants students to write long papers or diagram sentences or write on only one side of the page, that's fine (or stupid); but leave me out of it. I have my own things I want to do. [1973]

In effect, Cox argues that specific preparation for college writing tasks is impossible, that the best preparation is indirect: Teachers should concentrate on meeting immediate needs, not trying to anticipate writing forms for the future.

Suzanne Jacobs, who has taught a good deal of freshman English in both California and Hawaii, carries this concept one step farther:

Most of us need to take a writing course just at the time when we discover how difficult it is to express those things we really have some reason or desire to say (e.g., when we have papers to write, a cause to push, or a complex set of events to analyze). Adult courses and on-the-job courses are often more successful, because for most of the enrollees the "moment of discovery" has already come. The writing course should be offered to students on all levels, and it should be *essentially the same course*. A student should be encouraged to take the course as often as he feels that his growth in reading and experience has outpaced his growth in writing. [1975]

On the surface, the concept of a writing (or reading) *course* offered whenever one needs it may seem impractical, and it certainly seems inconsistent with the current school structure. But if we simply take "course" as a synonym for "instruction," it is clear that teachers can, in fact, offer courses whenever students encounter new literacy situations. It is simply a matter of saying, "the buck stops here." It suggests that colleges should welcome freshman English rather than treating it as drudgery, that high school teachers should teach the skills of writing and reading that are required for success in their courses, that the junior high and elementary teachers should concentrate on the reading/writing needs of the moment rather than preparing students for unpredictable future requirements, that elementary teachers should offer the fullest set of reading/writing/listening experiences they can without undue worry over the demands of the next grade.

Nor should this attitude of teaching what's needed when it's needed be limited to the college-bound student. Obviously, the non-college-bound also encounter new literacy situations regularly and need to be given help at crucial times. Too, the idea has implications for community-based and lifelong education programs. It is not unrealistic to consider that communities can create reading/writing opportunities which offer "the course you need at the time you need it" at any time during a person's life.

VI. English Across the Curriculum

The teaching of literacy must be a school-wide concern, not just the responsibility of teachers of English. The call for "every teacher a teacher of English," is one that has been issued frequently. Yet as often as not, the subject teachers have responded, not by teaching reading and writing, but by asking "Why don't English teachers do a better job?" It seems that everyone in the schools values literacy (or at least goes to the trouble of paying lip service to it), yet by and large, few are willing to take on the responsibility for teaching it. Thus, English skills become locked into English courses, and students fail to see application in other courses. When asked to write in history, they promptly forget everything they ever learned and write badly; when assigned science reading, they struggle. Even in the elementary grades, where single classrooms and multi-subject teaching are common, the skills of English—vocabulary, reading, penmanship—have been allowed to drift off into isolated components.

I suggested earlier that a "learn by doing" literacy program can comfortably be expanded into subject matter areas. I want to expand on that idea just a bit and offer a proposal for interdisciplinary teaching responsibilities, describing, first, the responsibilities for English, and second, the role for subject teachers.

Interdisciplinary Literacy: A Proposal for English. I propose that English teachers perceive themselves as teachers of literacy in the broadest sense, teaching language as it is bound up in the whole human process of living. English teachers are not principally teachers of isolated skills. English at its best will offer students an array of reading/writing/listening/speaking/media experiences on subjects ranging from exploring personal values and concerns to learning about the world around them. English teachers must take responsibility for the core—the basics—of literacy, not perceived as sounding out words, spelling correctly, or "talking right," but as using language broadly, flexibly, creatively in all manner of situations.

Further, English teachers should see their subject as interdisciplinary. English is not just literature and grammar; it is history, anthropology, psychology, biology, chemistry, physics, home economics, shop, humanities, and art. Though the English faculty should seek the cooperation of other departments in "going interdisciplinary," there is nothing to prevent, and everything to encourage, approaching English itself from an interdisciplinary point of view. The dimensions of English must expand.

I suggest that English teachers teach practical discourse, not by trying to prepare students for specific assignments they may encounter in other courses, but by helping them use language in real situations as often as possible. In a "real" English assignment, students consider the aims for their reading and bring their own experiences to bear on it; as they write "for real," they think about their own purposes in writing and the interests of their audiences. As students read and write in more and more sophisticated situations in a developmental program, they quite naturally increase their ability to deal with practical discourse and to anticipate and respond to the demands of unfamiliar tasks. The job of preparing students for work and/or college is thus subsumed under a broader, yet in many ways simpler, purpose: that of helping the students become fully literate.

Essentially, I am proposing that English teachers see their subject as central to the entire schooling process. Language, as I have stated, is a part of the processes of learning, knowing, and growing as a human being. A good English program will not just indoctrinate students into the values of classic literature or teach them linguistic table manners. It will ensure that young people are fully prepared to function as literate people in school and society.

For other subjects. I propose that subject teachers see reading and writing not just as tools to apply to the "material" of a course, but as a part of the process of learning the subject itself. Literacy is not something that is used just for homework reading and test writing; it is a part of every class, every experience. In being concerned about the quality of literacy, then, subject teachers take what for many is a new view of their subject in terms of the language it employs.

Subject teachers should (gradually) increase the formal use of literacy in their classes. In reading, this means expanding the use of non-text reading by making available more and more books— especially inexpensive paperbacks—and supplying appropriate magazines, newspapers, and journals related to their subject. In writing, it means assigning more than just notes and short answer questions. It requires employing the written word in all phases of learning.

The cause of literacy will not be advanced, however, if subject teachers simply find themselves trying to correct what they regard as the deficiencies induced by the English department. In assessing the students' reading and writing, subject teachers should talk about and respond to what they know best: the subject itself. Of course the teacher will, from time to time, correct spellings (especially words in the subject area) and help students with reading problems. But what students need most of all from the subject teacher is a sense of how the language shapes and is shaped by thinking in that field.

Thus it seems appropriate that subject teachers take responsibility for exposing students to the forms of reading and writing particular to that discipline and particular to the requirements of the course and the individual instructor. Science teachers best know what science writing looks like and can, without having a Ph.D. in English, tell students about it. Further, subject teachers must take responsibility for explaining and teaching the kinds of reading and writing they require. If a teacher wants papers typed with footnotes at the end, or, more substantially, if the teacher wants original perceptions rather than regurgitation, it is his or her responsibility to make those requirements explicit and, if necessary, to teach the forms required. If the students are to read a chapter in a textbook, the subject teacher ought to offer an explanation of how the book is put together and show students the necessary reading tricks and study skills to get the most out of it.

Finally, I want to propose that subject teachers recognize and exploit the creativity and subjectivity inherent in all language use. It is not correct to say that scientific writing or historical research is purely objective and that literary works are subjective and creative. In fact, even the plainest bit of prose—written under the guise of objectivity—is a reflection of personal experience. I suggest then, that subject teachers include literary works and good contemporary nonfiction in their rooms along with textbooks and references. They should allow and encourage students to compose their ideas in a wide range of discourse forms, in poems, plays, editorials, and satire, not just in expository essays or test prose.

VII. Administrative Support

New literacy programs require the active support of the administration. It is axiomatic that new programs will require the cooperation and assistance of the school administration, certainly at the building level, and ideally at the district or community levels as well. What is most frequently at issue is the kind and quality of administrative leadership that is offered. Simple administrative mandates to "do something or else" will only lead to change that is of poor quality and to a buildingful of teachers with low morale. Rather than adopting "the stick," school administrators are far more likely to achieve the kinds of change they want if they offer "the carrot"—by making change as easy and inviting as possible.

It should be obvious that the kinds of program changes I am recommending here will in the long run lead toward breaking down many school traditions. The isolated classroom might gradually give way to teamed, open-space, or workshop classes taught by several specialists. The rule of the class period—the fifty-minute time space punctuated by bells and buzzers—may need to be broken to allow for interdisciplinary studies. The schoolhouse walls will need to be breached, both to let children out and to let community members in. Such changes do not make life easy for administrators, and it is important for teachers to recognize the difficulty that new programs cause for the boss and his or her staff.

At the same time, it is important to recall that school is—ostensibly—for the benefit of the *learners,* and it is thus appropriate that administrative structures—bells, buzzers, and the like—serve the purposes of the clients, not just the system itself. In *The Revolution of Hope: Toward the Humanistic Uses of Technology* (1968), Erich Fromm has asserted that apparent conflicts between technology and human values spring up, not because of some sort of anti-humanistic element in technology, but because human beings fail to use technological advancements for the benefit of people. Rather, these advancements are used for the ends of the system itself. The same applies to administrative structures and the needs of students. If literacy programs are going to change, someone in the administration will need to see that the system itself is altered to facilitate that change.

What's needed are administrators who not only support literacy instruction but who are willing to put the administrative structures of the school to the humanistic uses of providing better reading/writing instruction. This might mean, for example, scheduling half the science faculty and half the English faculty with a common planning time. It could mean recalculating the school textbook budget to include paperbacks for history and economics classes. It could be putting the computer to work keeping track of a rapidly growing paperback collection. It might even involve discarding reliance on standardized test scores while including provisions for more complicated use of teacher-developed assessment measures.

Administrators, too, can do much to support the growth of their teachers as professionals. Certainly every department and, ideally, every member of the department ought to have a membership in the appropriate national professional group (in the case of English, the National Council of Teachers of English). Statewide organizations meet regularly as well, and teachers can be given released time and travel money, not just to attend these meetings, but to give talks about the district's new literacy program. Department meetings and faculty decisions must be treated with respect and, above all, not turned into sessions that dwell on operational matters rather than concern for the content of the courses. Teachers can be encouraged (if not given financial support) to take university courses and summer workshops to strengthen their competence in teaching reading and writing.

Nor is this kind of administrative support unheard of. For instance, in the 1960s and early seventies, many school leaders took great pains to let English teachers replace the relatively convenient classification of high school English into four courses, numbered I,

II, III, and IV, with more complex elective systems, which involved scheduling students into twenty-five or more different course offerings. Although the back-to-basics movement has cast some doubt on the wisdom of offering a multitude of electives (a doubt shared by some of the designers, not just the public), nevertheless, that era was one of growth for English teachers, who thought hard about crucial issues, who designed new courses, who acted as complete professionals. Administrators who supported that movement deserve a good deal of credit, and one hopes that despite tight budgets, the coming years will see renewed support for experimentation and growth in English.

VIII. Community Involvement

Members of the community need to have a hand not only in planning programs but, where appropriate, in conducting them. Community participation in curriculum decisions is one of the most frustrating areas of education, both for community members and teachers. To parents it often seems that their wishes and interests are ignored while educators experiment on children at taxpayer expense. From the point of view of teachers, it seems that the community is unwilling to trust their judgment, and in the case of English, that parents uniformly consider themselves qualified to comment on how it should be taught, even when their own skill in English may be minimal.

Community involvement is further complicated by being sporadic, keyed to crisis situations. Nobody worries much about community involvement when the school system is operating successfully. Only when things go awry—when young people get into trouble, when test scores decline, when the son or daughter of a distinguished community member is put into a remedial class—do parents demand and administrators begin to talk of community involvement.

Community involvement is more than a matter of public relations, of informing parents of what is already happening in the schools. Any time a curriculum is changed, the community ought to be represented on planning boards, task forces, curriculum and textbook review groups.

But in this area other communications problems assert themselves. I am reminded, by way of analogy, of the time my car had a chronic sputter and I had difficulties in communicating with the mechanic. At first I told him I thought it needed a tune-up (since I fancied I knew a bit about cars). Seventy-five dollars, six plugs, a set of points, and a condenser later, my car was tuned up gorgeously . . . but still sputtered. "Fuel pump," I diagnosed, and brought in the car to have that checked out. The fuel pump was fine; the bill was twelve dollars for labor; and the car sputtered. Finally I gave up amateur diagnosis and in the plainest, most ordinary language that I could, gave not the diagnosis but the symptoms, and the car was fixed (for another thirty-seven dollars).

In education, it is helpful for parents to explain their concerns: that they want their kids to be literate, that they're worried about a test score decline, that they disapprove of the kind of literature being taught. It is counterproductive for parents to try to make a diagnosis: that the schools don't teach "anything" nowadays, that we ought to go back to sentence diagramming, or that teachers are incompetent. As participants on planning boards, parents and community representatives should concentrate principally on describing perceptions of problems and on outlining goals, objectives, and expectations, not on trying to tell English teachers or administrators what ought to be happening.

At the same time, to return to my analogy, few things are more frustrating than a mechanic who treats the insides of your car as his own special domain of expertise and mystery and won't tell you, except in the vaguest terms, what's going on. "I pulled the glabatrator valve and cleaned the intake credenza," says the mechanic, handing you a bill for seventy-five dollars, and leaving you largely mystified.

English teachers, in particular, and the schools, in general, have been guilty of not telling the public what's going on and why.

Parents have little understanding of the aims of new methodology, and teachers must take on some of the blame for bitter public criticism. The public hasn't been told why grammar study doesn't change writing habits and people thus assume—not foolishly— that deemphasizing grammar means ignoring writing. No one has offered an explanation that "free" reading means "guided, independent, monitored" reading, so parents—not unjustly—assume that the English department has replaced substantive, disciplined literature courses with a student-selected smorgasbord. Like a mechanic, then, teachers need to explain where a proposed action will represent an improvement, and how they—the teachers—will take responsibility for seeing that it works.

Finally, I want to suggest that many traditional parent/teacher conflicts can be resolved if parents are brought in on Priority III in this chapter, "Knowing Students." By centering attention on learning more about young people—something that is obviously of as much interest to parents as to teachers—both groups can work together to shape the direction of the educational system. Thus parents can serve as experts in their own right by helping teachers understand what happens outside the school walls, how the students perceive their own goals and plans, what they have to say about their education, how they spend their time, and so on.

IX. Journalists and the Schools

We need journalists who are willing to look at and write about the schools as they are, not as they are imagined to be. A friend of mine once commented that journalists seem to be liberals who have a conservative streak when it comes to language and education. Certainly that idea was borne out in the back-to-basics uproar in the 1970s, when, if you believed what you read in the papers, schools had abandoned all discipline, language standards, and the teaching of "good grammar." But as several independent surveys pointed out, there was no wholesale abandonment of standards, and in fact, it seems that all too many English teachers clung to or retreated into practices that had long been proven valueless.

The press may well have taken its stand in response to the announced decline of college entrance examination scores. An explanation was required, and the press found one, in the alleged decline of morals, language, family life, and teaching. Yet the press could just as easily have launched an attack on the college entrance examinations themselves. The liberal press could have had a field day pointing out the obvious flaws in exams like the SAT, objecting to the control exerted by the Educational Testing Service and corporations like it, investigating the Big Brother aspects of mass testing, and publishing the corporate income of testing companies in America.

In fact, the schools have become neither permissive dens of iniquity nor test-bound factories of oppression. The journalists of this country could be of service rather than a hindrance to education simply by taking an open-eyed, unbiased look at the schools, by visiting schools and classes, talking to students, teachers, parents, and administrators, with an aim, first, of finding out what actually happens in the schools and, second, providing analysis and commentary.

I'm quite certain that if they visited the schools, journalists would not approve altogether of what they see; nor would I expect or even want them to. But they might be surprised by what they see. They might be surprised by the conservatism of some teachers and the imaginativeness of others; they might be surprised by the regimentation of the schools; they might be surprised that the schools haven't changed since they went to school; or they might by surprised that school has changed its face completely since their day. To be surprised by reality and to write about it would prove far more productive and would certainly be truer to the traditions of objectivity and inquiry in journalism than the scandal-sheet analysis of American education to which we have been subjected in the past.

X. The Hidden Priority

I presented many of these ideas in a speech to a gathering of English teachers. Afterward a member of the audience came up to me and said, "You know, the whole thing is political. Without a change in the social/political structure of this country, program changes in English will all be superficial." He agreed that one can talk comfortably of setting priorities, involving parents in the education of their own children, and engaging administrators cooperatively in efforts to change programs; yet all this will simply change surface appearances in education without fundamental changes in attitudes and values. He was quite right: In the final analysis, the shape of the educational system reflects the values and commitments of the people who pay for it.

It has been argued that schools are predominantly upper-middle-class institutions, which serve to ensure that the rich get richer and the poor are kept in their place. That analysis is correct in many respects, and there is no question that literacy instruction has been employed as much as any other aspect of the schools to keep class distinctions in mind. As Mina Shaughnessy (1977) of City College of New York has argued, America has constructed a society that depends superficially on literacy and has then denied many members of society the kind of literacy instruction required to operate in it successfully. Martin Nystrand (1975) of the University of Illinois, Chicago Circle, has shown that standardized tests, which are, in effect, tests of literacy, effectively preserve a classed society.

It seems apparent, too, that the back-to-basics movement of the 1970s had its origins, to a large extent, in concern over preservation of the schools as a middle-class enculturating/sorting device. The turbulent 1960s saw minority groups demanding new rights: first blacks, then Chicanos and Indians, and finally, the majority minority—women. The schools, which have traditionally held out the best education and best positions for white middle-class males, first recognized, then responded to the demands of these groups

for equal treatment. Further, as the college riots and rebellions—
Berkeley, Kent State, Columbia—demonstrated, much of the
unrest was coming from within the educational system. Even the
high schools were involved through student pickets, zaps, protests,
and sit-ins.

It was natural (if not entirely logical) for the taxpayers to complain about what they thought the schools were doing, and they
then began calling for back to basics. When the SAT test score
decline was announced, even more ammunition was supplied, for
not only were the schools apparently breaking down values, they
were no longer ensuring the children of the middle-class supremacy on standardized tests, which would guarantee preservation of
a way of life.

Thus the ambivalences to which I referred in Chapter 1 continued in yet another vein. Committed to something called "equal
opportunity," but threatened by it; committed to teaching literacy,
but believing that some people deserve to be more literate than
others; the public attacked the school system for failing to do
what it has always done so well: keeping the middle class exactly
where it is on the power spectrum.

Ironically, the minority groups also joined in the fray, not to
preserve a class system, but because they felt the test score decline,
the departure from the traditional curriculum, was somehow cutting them out of the picture. Having gained a foothold in the system, they wanted what the middle-class parents wanted: lots of
basics.

I think neither the middle class nor the minorities need fear a
change in the *status quo* of literacy instruction. Nor need they fear
that the kind of program I am recommending, based solidly on
reading and writing experiences rather than on grammar drills, is
neglecting basics or giving somebody the short end of the stick.
Further, neither group need fear a literate culture. All things considered, growth in society is healthier, faster, more productive,
and more in the interest of all citizens when people handle their
language successfully than when they don't.

In the 1970s the public, school administrators, and teachers made it clear that they are concerned about the reading and writing dilemma. But they only flirted with changing the system with which they were dissatisfied, often relying on superficial newspaper accounts of the problem and tampering with the system in obvious and often equally superficial ways. As I stated at the beginning of this book, nothing less than a major, dramatic change in the school system will produce a more literate society. But even before that happens, all concerned with education must consider the "hidden priority," on the surface, a simple statement, but with profound implications for reading, writing, and schooling in America: *The schools and society must reassess their interest in literacy; they must reaffirm their belief in the value of teaching reading and writing; and they must make a commitment to teach reading and writing, thoroughly and carefully, at whatever cost, to all children, regardless of race, class, or sex.*

5

One Hundred Projects
for Improving Literacy Instruction

This chapter is admittedly a potpourri. Having already presented theoretical backgrounds, I now want to list a number of projects, all of a practical sort, that suggest some first steps in developing a literacy program.

This is not the place to dwell at length on the dynamics of educational change or the "how-to" of organizing schools and districts to implement specific projects. Many of us have memories—too often unpleasant—of aimless Blue Ribbon Committees and Task Forces, of hollow subcommittee meetings and caucuses, of trivial conferences and debates, of leaderless meetings to "prioritize" issues, of problem-solving groups that create more problems than they solve, of groups and individuals who are more interested in promoting their own interests and causes than in producing worthwhile change. My approach here will simply be to present some specific strategies that will help schools develop a Plan A and realize a Plan B as described in the preceding chapter. I have divided these activities into four sections, addressed to *School Boards and Administrators, Parents and Community Members, English Teachers and Librarians,* and *Subject Teachers.* However, there is considerable overlap among the sections so that all groups ought to read all four sections. Further, the suggestions are phrased in the "impersonal imperative," which is grammar talk for "commands addressed to no single person." In other words, most of my suggestions are addressed "to whom it may concern," and can be undertaken by small or large groups, by individual teachers, by whole departments, by several departments working in concert, by an entire school, or by a school district. To this end, I conclude the chapter by suggesting some ways in which the individual can gain perspective on his or her role, working alone or with others, in promoting change in the schools.

For School Boards and Administrators

1. *Declare a commitment to improved literacy instruction; then act on it.* The first clause in that sentence is easy to do, the second, more difficult. In the past decades, many school districts have publicly pronounced their interest in improving the teaching of reading and writing, yet very few have taken substantial steps to achieve that goal. As often as not, reform has resulted in little more than adoption of a new set of textbooks or the inauguration of a new testing program. The result is that the curriculum itself changes very little. The projects that follow suggest some ways the commitment can be translated into action.

2. *Form a committee to write Plan A.* Who should serve on a Plan A committee? One possibility is simply to constitute a committee of anyone who cares enough about the problem to participate, a scheme that will create an enthusiastic, but possibly unwieldy group. More realistically, you might choose a workable committee of a dozen or so from the list of volunteers. The heart of the group probably ought to be experienced, imaginative, committed teachers and administrators—the paid professionals—and, to demonstrate the commitment to literacy, the superintendent might even serve as chair (or, at least, titular head) of the group. But parents and students need to be represented, too, and by more than a token representative.

Plan A might be a rather lengthy committee report compiled over a period of years, yet because of the importance of moving toward possibilities and practicalities (Plan B), a tentative Plan A should be formed more quickly. The committee, then, might produce practical ideas and suggestions from the very beginning, offering a starting point for small, task-specific groups. The committee should think about the distant future as well. August Franza, English Department Chair in Miller Place, New York, suggests that every community ought to have a group assigned to the task of thinking about community needs for the year 2000 and beyond (1978).

3. *Make a formal needs assessment of the community.* What do parents and community members see as important in teaching literacy? What do they value about their schools as they presently exist? What do they feel is wrong? In what ways do they feel satisfied with literacy instruction? In what areas does it need to be improved? The services of a good survey maker or research specialist may be required to create an instrument that will elicit the kind of information you want. Surveys of this kind have been based on diverse forms: parents might be supplied with a list of goals to be ranked in order or an open-ended questionnaire that allows write-in suggestions. Surveys can be distributed by mail, sent home with students, published in the community paper, or even based on sophisticated sampling techniques.

It is important to stress that a needs assessment should attempt to elicit feelings and values, not specific suggestions for instructional techniques. That is, if asked "How should we be teaching reading and writing?" a majority of parents will reply by describing the way they were taught. (It's all they know.) Rather, ask them to describe the areas that need more attention. Don't describe or present literacy so narrowly that all the responses seem to point in the direction of a basics program. Ask parents what they think of interdisciplinary programs as well as grammar. In other words, give parents an opportunity to request the best, the most fully dimensional program you and your staff can think of.

4. *Assess student interests and needs.* Do not limit the needs assessment to parents. Give students a crack at describing what's important to them as well. As educators learned in the 1960s and seventies, involving students in their own education means far more than simply asking kids, "whaddya wanna do?" A good research person can probably suggest a useful combination of, say, interviews, questionnaires, and small group discussions as a way of having students comment on their needs. Don't ask questions like, "Why are reading and writing important?" which are guaranteed to bring inflated, teacher-influenced answers. Rather, try to learn how students use literacy inside and outside school. (See the discussion of research conducted by Edna Saunders and Kathleen Lampert described in Chapter 4.) Find out what they write about when given a choice. (See Dyer's research, also in Chapter 4.) Learn about their TV watching, their reading and study habits, and their patterns of speech and conversation, so that you know how they use language outside of school.

In addition to questioning the current crop of students, go to the alumni lists and talk with recent and not-so-recent grads about their own uses of literacy. Other cautionary notes are important here. It is axiomatic, for example, that college freshmen will blame their high school training for any of their current academic problems. While that fault finding is sometimes appropriate, often it is simply a transference of present difficulties to a convenient scapegoat. A good survey will separate the real from the imagined failings of the schools, and, more important, will give you a realistic picture of what students do with the literacy education you give them.

5. *Evaluate the existing literacy curriculum.* "Curriculum" here is an extremely broad term. It may mean a system-wide, K-12 description of objectives and skills, a two-hundred-page volume passed out at teacher orientation meetings, or it can be broadly conceived as the sum total of what teachers and children do in the schools. The basic questions to be answered are: "Are we doing what we want to do?" "Are our current practices carrying us

toward or away from our goals in Plan A?" As most administrators know, curriculum evaluation is frequently perceived as a threat by teachers, who fear (perhaps rightly) that their own special interests are under attack. While the purpose of an evaluation is, obviously, to eliminate ineffectual programs, it seems clear that evaluation proceeds much more smoothly if its focus is the positive. What exemplary courses, classes, teachers do we already have as a starting point? How can we get our curriculum to include even more reading, more writing? What potential does the curriculum already hold for interdisciplinary studies? How can we modify existing programs to make them do what we want them to do?

6. *Write Plan B.* Plan B should be a natural evolution from steps 1–5 above: You have described your ideal, assessed the feelings of parents and students, and described the actual, existing program. Perhaps the best form for a Plan B is not a sustained document or master plan, but a series of projects that the administration and the Plan A committee think might help to realize the school's long-range goals. Projects might be as simple as articulation meetings between school levels, as complex as overhauling the existing high school curriculum, or as expensive as sending every English teacher in the district to summer workshops. The projects, however, ought to approximate your Plan A; that is, if all your Plan B projects are completed successfully, the school will have moved as close to its ideal as it possibly can.

7. *Invite groups to develop portions of Plan B.* Publish the Plan B projects and encourage interest groups to bite off an appropriate chunk and begin work. Start a group of parents working on, say, community-based learning resources, a physics-English group on science writing, a cluster of elementary teachers on increasing creative writing opportunities. Correlate and publicize the activities of these many committees and subgroups.

As a way of cutting down on the aimless proliferation of committees and study groups, build "self-destruct" mechanisms into committees. This idea grows from a splinter organization of English teachers that, several years ago, provided in its constitution that it would go out of business after three years unless its members could think of a good reason for continuing its existence. (It ceased to exist.) To avoid a network of inactive committees, center each group on a specific task with a reasonable set of deadlines. Once the committee finishes its task (or fails to), it automatically goes out of business (unless, of course, the committee can find some new, valid reasons for continuing its work).

8. *Provide funds for study groups and committees.* The kinds of committees I am describing here are not terribly expensive to support, and in most cases, the materials they need are already available within the school or community. However, the work of most study groups will be greatly enhanced if they have a few dollars to spend on a book or two or on a pot of coffee. Establish a petty cash fund of $50 or $100 for each committee to allow it to obtain needed resources, to conduct a survey, or to publicize its results. This is an effective, yet relatively inexpensive way for the school administration to show its support.

9. *Assess the existing school budget in terms of the goals of the literacy program.* Given the many tax limitation propositions that have been passed in the states, it seems unlikely that future school budgets will be dramatically expanded or that school administrators will find themselves with new sources of funding for programs. Indeed, with inflation jacking up the price of everything from coal to chalk, it seems as if the schools will find more and more difficulty even sustaining old programs.

Nevertheless, a great deal can be accomplished simply through realigning the ways in which the school spends its dollars for literacy. For instance, a traditional literature anthology costs the school district in the neighborhood of $7.50; a class set thus runs about $250. The common practice of adopting sets of these books for the entire system gobbles up the book budget, locks in the curriculum, and even commits future funds, since replacement copies must be purchased. In contrast, many schools have found that the same basic expenditure of $250 will purchase well over one hundred paperback titles and create the basis for an individualized reading program. These programs have the additional advantage that they can be added to in small or large numbers as funds permit. Despite attrition due to paper covers, the net effect is to allow for a natural accumulation of large quantities of books over a five-year span. Similarly, a gimmicky film on teaching the comma (16 minutes, color) costs $295. While some media resources are genuinely useful, a great many are pedagogically unsound and hopelessly overpriced. Offer teachers the option of spending the cash to buy more reading materials: books, newspapers, magazine subscriptions.

10. *Support teacher development of curriculum and pilot projects.* Sometimes the red tape involved in getting a new course or program established is so great that teachers feel that curriculum development is hopeless. At other times, so much stress is placed on the common textbooks or a central curriculum guide that teachers fear to do any innovative work on their own. Cut through the red tape by setting up simple procedures for "pilot" or experimental programs of limited duration. If the pilot project proves itself successful, then it can be sent through the more formal procedure required for permanent approval. Having numbers of experimental programs going on in a school seems to add considerably to school morale.

As an incentive, offer limited funds to support experimental programs. A small petty cash fund similar to that suggested for committees will allow the innovative teacher or faculty interest group to purchase a needed book or two, to obtain a few extra materials, to do something special or interesting for the students. Naturally such expenditures need to be justified and adequately documented, but even here the red tape of accounting can be minimal.

11. *Provide time for experimental course and program planning.* Use in-service days to give pilot program teachers time to work together. Provide pilot teachers with a common lunch hour or give over the monthly faculty meeting for gatherings of interest groups.

12. *Get the district grantsperson to find funds for literacy programs.* Explore fundings sources—U.S. Office of Education, State Department of Education, Council for the Arts, local businesses and industries—and then encourage teachers to write up proposals. Most teachers have never written a proposal and won't do it without encouragement and support. Make it a priority item to match the interests of good teachers with existing funding categories. Too often grants go only to the "haves," the school districts with prestige and muscle. If you're a "have-not," change your status.

13. *Sponsor articulation meetings.* Get together groups of people who ought to talk to each other but don't: junior high and elementary teachers, senior high and junior high teachers, parents and teachers, teachers and principals, students and parents and teachers. Encourage interdisciplinary gatherings within school buildings. Bring in representatives of college and industry who can talk sensibly about the literacy needs in their areas.

14. *Involve the community.* In addition to simply endorsing the cooperation of the various parent/teacher organizations, actively seek community participation not just in understanding the program but in developing it. Include:

The Press. School press coverage is often bad because it grows from negative reaction, responses to "crises." Instead of waiting for attacks, invite local journalists to join in the process of evaluating the school system. Get the paper to run a series of articles on what's new in literacy education, to visit and write about existing programs, to pick up and publish sensible national stories related to reading and writing.

Service Clubs. These groups spend much time and energy on community action programs. Why not on literacy education? What of a Rotary- or Lions-sponsored book drive or fund raiser for the library? Or an Elks scholarship to send a senior to journalism school?

Community Experts. Draw on them as free consultants: the education professor, the attorney, the carpenter, the poet, the psychologist. Find ways of exploiting their knowledge, information, and interest.

Parents. Place parents on committees of all kinds. Ask them to help select books for school libraries and free reading programs. Develop a corps of volunteers and aides for use in English classes. Bring parents in as speakers and discussion leaders, as co-editors of the school/community newspaper or newsletter.

15. *Celebrate the accomplishments of student writers.* Publish an "honor roll" of student writers and get the local paper to publish some of their work. Hold readings and dramatizations of student writings in the auditorium. Establish a system- or city-wide literacy week. Award prizes for young writers just as you do for young atheletes.

16. *Have lunch with the area paperback book distributor and discuss ways of getting more inexpensive reading material into the school.* See Daniel Fader's *Hooked on Books* (1976) for a description of how one Detroit distributor has sponsored and supported a wide range of literacy programs.

17. *Support smaller class loads for teachers of literacy.* This is unquestionably the most controversial topic on my list of projects for administrators. For decades the National Council of Teachers of English has argued that the class load for English teachers should be no more than one hundred students and four classes per day; yet all over the country English teachers regularly face 150 or more students in five or more classes. Given such loads it becomes nearly impossible for teachers to assign as much writing as they would like or to create a truly individualized reading program.

Obviously many departments have claims of "unusual circumstances" that they feel require smaller workloads as well, and to decrease the load for English teachers will obviously complicate union negotiations. The discussion has been confused, too, by the wide publicity given to some generally nebulous research that has, in the past, revealed "no significant difference" on standardized test scores when class loads are reduced.

One reasonable approach is for administrators to experiment

with pilot programs that offer a temporary reduced load—e.g., teamed, workshop, or interdisciplinary courses that include fewer students than usual. What happens? Are the results positive? Specifically, do teachers assign more writing and do students read more books when the teacher load is reduced? If they do, then perhaps the reduced load is justified.

For Parents and Community Members

William Cushman of the Baylor School, Chattanooga, Tennessee, asked his faculty members to brainstorm for ways in which parents could help their children become more successful users of English. The list, sent home as part of a letter to parents, is so detailed that I simply want to add it to my own, as Projects 18–52.

18. Create situations in which conversation is likely to occur. A family watching television together is very likely not together at all, for often no communication takes place. On the other hand, a family playing a board game may be significantly together. Even talk about the game is talk.

19. Ask children questions which require more response than "yes" or "no" or "I don't know."

20. Be willing to let a child express himself on the subjects that interest *him*. This usually means lengthy retelling of games you viewed together or maddeningly detailed retelling of stories he has read or movies he has seen, but it does let you know what he is interested in and it does get him to talk, to use the language.

21. Play word games. Have spelling bees.

22. Try to find ways to place your child in the company of older adults who are good talkers. Children are often fascinated by the stories of old timers—and that's what it's all about: getting them interested in stories.

23. Consider the possibility that there is a priceless by-product of reading to a young child: a closeness and affection between parent and child that can develop in almost no other way. Talking

together about problems faced by characters in stories can perhaps lead naturally to the child's feeling comfortable about coming to the parent with his own problems.

24. Read stories to children. Examples: Bible stories, Richard Adams' works, *Winnie the Pooh*.

25. Parents should read to their children at first and with their children later, but they should read together all the time.

26. Seek opportunities to read aloud to your child and encourage him to read aloud to you (maybe just a brief passage that he thought funny).

27. By showing delight at learning a new word or liking a new book show your child that verbal development and verbal fun are life-long processes, not ones limited to the school-going years.

28. If parents read, kids will.

29. Consider this: it makes little sense for one to expect his children to read if they don't frequently see him read.

30. Parents should be interested in anything their child writes. They should encourage the child to write letters, stories, poems, notes, diaries—anything. They should be interested enough to read the material, if the child doesn't mind.

31. Parents should demonstrate an interest in the child's homework not only to encourage neatness, thoroughness, and promptness, but also to imply that the skills being learned were important in the parents' development.

32. Every home should have a reference library (dictionaries, Bartlett's *World Almanac and Book of Facts,* and the *Columbia Encyclopedia,* etc.) and it should be used by everyone. Children should be encouraged to "look it up" every time their curiosity is aroused and every time an unfamiliar word or phrase is encountered in conversation or daily reading.

33. Institute an "open dictionary" policy. If a dictionary is kept in a prominent place and if parents may frequently be seen using it, many children will develop the "look it up" habit.

34. Be sure that your child is familiar with the pleasures of a good public library.

35. Keep good and fun reading material in almost every room in the house.

36. [Cautiously and critically] Read together Edwin Newman's *Strictly Speaking* or his *Civil Tongue*. . . . they help us think about the present state of our use of the English language.

37. Subscribe to some periodicals in addition to the usual *Time, Newsweek, Sports Illustrated,* etc. Some very worthy ones are *Harper's, The Atlantic, Commentary,* and *National Geographic.*

38. Talk together about political cartoons.

39. Allow the child to stay up thirty or so minutes after "lights out"—if he is in bed reading.

40. Show a gentle interest in grammar and pronunciation.

41. Try to keep corrections and recommendations friendly and humorous. Communication on this subject is difficult even without anger.

42. One should try to avoid giving his children the impression that he advocates only "good" books. Otherwise, a hopeless dichotomy often emerges, in which the parent wants the children to read only the classics and the children want only not to read them.

43. Give carefully selected books to friends whom your children know you value. Give books to your own children!

44. Try to be well read enough to be able to suggest books to your children.

45. Actively discourage television with the exception of intelligent shows designed for children. Encourage the belief that there should be a reason for turning the television on and that there should be a sequence of other reasons for keeping it on, that its natural state should be "off." Discourage turning on the television "to see what's on." Keep listings handy and consult them "to see what's on." Once on, a set is hard to turn off.

46. Treat television as a reward for time spent in reading. This approach enables the parent to avoid seeming always against television. He can agree that it is fun and sometimes useful but that it needs to be balanced by the entirely different world that only reading can provide.

47. Selectively discourage the use of television rather than issuing blanket condemnations.

48. Forbid the watching of more than eight hours of television per week.

49. Permit no watching of television after supper, except for "special" shows that are of particular interest to the child.

50. Help young people develop and maintain a sense of detachment from the characters they see on television. Of course, this issue is profound when viewed in terms of the content of programs, but here we are concerned primarily with the quality of English that is spoken on television. *The Adventures of Huckleberry Finn* has often been condemned because of Huck's terrible English. However, young people seldom fail to perceive the conditions out of which that language emerges. One who watches much television may, though, fail to notice that the slang-filled, ungrammatical English he hears is not the English he should speak, so inundated is he by that language.

51. Television is a problem not so much because of its content as because of the passivity it produces in the child. Children should learn to seek answers, not simply to wait for them to appear on the screen.

52. Let your children know that you pay careful attention to excellent television programming for adults as well as children.

Although the Cushman/Baylor list is detailed and useful, there are additional ways in which parents and community members can become directly involved in the development of the literacy program itself:

53. *Declare your support for development of a comprehensive literacy program.* Don't be satisfied with a back-to-basics program that concentrates on nothing more than grammar drills and raising standardized test scores. Ask for a program that actually involves students in reading, writing, speaking, and listening. Write letters to principals, school administrators, and board members letting them know where you stand. Support smaller class loads for literacy teachers.

54. *Find out more about the schools.* Don't base your assessment of your own schools on what *Newsweek* or the State Department of Education might tell you. Visit the school. Volunteer as a parent aide. Go to parent/teacher nights. Meet and talk with the principal. In visiting the schools, don't cast yourself in the role of spy or investigative reporter; simply go to find out what you can do.

55. *Find out where you fit into Plan B.* Join a curriculum-planning or parent interest group and work on one of the specific projects for changing instruction in reading and writing in the district. Don't underrate your qualifications or stay away because you don't feel you know enough about English. Your interest and energy are more important than literary credentials.

56. *Volunteer your time.* The schools can use community support in the form of teacher aides, tutors, theme readers, members of book review committees, activities leaders, public relations experts, publications advisors, club advisers, outside speakers, consultants, and so on.

For English Teachers and Librarians

57. *Saturate the school with materials of literacy.* Arrange for a supply of paperbacks, magazines, and newspapers in as many classrooms as possible. Avoid adopting class *sets* of books (paperback *or* hardbound) and concentrate expenditures on individualized reading programs. Look for commercial programs that take an interdisciplinary, multitext approach. Establish a paperback bookstore inside the school (staffed by and with proceeds to, say, the senior class).

58. *Use the library as more than a repository of books.* The best libraries no longer fit the stereotype of dark, tomb-like halls where people read silently under the eagle eye of the librarian. No longer are librarians more concerned about neat shelves and clean covers than about the circulation of books. A good school library can provide such services as:

—Book and reading lists for teachers and students.

—Book carts on selected topics that can be wheeled into a room and from which books can be checked out.

—Films, filmstrips, and other audiovisual materials.

—A listening library, where students can hear anything from a symphony to a novel.

—Book talks: informal reviews of current books of interest.

—Used paperback exchanges, where students can bring titles they have read to trade for something new.

59. *Make individual rooms conducive to the uses of literacy.* Display books attractively on shelves and racks, either provided by area book distributors or hand crafted in the school shops. Set up a comfortable reading area in one corner, complete with a throw rug, an overstuffed or beanbag chair, and a space where kids can stretch out and enjoy free reading. Line the bulletin boards with book jackets of good children's and adolescent novels. Create a writing center with a supply of the tools of literacy—pens and pencils, paper, reference materials, typewriter, bookbinding materials, and so on.

60. *Create English programs that are based on the actual use of language.* To learn to read, students must read, not just study about reading. To write, they must write, not just do exercises and drills. The essential questions to be answered then, are "How often do the students read and write?" How often do they use oral language?"

61. *Involve the department in Plan B.* Sketch out a series of projects for the near and distant future. How will the curriculum grow/change/evolve this year? Over the next four or five years? Start a series of pilot programs and experimental courses. Explore new connections between the English classroom and the library. Publicize the plans throughout the school and seek the support of other faculty and the administration.

62. *Extend the dimensions of literacy.* Second in importance to the question, "How often do students use the language?" is "In

how many *different ways* do they use it?" Open up the English classroom to the full range of human discourse. Make certain that students write stories and plays as well as essays and tests, that they explore film and video as well as print, that they learn about talk, discussion, drama, improvisation, and theater as well as literature.

63. *Teach the structuring of writing, not writing structures.* That is, instead of filling students' heads with ideas about paragraphs, topic sentences, transitions, theses, and clinchers before letting them write, focus writing instruction on helping students find interesting things to say and audiences to whom they can be said. In the process of writing, students themselves will come to discover the kinds of structures they need to use to find success with an audience.

64. *Teach reading, not reading patterns.* Base reading programs on having students put nose in book to read, not on studying word parts, sentence parts, story fragments, book fragments.

65. *Read and write with your students; listen and talk to them.* It's an old axiom that English teachers should write some assignments along with their students, both to understand the problems students encounter and to show the kids that the teacher, too, struggles with the written word. Many new reading programs include time for the teacher to read during silent reading as a way of showing that adults read and find books interesting and useful. A teacher can join in oral work as well, not so much as a "teacher," but as an adult participant, one who can add to and learn from discussions in productive ways.

66. *Base the language arts program on a thorough grounding in the nature of language.* In lieu of grammar and correctness drills, help students understand how language functions. Explore the ways language is used in society for persuasion and communication of information. Examine dialects to see where they come from and what they do (or do not) say about their users. Explore the concepts of "good" English and the origin of language standards. Look at the differences among written and spoken vari-

ations of the language. Study "silent" languages—body talk and other non-verbal systems. Look at the past and future of English.

67. *Base the program on the drama inherent in literature and language use.* The English program can explore the drama in both student writing and literature by using such dramatic techniques as improvisation, pantomime, reader's theater, scripted theater, and by perceiving literature as a dramatic exchange, first, among characters or ideas on the page, and second, between the writer and the reader.

68. *Teach oral English.* Although talking comes to human beings almost as naturally as eating, *good* use of talk is quite difficult and needs to be fostered by the schools. Include an oral component in the English program. Show students how to engage in group discussion productivity; teach them about brainstorming; show them how talk can help them shape their writing; introduce them to some of the informative uses of oral English: speeches, panels, debates, interviews, and so on.

69. *Teach students to serve as their own editors.* The traditional English program has always thrust the teacher into the role of theme-corrector and editor, taking on responsibility for finding the flaws and errors in students' work. This not only creates an intolerable theme-correcting load, but is ultimately harmful to students, who never develop the capacity for revising and editing their own work. Instead, build in provisions for small group and individual analysis of papers at every grade level. As students mature, their editorial skills will grow as well. Make it clear to students that once their twelve-year hitch in school is up, *they,* not their teachers or employers, will be responsible for the final copy of their work.

70. *Use collaborative learning projects.* Students can learn more than just editing from one another. Use collaborative projects as a way of helping students learn to share skills and ideas. Through working together students marshall their language abilities and show each other—informally, of course—how to employ those skills in a new setting.

71. *Publish student work constantly.* In this context "publish" means "make public." In other words, provide audiences for student work. Papers can be published through informal class newspapers and magazines, as individual hand-bound books, as part of a bulletin board display, as part of an oral or dramatic reading. Provide for dramatic readings and renderings of students' stories, plays, and poems as part of Literacy Week. (See Project #15.) As students write for audiences—for each other as well as audiences outside the class—their sense of the language and its use will evolve.

72. *Subsidize student publications.* The traditional school newspaper or magazine serves very few students and consumes a good chunk of departmental money. Consider replacing (or at least supplementing) the school paper with subsidized student publications. Make it easy for a group of students or a language arts class or a science class to get their best work into print, be it an inexpensive, mimeographed, one-page broadsheet or a more elaborate printed book. (Remember the days of underground student newspapers? Although such publications caused administrators and parents a lot of anxiety, the fact is, a great deal of writing was learned in the process of putting out a student-created publication.)

73. *Treat young people's writing as part of the literature of a class.* What students write will obviously not be as skillful as professional writing; nor do we want to give young people the idea that their work is somehow equal to that of Faulkner or Balzac. Yet student writing is built of the same raw materials—emotions, ideas, words—as classic literature, and it merits the kind of serious response that we give to adult and professional writing. In the language arts class, then, the work of young people deserves to be read and discussed on a regular basis, as literature, not just as composition.

74. *Establish literacy help centers.* With parent or student volunteer help, create a place where students can go for help with their reading/writing. Such centers simply supply the student with

tutoring whenever he or she needs help. Centers can go a long way toward eliminating the need for remedial classes and the stigma attached to them.

75. *Create supplementary literacy activities.* The schools draw hordes of kids into after-school activities like sports, arts, and crafts. Why not literacy as well? With the aid of parent volunteers, create a Poetry Club, a Journalism Society, a Group of Mystery Readers, an Author's Fan Club.

76. *Assign subject-matter reading and writing in English class.* Extend the dimensions of literacy by offering subject-matter options in assignments. Build in possibilities for the student who is interested in astronomy or civil war history or shopcraft or cookery. Encourage students to read in their interest areas and to write papers about their knowledge.

77. *Develop interdisciplinary and team-taught courses and units.* As a first step toward interdisciplinary studies, find interested souls in other departments and offer to team with them for a period of time. (Such courses need not involve complicated scheduling or credit arrangements. For a starter, simply work with people who teach or have lunch at the same time you do.) Use these pilot ventures to provide support for more complex, formal programs.

78. *Develop an interdisciplinary consultant system.* Assign members of the English department to consult with teachers in other departments. When a subject teacher is about to assign a test or a paper, he/she consults with an English teacher for ideas on how to make the assignment a good one (i.e., one that encourages rather than discourages good writing). If the subject teacher has doubts about the suitability of a book or reading assignment, he/she seeks help. Thus instead of trying to teach subject reading, the English teachers help others learn to do it in their own classes.

79. *Seek real world connections in the English program.* Send students outside the school on assignments to see language as it is actually used in non-school situations and to draw on the wealth of language/information sources available outside the school. Use

newspapers and magazines as a base for instruction. Encourage the students to write from their own experiences and observations.

80. *Develop alternatives to conventional English programs.* On a pilot basis, experiment with internships, "city-as-school" experiences, and work-study programs. If these approaches work, make them a regular part of the English offerings. Whether or not full-scale alternative programs are practical, incorporate some of their features into conventional English classes.

81. *Open up the English classroom to the community.* Invite parents to see what is happening in your classes, during the week, not just on Parents' Night. Create a newsletter for parents so they know what is happening even if they *don't* want to come in. Ask parents to serve as tutors, volunteers, and book selection aides.

For Teachers of Other Subjects

82. *Stock the classroom with books related to your subject.* These may include fiction and nonfiction, autobiography and biography, informative books, "how to" or craft books, and, for older students, professional contributions to your field. For students in elementary and junior high years, an invaluable guide to resources is May Hill Arbuthnot's *Children and Books* (1972), a detailed discussion of books for young people, including resources in historical fiction, biography, the biological sciences, the physical sciences, the social sciences, and religion and the arts. Three annotated bibliographies by the National Council of Teachers of English can also provide guidance to a subject teacher looking for books: *Adventuring with Books* (Patricia Cianciolo, Editorial Chair, 1977) is a K–8 list; *Your Reading* (Jerry L. Walker, Editorial Chairman, 1975) covers the junior high years; and *Books for You* (Kenneth Donelson, Editorial Chairman, 1976) presents materials for the senior high years. NCTE also publishes *Book and Non-Book Media* by Flossie L. Perkins (1972), a "bibliography of bibliographies," which guides teachers to specialized booklists.

However, subject teachers should seldom have to "go it alone" and should have the assistance of both the school librarian and members of the English or language arts faculty. In making subject-matter books available to the students, the teacher will go a long way—fairly effortlessly—toward teaching reading in his or her content area.

83. *Include popular magazines in your classroom.* Bring in copies of trade magazines that touch on your field: *Road and Track, Scientific American,* or *The American Historian.* Better still, get the principal or librarian to sponsor subscriptions so that the fresh copies go directly to your class. Start a bin file of newspaper and magazine clippings of articles that relate to your field. Use these for assigned or free reading, or simply for browsing.

84. *Teach the writing and reading skills required for your class.* This does *not* mean that the subject teacher must begin teaching phonics or vocabulary or paragraphs. Rather, teach literacy through the subject itself, through example rather than rule. Pre-read difficult selections with your students, helping them see the overall pattern of the text information before they plunge in. Help them see how the results printed on the page grow from actual research or other kinds of studies. Explain the specialized conventions of writing in your field (e.g., codes, symbols, special research forms) and show how they are necessary to clear communication. If you have particular demands for the form of written work, describe and help the students master them. Teaching writing and reading in the subject area is, in large measure, a matter of demonstrating that you are concerned about the use of language and offering students assistance when they need it.

85. *Offer many alternatives in written assignments.* Get help from English teachers so that you can offer students creative as well as expository writing assignments and can draw on media forms as well as print. Why not let students demonstrate competence through a slide-tape or other audio-visual presentation? Is it possible for them to show what they know through a short story or play rather than a piece of explanatory prose? Most subject teachers who have tried offering alternatives feel that enlarging the

range of discourse considerably enriches students' understanding of the subject itself.

86. *Include "purpose" and "audience" in written assignments.* This is a simple trick, but one that will immeasurably increase the quality of your students' writing. Instead of simply asking for explanations to reveal mastery, have students write *to* somebody (to each other, to a person unfamiliar with the subject, to the president of a manufacturing company) *for* a purpose (to persuade somebody, to teach somebody something new, to explain a bright idea to someone in power). Whenever possible, make these real audiences—that is, have the students actually write for someone other than you.

87. *Introduce journal writing in your class.* The journal can be used in almost all subject areas as a place where an individual can write down, not just observations, but responses to what he or she is experiencing. In lieu of subject notebooks—often little more than routine gleanings from textbooks and lectures—have students write about their reactions and responses: to class discussions, to experiments, to people in the subject area. Most English teachers who use journals do not grade them, but rather, simply read the material from time to time to study responses and send reactions back to students. See somebody in the English department about this technique.

88. *Present writing in your area as an example of personal narrative.* Most scientists, historians, critics, philosophers, craftsmen have a *story* to tell. Whether they cast their writing in first person pronouns or present it as an objective essay, their writing tells a story. Perceiving subject writing in this way—even the writing of formal articles—helps students see the man or woman behind the printed page.

89. *Encourage interviews as a way of learning.* Children can successfully interview each other and adults from the early school years on. Interviewing develops oral language skills, "thinking" and synthesizing skills, the ability to transcribe and write, and finally, the editing process.

90. *Use oral English as a mode of learning and sharing.* Set up panels, group discussions, reports, debates, and even oral examinations in your class. Stay away from traditional, formal speech situations such as the "five-minute report" or the "pop oral quiz." As with the teaching of writing, you need not be an expert in speech to draw on oral English successfully. Concentrate on helping students know their subject and find occasions to speak, with purpose, to an audience that cares to listen.

91. *Respond to student writing as a subject-matter reader, not a theme grader.* That is, when student writing comes in, don't perceive yourself in the role of freshman comp grader and start red penciling every error you see. First read the piece as you would any piece of writing in your field and respond to the student in terms of its content. If you like the way the material is presented, say so. If the facts are wrong, point that out. At least initially, react to grammatical and spelling problems only as they genuinely interfere with your reading of the paper. If, as you receive more writing from students, you want to go into more detailed commentary about structure and style, there's no question English teachers will welcome your efforts. But you need not be a theme grader or editor to respond helpfully to the writing you receive.

92. *Find publishing forms for student writing in your subject.* Collect the better papers of the term and have them duplicated in a booklet. Display student work on bulletin boards in your class or the hallways. Have students send good writing to the school paper for possible publication or have them write up interesting class projects for possible use as a feature in the school paper. Let students collaborate on a book about your subject. Search out talent fairs where students can display and write up their project work.

93. *Have your class create a guide to writing in your field.* As students learn more and more about reading and writing in your area, they will be able to share some of their learning with future students. Have them put down what they know about how to write a good paper in your class—including matters of form as

well as style and content—and duplicate it as a guide for next year's students. Then have next year's students prepare the revised second edition for their successors.

94. *Explore the literary forms connected with your subject.* While the bulk of subject-matter reading and writing will be directly connected with informational prose, students can gain new insights into the subject by reading literary materials as well. Most subjects have short stories and novels that have been written about them. Science, for example, has science fiction and novels of scientific criminology. History has the historical novel. Social science can draw on numerous plays, short stories, and dramas. With the help of the librarian or the English department, stock a related reading or extra-credit reading bookshelf in your classroom.

95. *Bring in literary works written by subject-matter people.* Loren Eiseley, an anthropologist, has also written powerful poetry; Isaac Asimov has written fiction as well as informative books in science; John Kennedy wrote biography; Winston Churchill wrote history. Place these kinds of books on the extra-credit reading shelf.

96. *Bring in biographies and autobiographies of major figures and personalities in your field.*

97. *Study the origins of specialized vocabulary in your area.* Why is "mitre" a term for a woodworker's joint? Where did the term "carapace" come from? Why are those purple spiny sea creatures called "urchins"? In addition to unusual expressions, you can examine the jargon and argot ("secret" languages) of your profession, along with the origin of terms.

98. *Compare the language used in popular and technical articles in your field.* Show students a professional article, a magazine or newspaper article, and a textbook discussion on a single topic and ask the students to compare the forms of language. How do language and content differ as writing is more or less specialized, more or less formal?

99. *Have students translate technical reports or textbook stud-*

ies into "lay" language. Also invite students to put their own knowledge of the subject into language that can be grasped by a younger brother or sister or a group of younger children.

100. *Team teach a course with an English teacher.*

What Can One Person Do?

The projects outlined here are, for the most part, ideas that can be initiated in almost any school and can be done in the not-too-distant future. They are not extravagant, and they can be initiated with existing funds rather than new money. In contrast to the sciences, manual arts, and even the fine arts, literacy instruction requires very little hardware. The basic resources—books, pens, paper—are cheap. Thus schools and districts need not wait for federal or state funds in order to launch a substantial, creative, exemplary literacy program. (Nor need they become locked into the testing/reporting bureaucracy accompanying such money.)

At the same time, as I have discussed these ideas for change with teachers, administrators, and parents, I have encountered a frequent worry: "All this is well and good, but I feel I'm working alone." Teachers, for example, often feel that they are the only ones in the building that have a given concern, that they'll have to "go it alone" without the support of colleagues. Further, teachers often sense a discrepancy between their aims and those of the school administrators. Because of concern with public relations and making ends meet, the administration seems to place concern for curriculum into a corner. Administrators, in turn, just as often feel isolated from their teachers. Principals frequently feel that the faculty doesn't appreciate their position and tries to undercut it. Further, parents have a great deal of difficulty agreeing on what "ought" to be going on in the schools, so opinions differ from neighborhood to neighborhood. (In a recent survey in a Michigan community, parents described "curriculum" as the area of the school system with which they were most satisfied. However, they were also *least* satisfied with "curriculum" and when asked to describe the area they knew least about, they responded "curriculum.")

The feelings of being alone are created by the traditionally closed communications channels in the schools. Teachers don't talk to each other except at lunch hour and then only to gripe about kids; the administration talks with teachers only through memos or formal faculty meetings; parents are invited in only on special occasions or when something goes wrong. Sponsoring articulation meetings (Project 13) can go a long way toward both eliminating the symptoms of loneliness and making it clear where people stand on basic issues and where the disagreements lie.

It is curious, for example, that in the uproar over student writing skills in recent years, each group offering opinions—parents, teachers, the press, college professors—has acted as if it is the *only* group that cares about preserving and developing literacy. Thus we had the phenomenon of people *acting* as if they were alone and alienating each other in the process. In fact the differences among those groups center, not on basic aims (*everybody* wants kids to write better), but on matters of methods and means.

Second, individuals and splinter or minority groups should not underestimate their effects and their power. There's nothing wrong or ineffectual about a good teacher—working alone—doing something new, interesting, and vital for a group of thirty students. There's nothing wasted when a parent tutors a group of four or five kids in writing, even if he/she is the only parent in the school doing it. Further, educational changes created by individuals have a way of infusing themselves throughout systems. The "good works" of individual teachers, parents, and administrators are imitated by people who know a good thing when they see it.

Third, and finally, individual efforts—on which all larger movements are ultimately based—are considerably strengthened if the individual can gain a clear perception of where he or she stands and what kinds of skills he/she can bring to bear on a problem. Each person has avenues of action that he or she can ply more or less successfully. For some people, pounding on a superintendent's door will bring positive results, but for others it will bring a pink slip. The individual needs to develop the sense of how and where he or she can work successfully. Just as school districts need a Plan A and Plan B, parents, teachers, and administrators need individual plans: a Plan A, which sketches out their own ideals for participation in change in education, and Plan B, a realistic, considered plan of action for their role in reforming reading and writing in America.

6

Testing and Measuring
Growth in English

A while back I had an opportunity to participate in a conference held at the University of Chicago on the topic, "The English Curriculum Under Fire." Participants came from all parts of the country to discuss the back-to-basics movement and to hear about ways in which English teachers could respond to the widespread criticism of their work.

I led a discussion group, and to begin the session I asked participants to describe the pressures they were experiencing: "How is the back-to-basics movement affecting your school or district? What are the complaints, and how are they being conveyed to you?" I had expected a range of answers, to hear that English teachers were under fire from parents, administrators, college professors, and even from their own students. But I was surprised, for a single topic—testing—absolutely dominated the discussion. Teachers in both colleges and high schools reported that they were increasingly being involved in testing programs. State departments of education were expanding assessment programs; competency tests were being developed for college freshmen; exit-level or graduation examinations were being introduced for both secondary and elementary schools; and in many areas, basic skills tests were in the works at every grade level. One teacher even reported that sequential tests were being proposed on a term-by-term, course-by-course basis for her high school, so that an English student might be tested as many as sixteen times across four years of high school, in addition to taking a diagnostic test upon entering and passing a test in order to graduate.

Why all this testing? One conference participant remarked that Americans seem test happy. "We like to be tested," he observed, "we want to know how we measure up." He pointed out that popular magazines are filled with self-analysis and self-help tests of personality, vocabulary, sexual prowess, and so on. But the mania for testing is more than simply *liking* tests or wanting to know how we compare to others. As a matter of fact, a great many people fear and abhor testing, perhaps because with most tests, there have to be as many ranked "below normal" as "above," as many losers as winners, as many deflated egos as ego trips. It seems axiomatic that those people who do well on tests will be ones who enjoy them most.

The current interest in testing, however, seems to go much deeper, for as often as not, the development of a new test is seen as solving a problem. If a child can't read or write well enough, we test until he or she can. This impulse comes, in some cases, from highly publicized lawsuits in which school graduates have sued the district for failing to teach them to read or write. If the children had been tested and failed, the play-it-safe response goes, the school district would never have gotten itself into a jam. (Whether the child would have learned to read, or, more likely, simply been detained at grade level until school-leaving age, is seldom discussed.)

Further, testing programs create the impression—a false one, I think—that standards are being maintained. After all, if tests maintained standards, the quality of college freshmen would long since have been ensured, since colleges have tested their applicants for over one hundred years. Whatever it does, college entrance testing does not ensure that the product received by the colleges will be "quality."

In the meantime, tests have increasingly come to exert what Banesh Hoffman (1964) labeled as "tyranny" over school programs. While intended to improve instruction and raise standards, they frequently have just the opposite effect. Teachers are forced to concentrate their energies on preparing students to face examinations that, in many cases, have very little to do with real life skills. While some would argue that teachers need this kind of pressure, testing, in fact, seems to be a short-sighted and ineffectual way of bringing about change.

The teachers at the Chicago conference were not opposed to testing in moderation; in fact, most felt that some kinds of standardized tests were quite appropriate as measures of student and teacher performance. Yet it was clear that in most cases the goals and objectives being set by examinations were narrow and fragmentary, focusing on a handful of "minimums" and letting the "maximums"—the essences of quality education—take care of themselves. "The problem with tests," one teacher said, "is not that they *measure,* but that they measure *so little.* They restrict the curriculum rather than opening it up."

Coincidently, while the conference was in session and all this discussion of testing was taking place, the Chicago Board of Education released some test score data. The response of the press helped to demonstrate both the tyranny of the tests and the mindlessness of letting them dictate standards. The announcement was positive rather than negative (for a pleasant change): Chicago children, while on the average reading below grade level, had shown dramatic improvement since the last testing three years earlier. The children now seemed well on the way toward coming up to national norms.

The press was delighted with the news. The staid *Chicago Tribune* made it a front-page headline on the Saturday edition. The newscasters on Channel 2 seemed equally pleased and paused in their formal delivery to engage in an impromptu discussion. One announcer suggested that the test score rise made the Chicago schools a model for other cities, and another agreed, making a quantum leap to exclaim that it was now clear that the large cities of America could save themselves!

Asked to explain the score increase for the benefit of TV cameras, a tests-and-measurements man for the Board of Education first said in a kind of educationese that it was due to increased clarity and specificity of objectives coupled with an improved, more efficient delivery system; but then he also said that it was a result of the commitment, dedication, and enthusiasm of Chicago teachers.

Those teachers had in the past been lambasted by the media, and obviously the praise had to be good for their morale and self-esteem. But whether the teachers should willingly have accepted that kind of praise seemed to me problematical. Without wanting to be a wet blanket, I had to observe that in these proceedings nobody had bothered to describe what was on the test itself. Most good psychometricians will tell you that "reading grade level" is an arbitrary concept, so it was not clear exactly what was being taught and learned more effectively. Further, given the Board administrator's inconsistencies, it wasn't even evident that the changes were due to better teaching. I was thus reminded of Woody Allen's refusal to come to Hollywood to accept his Oscar for *Annie Hall*. When asked why he wouldn't come, he explained that he had not particularly valued the Academy's choices when it did *not* recognize his work; it would be inconsistent to accept its praise now. In short, should the Chicago scores *decline* next time around, due to failures in the "delivery system" or "teacher dedication" (or, more likely, to the social, cultural, and economic conditions that are known to affect test scores dramatically), Chicago teachers might once again be forced to accept the condemnation and amateur educational analysis of the *Tribune* and the six o'clock news.

Most important is to note that an entire school system (indeed, an entire city) was being judged on an arbitrary construct—"reading grade level"—which was probably determined by having children read short passages selected from textbooks or encyclopedias, remember information, and make marks on a machine-scored answer sheet. The realities of instruction—teachers working with children, children reading books and talking about them—were ignored and, one can assume, will continue to be ignored, as long as test scores are allowed to substitute for reality.

The Dimensions of Testing

At this point it is probably useful to introduce a bit of terminology. Discussions of tests are filled with jargon: "age norms," "alternative form reliability," "culture fair" and "culture free" tests, "percentiles" and "stanines," and the "split-half reliability coefficient." We can ignore most of that and focus on three central distinctions:

> *Standardized tests* vs. *non-standardized tests*
> *Objective tests* vs. *subjective tests*
> *Formal examinations* vs. *informal assessments*

(Just so you will have some idea where we are going, I will come out acknowledging the need for limited amounts of the kinds of tests on the left of each equation and advocating more extensive development and use of the tests on the right.)

Standardized tests are designed to be administered to large numbers of people at different times and places, but under common conditions so that the results of groups can be compared validly with one another. The tests are standardized in terms of content (frequently the test will have several different forms with different questions, but the forms will have been shown to be equivalent statistically) and conditions of administration (the time for the test is precisely controlled; the instructions must be read aloud from a standard sheet to the test takers; no questions may be asked of the supervisor). Because they are meant to be given to huge numbers of people, most standardized tests are multiple choice tests that can be machine scored by a computer. Many standardized tests are "norm-referenced": The individual's score is either compared to results achieved by a carefully selected "norming population," a group of initial test takers who set the base-line standard; or compared to the level of achievement of all people taking the test at once.

Non-standardized tests, by contrast, are not so tightly controlled and are usually designed for use with a single group on a one-time-only basis. Non-standardized tests may be multiple choice, but they can also accommodate other answer forms, including the writing of essays that will be graded subjectively.

Objective tests have right and wrong answers; *subjective tests* are graded or scored on the values or perceptions of the reader or grader and frequently involve gradations of quality. Essay tests are the most common form of subjective exam, while multiple choice or short answer tests are generally objective. Nevertheless, one can create essay tests that measure fixed content and are therefore objective, and the following clearly shows that you can write multiple choice questions that are highly subjective:

Whom do you love?
    A. Mary
    B. Bob
    C. Mother
    D. Father
    E. None of the above

Formal examinations take place under controlled conditions, frequently using paper and pencil as the medium. *Informal assessments* can happen at any place at any time and involve a variety of methods of measuring and observing.

Where a great many educators are at odds, if not at loggerheads, is over formal, standardized, objective tests, such as the reading test administered to Chicago children, the Scholastic Aptitude Test and other college entrance tests, most IQ and aptitude tests, and many state and national assessments of pupil growth. There exist a good many solid and fair critiques of these kinds of tests, and the reader may want to look into some of them further (Hoffman, 1964; Dyer, 1974; Hawes, 1974).

As proponents have long argued, standardized, objective tests are unquestionably efficient if one wants to assess large numbers of people. There is, in fact, no apparent alternative in mass testing. It is also argued that standardized tests are relatively inexpensive. Because of the very massiveness of the test programs, test makers are able to spend much more time and money on item development and analysis than could a school district developing its own tests; at the same time, the price of individual administrations is kept reasonably low. Further, the establishment of norms is seen by many to be an advantage, establishing a set of checkpoints, benchmarks, or standards against which schools, individuals, and entire generations can measure themselves. Current computer technology also plays a role in standardized testing, because with sophisticated programs and millions of scores to work with, a computer can come up with analyses and comparisons that are much more informative than raw scores from a small group of test takers. Finally, it is argued, the scores of standardized mass testing are required by industries and colleges as a means of assessing the quality of applicants.

On the other hand, standardized, objective tests are subject to criticism because of the number of flaws inherent in the very nature of mass testing. That is to say, the mass-ness that gives the tests their value also builds in weaknesses that, in many cases, cannot be remedied. Among the most frequently cited problems are the following:

1. *Standardized tests are one-shot measures.* They examine performance at one time only and are thus subject to considerable variation. The day-to-day inaccuracy of the SAT is about ±30 points on a scale of 800, which means that a student scoring as high as 630 one day might drop to 570 the next taking the same or a parallel form of the test, a variation that would certainly make an extraordinary difference in his odds of getting into college (Brill, 1974). Perhaps sensing this, many students take the

Boards over and over until they get a set of scores they like. However, in many standardized tests, the candidate must ride with whatever set of scores he or she earns on a single testing.

2. *The items are frequently ambiguous.* The strongest point made in Hoffman's *Tyranny of Testing* is that many multiple choice and other objective test items actually have more than one answer. The "thinking" test taker may actually come up with wrong answers if he/she mulls over the choices. Thus it is a standard rule in test taking that one should go with the "impulse" answer, the first answer that comes into one's head. The tests thus encourage simplistic thinking.

3. *Testing experience, not just knowledge, helps to determine test scores.* Some people become "test wise," and there is no question that a person who has familiarity with the form of items on a test has a big advantage over one who doesn't. Thus a "practice effect," frequently ignored or denied by testmakers, can artificially inflate scores or harm the inexperienced test taker.

4. *They are subject to racial, cultural, and ethnic bias.* Work has progressed in the development of so-called culture-free tests, but it is extremely difficult to create a standardized test that does not favor the middle-class, standard culture. Thus for many years blacks, Mexican-Americans, and Indians have routinely scored lower on the major standardized tests, not because they necessarily knew less, but because the tests were based on the values and experiences of white Americans.

5. *They fragment knowledge and measure only a portion of what is known.* In literacy, this means that only a few language skills are measured on any given test. Something like the SAT "verbal" test is properly described as a test of vocabulary items, sentence correction, and skill in answering prescribed questions about short passages of reading. It is not, in any sense, a global or comprehensive test of verbal skill.

6. *They test weaknesses, not strengths.* In order to create a "curve" or distribution of scores, test makers search for items some people will get right and others will get wrong. If 100 percent of

test takers got an item right, the test maker would remove it from the battery because it would not produce any useful information. Thus tests literally seek out weaknesses and ignore competencies or knowledges that are possessed by a majority of test takers. While this may be useful if one wants to use a test for diagnostic purposes, it slants results on the negative side and shifts the tests themselves into little known or obscure areas of a discipline.

7. *They are designed for the convenience of test makers, psychometricians, and computer programmers, not the test taker.* What will fit in the computer becomes a major criterion for a good test item. In other words, items that lend themselves to analysis on existing computer programs are favored. Most obviously, this has led to writing skills being measured by multiple choice items rather than a writing sample, to reading comprehension being gauged on short answers to questions rather than, say, a summary of a passage, which would better demonstrate understanding.

8. *They are locked in time.* Because many standardized tests place much emphasis on having each successive testing comparable to the norming exam, the tests cannot substantially change. Whatever skills or knowledges are deemed important by test makers when the test was first created become immemorial. Changes in content are not possible because that would destroy the standardization of the test itself. Many tests currently in use were created in the 1940s and fifties (the SAT, for example, reached its present form in 1948). Thus a phenomenon like the evolution of television is completely ignored by most existing standardized tests. Further, through a phenomenon known as "skyhooking," many standardized tests are validated against one another. Thus a new test achieves credibility by demonstrating that its scores are comparable to an older test. The obsolescence of existing tests is thereby "cloned" into new ones.

The items listed above are flaws inherent in the tests themselves, but the most damning indictments, to my mind, have to do with the fact that, in the end, standardized tests don't do what they claim to do:

9. *They are not cheap.* Standardized testing has become a multi-million-dollar industry, with competing firms scrambling for supremacy and big dollar contracts. While cost-per-pupil figures may seem low, testing every kid in a school, district, or state is staggeringly expensive. Since tests typically cost up to a dollar per child, any district-wide test administration quickly runs into thousands of dollars. In some experimental programs, the obsession with proving results is so great that more money is spent on testing than on program materials. By contrast, a good teacher-constructed test may cost no more than the paper on which it is written. So when someone says that standardized tests are cheap, we must ask, "In comparison to what?" As a matter of fact, no form of testing is probably *more* expensive than the standardized test.

10. *They are not especially good measures.* Because of their very size, standardized tests measure only common skills rather than specific ones; individual or unique skills are completely ignored. In searching for common-denominator skills and knowledge, the test makers must ignore individual traits. Thus, the results of tests might be useful in evaluating groups of people, but not individuals. For example, a single student's score on a college entrance examination is *not* a particularly good indicator of how well he or she will do in college. The college entrance tests "work" only in the sense that the colleges know that if they accept ten thousand students with a score of X or above, a certain percentage of them will make it. Of Jimmy or Sally, both of whom scored X, we can say very little. Lastly, because of the fragmentation of skills and knowledge, standardized tests seldom provide the kind of information that teachers need to teach successfully. Test scores cannot be easily translated into instructional programs for individual children.

Finally, it is important to note that standardized tests and their results are easily subjected to abuse. This is not a problem with the tests themselves; it is something for which the *users* must take some responsibility. Yet these abuses are so pervasive that they seriously limit the uses of the tests:

11. *Standardized tests are used to pigeon-hole, label, and classify students.* Test scores are easy to use as a substitute for actual observations of students. On the basis of test scores young people become labeled: *gifted, remedial, educationally disabled, handicapped but educable,* and so on. Given the weaknesses inherent in the tests, such labeling is obviously chancy, and most teachers and parents know of children who have been misclassified. More important is that such labeling serves no useful purpose in a school that cares to individualize its program, and labeling frequently leads to a sorting and grouping of children that is inefficient, limiting, and downright immoral.

12. *Norms and averages are confused with standards.* Reading "up to grade level" is a limited goal. There is no real world correlative of grade level, so even if a child reads up to this arbitrary par, he or she cannot necessarily handle real world literacy tasks. Because the tests present norms, the norms themselves are too often taken to be the end product of the educational process. Similarly,

13. *Minimums become maximums.* Because the tests examine only fragments and minimums, they provide an incomplete picture of a subject. Yet when teachers are held accountable for test results, the minimums and fragments become overwhelmingly important in teaching. "Teach to the test" becomes a motto—a sensible one if you want to keep your job—and quality education is left to fend for itself. In other words,

14. *The tests become the curriculum.* In no small measure that is happening in America today. As tests proliferate, teachers are spending more and more time prepping, more time teaching fragments and less time teaching reading and writing. The net effect could very easily become curriculum design by test makers.

Toward a Philosophy of Evaluation

If one looks to the history of mass testing, which begins at the turn of the century, one finds that two major educational movements were blossoming: the "scientific education movement" and the "child-centered movement." Initially these two were not in opposition to one another. The scientific movement was concerned with efficiency and precision in education, because American schools were growing at a rapid rate and school leaders needed to learn to teach children—particularly the children of immigrants—in large numbers. E. L. Thorndike of Columbia University is widely quoted for his belief that "Whatever exists at all exists in some amount," which formed the basis of the scientific measurement thrust in education. But in the mind of a man like Thorndike, measurement was principally a way of learning more about one's pupils; it was not simply a way of dealing efficiently with the masses of pupils, and it certainly was not designed for pigeon-holing and classifying them. Scientific measurement was of interest because it would presumably yield *better* information about children's needs and abilities. In this respect, the tests and measurements movement was not at all at odds with the work of a man like John Dewey, who was, in his own way, calling for a child-centered curriculum, where teachers would understand and respond to the needs of their students.

However, it is also clear that from the start, testing was subject to misuse and misapplication and often yielded inaccurate and incomplete data. In *The Abuses of Standardized Testing* (1977a), Vito Perrone shows that other pioneers in the testing movement— Lewis Terman, Henry Goddard, Robert Yerkes, and even Alfred Binet, "father" of the IQ test—had set ideas about eugenics and racial and cultural superiority, which resulted in tests being used to discriminate broadly against racial and ethnic minorities, even to the extent of excluding them from immigration quotas on the grounds of alleged intellectual backwardness. That the misuses and abuses have continued to our own time is obvious.

There is good reason for us to worry today that the tests will dictate the curriculum. As long as testing is allowed to set standards, change in the literacy curriculum will be exceptionally difficult. The tests being introduced into the schools today (and the movement is gaining strength, not becoming weaker) are, by and large, conservative, limited in their scope, with norms and standards that are decades out of tune with the reading and writing habits of Americans. These tests do not raise standards; they merely establish false norms.

I do not, however, mean to create a position that is anti-test or anti-evaluation or to say that schools do not need to measure or assess either students or teachers in any way. As Helen Lodge, a California teacher, wrote in *Uses, Abuses, Misuses of Standardized Tests in English* (Beck, 1973):

Evaluation is part of the teaching act. All good teachers evaluate, in one way or another, the extent to which they achieve the objectives they set for themselves.

The question is not *whether* teachers will evaluate growth in literacy, but *how*. A high school student, Cheryl Loudon, offers one suggestion (also in *Uses, Abuses, Misuses of Standardized Tests in English*):

It is inconceivable to me that a teacher who sees a student from 4–30 hours a week could possibly need a scanner sheet [a computerized printout of test results] to tell them where a student belongs educationally. If a teacher cannot tell where a student's mind is while standing there in his own environment, no multi-produced tests will do it for him.

Valid alternatives to the "multi-produced" test exist, allowing the individual teacher to observe, measure, and record growth. Although standardized tests are obviously here to stay, teachers need to be concerned with developing informal, non-standardized, subjective classroom assessment measures. These need not be idiosyncratic, sloppy, or so subjective as to be useless—charges often leveled at tests that are not standardized and machine scored. In fact, informal assessments are potentially quite scientific and fully in the spirit of E. L. Thorndike, providing ways for teachers to know their students better, to learn more of their needs and interests, to discover their achievements and weaknesses, and, ultimately, to teach students more efficiently *and* more humanely.

Alternatives to the Standardized Test

Vito Perrone has prepared a series of questions that teachers, parents, and administrators can apply to tests, both standardized tests and informal assessments. I suggest that these questions be applied to the alternative measures described here and to the standardized tests currently being used in the school or district where you live, work, or teach:

Are they [the test items] clear? Are they fair? Do they address the *particular* educational concerns of teachers of young children? Do the tests provide *useful* information about the individual children, about the class as a whole? Do they help young children in their learning? Do they support children's intentions as learners? Do they provide parents with essential information about their children? . . . Do teachers feel any pressure to teach to the tests? If the tests were not given, would there be fewer skill sheets and workbooks, a broader range of materials, more attention to individualized learning? Would teachers prefer to use the time devoted to . . . testing for other educational activities? Do teachers feel they can assess children's learning in more appropriate ways . . . ?   [1977a]

A good test, then, is something that directly serves the learner and his/her teachers, rather than being a barrier to better instruction. Although the public seems to have developed a kind of reliance on standardized test scores (the interest in "norms" described earlier), it is often the case that given the choice between good teacher-initiated evaluation and the raw score and percentiles of a standardized test, parents find the former more interesting and useful. In the remainder of the chapter I will present a "sampler" of assessment and evaluation techniques that are specifically useful in a literacy program.

Assessment of Solid Achievement

In the debate over standardized testing, it seems to have been forgotten that, in simplest terms, what students *do* is the best measure of what they are *capable of doing.* That is, whenever students write or read, whenever they make a verbal presentation or participate in a discussion, they demonstrate the skills and abilities they have mastered. When children write, they draw on literally thousands of language skills; when they read they do the same. If teachers (and parents) simply observe and record the language achievements demonstrated by young people, they have an assessment record that is far more comprehensive and specific than any standardized test of basic skills.

This method, in turn, reinforces my earlier arguments for literacy programs based on actual language use. How much does the student write? How much does she read? Does he use speaking and listening skills often? Does she engage in discussion frequently? These are crucial questions for parents and teachers to ask. In examining student-produced language—compositions, reports and reviews, presentations—we can come to know precisely how well students are using the language.

Many teachers supplement the traditional grade book with a range of reports of student achievement. For example, anecdotal records (sometimes called "twenty-six letter grading") are simply notes of a teacher's observations, recorded at regular intervals and shared with students and parents. These periodic summaries usually contain a listing of the work achieved by the student over a set period of time, along with the teacher's comments about progress, needed improvement, and so on. Student journals or work reports can also be used as twenty-six letter evaluation resources or even as attachments to the teacher's anecdotal reports.

At the University of North Dakota, Vito Perrone and his faculty have developed a system called "documentation," which offers another illustration of how concrete achievement can be assessed and recorded. As part of an experimental school program a "Documentation Committee" of parents, staff, and students was established.

A wide range of documents was maintained, including systematic records of individual children's learning, teacher journals, weekly and daily goal statements, anecdotal records, written evaluations prepared for parents, newsletters, field trips, interactions with parents about individual children, advisory council meetings, teacher, parent, child interviews, use of instructional materials center, parent participation in the classroom, maps of classrooms at various intervals, etc. Document samples and evaluative comments filled out the documentation booklet (247 pages in all). [1977b]

In an English program, the documentation for an individual student might include a year-by-year list of books read (a list, by the way, that can be maintained as easily by the students as by their teachers), and a sampler of student writing, say, five papers from each grade level. It would hold a description of some of the non-written projects—roleplays, dramatizations, discussions—in which the student had participated, along with the teacher's anecdotal descriptions of the student's work. For entire classes, the teacher would record his or her basic aims and objectives, a rationale or statement of philosophy for those goals, and documentation of successes and failures. Obviously the documentation package as described by Perrone is completely flexible. A documentation committee would want to select from the myriad forms of evaluation available a manageable number: enough to show the program's results, but not so many as to bury teachers in paperwork.

Implied in Perrone's description is something at least as important as the evaluation measures selected. It seems clear that the project participants saw evaluation as a tool for use in developing a good program rather than as a threat. Thus they wanted to do it as well as possible, developing their own measures rather than relying on prepackaged, inadequate, and at times threatening standardized tests.

Checklists, Criterion Referenced Tests, and Performance Mastery

For some, even the complex evaluation system involved in a good documentation program seems too informal, too subjective. Further, such devices as anecdotal records and periodic written reports are time consuming and, for teachers with large class loads, not an altogether practical method. In such situations a combination of checklists—which allow for "shorthand" records of performance—coupled with occasional anecdotal summaries may be appropriate.

For example, a teacher can take the basic course objectives and create a series of checklists or observation schedules. Objectives—broken down as finely and in as much detail as the teacher wishes—are listed in one vertical column and student names are written across the top of the page to form a grid. The teacher simply indicates through a simple grading key whether, how frequently, and how well the student met the course objectives.

An especially useful kind of checklist describes the basic skills that are demonstrated by the successful completion of a writing or reading project. The teacher lists five or ten skills that are "documented" or established when a student, say, writes an essay or reads a novel and reports on it. When the project is completed, the skills are simply ticked off in the teacher's or the student's logbook. Systematically kept, these records can reassure parents and teachers that the basics are being taught even in programs where workbook and drill are deemphasized.

Checklists can be used to measure affective behaviors that are far beyond the range of conventional tests. James Wilsford (n.d.) has developed something called the "Experience-Language Context Inventory," which is a checklist to assess whether or not students show such traits as self-direction, sensitivity toward others, open-ended questioning, and an ability to draw on past experiences.

Checklists can even be computerized. The East Lansing, Michigan, public schools allow teachers in the middle schools to prepare a series of statements describing the work done in school during a marking period. The statements are then entered into the computer. The teacher assesses whether or not students performed the required activities, and his or her observations are entered on a machine-readable scoring sheet. At grading time the parent receives a computerized printout for each course in which his/her child is enrolled, detailing precisely what was accomplished during the term. While this system obviously smacks of standardization and dehumanization, it is also a manageable scheme that gives parents an individualized report based on actual classroom observations, while not burying teachers in paperwork. Further, the cost is quite low for school districts using computers for such tasks as budgeting and inventory that use the same basic programs.

"Criterion referenced" and performance mastery tests are also checklists of a sort. The *criterion referenced test*, which in many areas is replacing the norm referenced tests, simply measures whether a student can or cannot achieve a particular task (rather than making comparisons between a student and a normative population). The test asks the student to demonstrate a skill by actually doing it. Thus, for example, if the goal of a program is for students to write a business letter, they write the letter and have it graded by specified criteria of acceptability; e.g., "Is it legible?" "Are the headings correct?" "Did it contain the essential information?" "Was it signed?" Courses centered on *performance mastery* simply outline the tasks or tests that need to be passed in order to demonstrate competence in the subject. The instruction can be centered directly on the activities involved in the test, rather than focused on fragmented or unrelated skills.

Evaluating Writing

Measuring growth in written expression is a matter that has plagued teachers and test makers for generations. The concept of "growth," for example, is a complex one, for people rarely write the same composition twice, and if they do, any changes are as likely to reflect changes in content as increased linguistic skills. Thus one can't easily have students write an essay once in September, again in June, and compare results. Further, defining "good writing" (and thus writing growth) is devilishly difficult. The research literature is filled with cases where raters were so divided in their opinions that they gave every conceivable grade from "good" to "bad" to each paper in a set. Often the only criterion of "quality" turns out to be handwriting, which merely means that theme graders give good grades to the papers they can read most easily. Multiple choice or short answer tests, which require students to correct errors, pick "the best" sentence, show knowledge of grammar or rhetoric, can produce a set of scores on verbal ability, yet no one has ever shown such tests to correlate well with the quality of writing people actually produce.

The best measure of growth in writing remains concrete achievement. That is, if you want to see how well or badly a child writes, ask to see his/her writing protfolio and read half a dozen pieces. Such analysis does not permit easy comparisons among children—since each child presumably writes on different topics—but gives you a very clear sense of the student's abilities as a writer and his or her range of interests.

Nevertheless, many schools are now searching for a more formal means of assessing writing, wisely wanting to use actual writing samples rather than a standardized test. Paul B. Diederich has developed one fairly successful procedure; in *Measuring Growth in English* (1974), he describes a school-wide assessment program that has been used with apparent success by a number of districts. It involves having essays written early and late in the term or year, then evaluated by two, and in the case of disagreements, several teachers. Diederich relies on what is called "holistic" grading, in which readers rank papers on the basis of general impressions of such matters as *ideas, organization, wording, flavor, usage, punctuation, spelling,* and *handwriting.* While a trait like "flavor" may seem hopelessly vague, Diederich finds that with some training readers show surprising consistency in rating.

At the same time, the process is very time consuming, and at least one large school district that tried the program decided that it simply wasn't worth the effort, that the information gleaned from the concrete "scores" produced by this method did not yield sufficient information to warrant the time and expense (Suhor, n.d.) Further, after all the work has been done, the school has only a measure of student work on two essays, rather than a broad assessment of his/her writing ability.

The outline of a more complex, yet more practical classroom scheme has been suggested by Charles Cooper (1975), who uses a number of different measures to evolve a picture of how well a student writes. Among the evaluation components he proposes are:

—*Writing quality.* This can be demonstrated several ways, from a review of an entire writing portfolio to the use of something like the Diederich scale.

—*Willingness to write.* This is revealed through teacher observations about the student's approach to writing tasks, coupled with the student's own journal comments about writing.

—*Valuing writing.* Using attitude scales, students indicate how they "value" writing in comparison to other modes of learning and expression.

—*Frequency counts.* Cooper recommends the limited use of formal counting measures as a means of assessing such matters as correctness (number of errors per selected number of words) and verbal fluency as determined through length of sentences.

To his measures we might add such means of assessment as:

—*Describing the range of composition forms.* (How many different kinds of writing does the student try?)

—*Competence on real world writing forms.* (Can the student write a business letter? an exam question?)

As these options suggest, for a teacher to make solid statements about students' writing (and even their attitudes toward writing) is not difficult. The abstract concept of "growth" is more difficult and in many ways misleading. Thus parents and teachers should aim at seeing student work described and assessed from many different points of view, rather than looking, as we have in the past, for some sort of single, all-encompassing "score" that will answer the elusive question, "Can this child write well?"

Evaluating Reading

"Can the child read?" is equally elusive, for "reading," like "writing," is a term that has many meanings. To some it represents the ability to translate symbols into sounds (reading aloud); to others, it is the ability to retell the contents of a passage (comprehension). For many years, those two concepts dominated the reading curriculum. More recently, however, research has shown that reading is vastly more complex than imagined. Good readers do *not* read every single word on the page; they skip and jump, picking up words and contextual clues. Good readers do not remember everything in a passage; they ignore material that is not related, directly or indirectly, to their purpose. Good readers do not passively absorb the fixed content of a printed page; they blend the message with their own experience to create new and unique meanings. Little wonder, then, that assessing reading skills defies easy measurement.

One simplistic measure, nevertheless widely used, is the concept of reading grade level, which is frequently derived by evaluating a normative population in a standardized test or by applying a readability formula to a selection (counting long and short words, sentence length, etc. as indicators of difficulty). But reading tests are often based on passages overloaded with information, passages chosen to meet a test maker's, not a reader's, purposes, with total comprehension rather than careful selection of detail at stake, all done under timed conditions rather than at one's purposeful leisure. Under those circumstances, it's not surprising that tests so often show that "kids can't read." Further, Frank Smith (1971), a reading specialist from the Ontario Institute of Education, has shown that comprehension tests may even be damaging to readers, forcing them to change their day-to-day patterns in order to remember facts from the passage.

To show some of the ways in which standardized tests can distort the reading act itself and to imply instructional needs that are themselves distorted, I proposed in *The English Journal* (1974) an alternative way of determining reading skill, drawing on the admittedly defective concept of grade level, yet allowing the students to be tested on their own turf, rather than on that of test makers. The instructions to teachers are as follows:

1. Ask your students (especially the ones whom you see as "problem" readers) to bring in a passage or reading material of their own choice, something they think they would especially enjoy and would like to share with other students.
2. Give the students time to read the material—as much time as needed—then ask them to share the ideas with another person. If the partner has questions, the student is free to go back to the text to look for the answers. The two students can continue discussing until both are satisfied that the main ideas have been shared. While this is going on, you can drift from pair to pair to check on the process. The question is simply this: Can the student read this self-selected passage well enough to share it with a friend?
3. Have the students compute the "grade level" of their material using a simple readability formula. The SMOG index of the Gunning FOG formula will work satisfactorily and you can find information about them in any basic reading test.
4. Compare the score to the students' regular reading scores as established by the school's tests.

The results of this form of testing are pretty obvious. In my own experiments, children regularly scored one to several grade levels higher on the self-selected, informal test than they did on a standardized test. Critics pointed out the obvious fact that testing kids on their own choice of material biases the test, making it "easy." To counter, I submit that what young people actually read is a better test of their reading ability, that standardized tests introduce a bias of their own.

At the very least, it seems clear that even if students are to be tested on material of someone else's choosing, that material should have some relationship to their own lives (e.g., they should be tested on a passage from an assigned history or science text, rather than a snippet from a totally unfamiliar work.)

Increasingly teachers have found that informal inventories of reading skills and reading difficulty can be done right in the class without reliance on standardized tests. Thomas A. Rakes and Lana McWilliams (1978) have described their work with two informal tests, *Cloze Procedure* and *Content Inventory*. The Cloze test simply blanks out _____ seventh word in a passage, and _____
$$1 \qquad\qquad 2$$
the reader can satisfactorily insert the _____ word or a reasonable
$$3$$
synonym, the _____ is probably not too difficult for __ or her.
$$4 \qquad\qquad\qquad 5$$
(Answers: 1, *every;* 2, *if;* 3, *right;* 4, *passage;* 5, *him.*) If a student is able to fill in the blanks—usually with the missing word or a close synonym—the passage is said to be "readable." No reference to age or grade level is required. In contrast to the usual readability formulae, the Cloze test recognizes that a good reader is a "meaning maker," that the difficulty of a passage is determined, not so much by whether the words are long or short, but by whether the reader can make sense of them in context.

Similarly, the Content Inventory described by Rakes and McWilliams draws on a selected passage from a book proposed for reading by the class, not just a short excerpt, but a several-page section long enough to have meaning of its own. The teacher then prepares a dozen content questions based on the material he or she wants to emphasize in the course. Students' answers are recorded on a summary sheet that allows the teacher to assess student competence on a one-to-one basis. The whole class score allows the teacher to judge subjectively but scientifically whether or not most of the children in the class can comprehend the book.

Informal assessment measures need not be limited to reading. Literary appreciation can be assessed and evaluated as well. For instance, Sarah Snider (1978) has adapted what are called Likert scales—assessing behavior on a scale from "frequently" to "never"—to measure five levels of response to poetry. These range from the student's perception of poetry itself ("How often would you sit in on a class session of poetry reading if you always had a choice?") to criticism ("When presented with two or more poems, how often do you decide which you like better?") to affective response ("When you read poetry about people, how often does it cause you to feel differently about yourself?"). Snider's test is a learning instrument in itself: Not only can the teacher learn about students' responses, the students can study how they react to poetry and strengthen their skills of appreciation. The instrument, then, provides a natural bridge from teacher evaluation to student self-assessment.

Self-Evaluation and Conferences

One reason Americans are so test happy—wanting to know how they "measure up"—is that the schools seldom teach them independent self-evaluation. Thus as adults they must frequently depend on the assessments of outsiders. For instance, one reason many students do badly in college freshman composition is that they lack the ability to evaluate and subsequently to edit what they write. Having depended upon teacher critiques of their writing in the schools, the students find themselves at sea. A good composition program, then, ought to place very high value on the skill of self-evaluation, and so should the literacy program in general.

To some critics of education, "self-evaluation" is a buzzword, resurrecting memories of programs in the late 1960s that "threw grades out of the window," where students were told that only "expressiveness and creativity" mattered, that they needn't worry about formal standards of evaluation.

However, focusing education on self-evaluation is a matter of having very high standards and expectations, both for oneself and one's students. Teaching students to serve as their own evaluators is time consuming and complex. One obviously can't just "turn kids loose" and expect that assessment will be satisfactory. As Peter Elbow has shown in his excellent book *Writing Without Teachers* (1974), helping students learn to critique their own (and each other's writing) must be done in gradual steps, first simply getting students to see and respond to what has been written, then moving on to more and more complex kinds of criticism.

Richard Beach (1975) has articulated a three-step procedure for self-evaluation based on stages of *describing, judging,* and *predicting.* First students learn to *describe* what they (or others) have done, whether in reading, writing, drama, or speech. Only after they can summarize their accomplishments objectively do they go on to make *judgments* about quality. Most important, perhaps, is that on the basis of their own judgments, the students then concentrate on making *predictions:* How can I do it better? If I do X differently, will Y occur? What will happen if I try it a new way? This kind of predicting is the skill that few of our school graduates possess, and it is quite difficult to learn as an adult. One has to wonder what the effect on the schools (and adult performance generally) would be if, instead of being immersed in a series of teacher-graded tests and compositions, young people were placed in a program that systematically developed their skills of self-evaluation. They might keep journals and logs of their work, engage constantly in peer evaluation and feedback, learn to edit their own writing, and, as they grow toward the end of their school careers, move into formal aesthetic and intellectual criticism. One has to guess that such students would not only be independent thinkers and users of language, but would be quite capable of functioning in the real world of employers, teachers, and even standardized tests.

Of course, in a self-evaluation program the teacher is neither neutral nor passive. The teacher knows (or ought to know) what good writing is and knows (or should know) the difference between an adequate and an inadequate reading of a poem. In self-evaluation, however, teachers allow their standards and knowledge to be learned through modeling rather than direct imposition; that is, teachers show their skills rather than imposing values, using marks or grades as a club.

Close interaction between students and teachers is important in self-evaluation, and having conferences together is a vital part of any self-assessment program. Each student should meet with his or her teacher to talk over the student's descriptions, judgments, and predictions and discuss their accuracy. Further, parents ought to be involved as well, meeting with the teacher once or twice a term, not just to hear about how well (or badly) Johnny is doing, but to participate in the evaluation and growth process, contributing perceptions along with those of the teacher and the child.

Grading

Of grading I will write only briefly. Grades are, by and large, an even less adequate measure of achievement than standardized tests. They condense a wide range of behaviors into a single score that communicates very little to the student or his/her parents. Further, the grading system is notorious for distorting the aims of education, forcing and cajoling students to work simply for grades. Indeed, given the dominance of the grading system, it is not surprising that so few of our students develop skills of self-assessment and self-evaluation.

But grades, like standardized tests, are with us and will remain with us for the foreseeable future. The colleges naturally rely on grade point averages as an entrance criterion, and the schools use marks for purposes of classifying and sorting. While neither of those uses is satisfactory (like college entrance examinations, grades are at best mediocre predictors of individual success in college), our school system is geared to their use.

Teachers, parents, and administrators concerned about the negative effects of grading ought to examine *Wad-Ja Get: The Grading Game in American Education* by Howard Kirschenbaum, Rodney W. Napier, and Sidney Simon (1971), which not only reviews the inequities of the grading scheme, but suggests a number of alternatives to grading (such as Pass/Fail and Credit/No Credit) and alternative ways of grading (like contract grading, performance mastery, point systems), which allow the teacher to document achievement as well as grade it.

In the meantime, if teachers develop a battery of informal assessments of the sort I have described here, the negative aspects of grading will be minimized. If a teacher uses a sound documentation system, coupled with work in student self-assessment, the actual grade, derived after other forms of evaluation that take place, will be made less important and its basis will be clear to the student. It is when grades stand alone without other kinds of evaluative measures that their interest and importance become all-consuming.

Evaluation and Teaching: The Teacher as Learner

Perhaps the most useful thing about an informal, teacher-developed assessment program is that it puts the teacher in the position of raising, and then answering, questions about his or her own teaching. While it is important for teachers to know the formal research in their field—research into the relationship between thinking and writing correctness, research into the reading process—the best research questions and the most appropriate answers will be found by individual teachers working with individual students. The professional literature simply doesn't provide much assistance when it comes to Johnny over there in the second row or to Jane in third period honors. It is through systematic collection of data and testing of informal hypotheses that teachers can grow in their teaching. Evaluation, in short, is useful for teachers as well as students, and both successes and failures need to be recorded and considered. Thus teachers might draw on informal evaluation instruments to involve themselves in a self-assessment cycle.

Describing. What is happening in the class? What is happening to individual students? What are they reading? What are they writing? How much and how often do they talk? What do they talk about? What are the dimensions of literacy in the classroom? How can I document the activities and achievements of the class?

Judging. How do I value what is happening to the class as a whole and to individual students? Are the students writing well?

What are the gaps in their reading experience? What teaching strategies work? Which don't? Why? What do my evaluation measures tell me about my students' successes and failures?

Predicting. What strategies, techniques, materials can I employ to bring about the changes I want to see? How can I evaluate whether or not my predictions are correct?

The case for the teacher-as-experimenter, for the development of teacher-designed assessment measures is, to my mind, a strong one. It is not, as some would say, a refusal to be held accountable for external judgments, and it is certainly not an attempt to avoid either hard work or the task of evaluating young people. In the long run, teacher-developed assessments of their own and their students' growth are more thorough, less expensive, and far more professional than the standardized tests that are being offered as a panacea to educational ills.

Further, as we approach century twenty-one it appears certain that the relationships among literacy, society, and the schools will become increasingly complex. We need to raise hard and thoughtful questions about the teaching of reading and writing. Evaluation itself will not provide direct answers to those questions, but a quality assessment program, with standardized testing kept in moderation and informal assessments as a mainstay, will help us see if we're on the right track toward a more successful teaching of reading and writing.

Interlude: English Teacher: 2001 A.D.

Paul Benjamin awoke with a vague feeling of unreality and an ache in his skull that told him he was hung over. He only dimly recalled being out the night before on a consciousness-altering binge, but he knew he'd have to pay the price: a day of slogging through his teaching schedule, feeling ill, and regretting the night before. Pine-tree alcohol (or "bark booze") created splendid hallucinations while you were drinking it; but it was raw stuff, and you could never tell when it would stop working on you. Sometimes Paul longed for the good old days when grain could be used to distill smooth, predictable, sippin' whiskey, not just to feed hungry millions.

He kicked off the covers and immediately regretted the sudden movement, then stumbled to the window to see what the day promised. Soot-colored rain fell from the autumn sky, turning the last of the chrysanthemums ash grey. A cloud of steam and smoke curled up through the drizzle, and Paul muttered a small note of appreciation that Tommy had remembered to stoke the wood fire in the boiler of the ancient 1975 Toyota. He groaned inwardly as he thought of what it had cost to convert the car to steam power last year. It had been bad enough back in 1990 when the government had offered tax incentives for the original conversion from gasoline to electric power. This time not only had there been no incentive, he'd been fined a pretty penny just for owning a foreign car in the first place. Furthermore, the wheels were beginning to splinter, which meant that he'd have to drive two hundred miles to a forest preserve just to locate a tree big enough to supply replacements. Then, as soon as the glass shortage was over he'd have to shell out at least a grand to replace the windshield that had shattered during last year's Deep Freeze.

He moved in pain to the bathroom and lathered his beard in the dark. Then he snapped on the bulb and had almost completed shaving sixty seconds later when it turned itself off. He thought about waiting for it to recycle but decided to scrape off the rest of his stubble in the dark. The energy saving incentive had worked once again.

Paul began to dress while checking over his schedule and notes for the day. First period it was History I. He groaned again; facing three thousand bored faces in the gym was more than he thought he could bear. He didn't know a damn thing about history anyway, but taking on this course had saved his job in the last round of cutbacks. Second period would be back in his speciality but only slightly more to his liking: supervising 250 graduating seniors in the English Remedial Skill Development Laboratory.

During third period he was due at the daily English Department Crisis Meeting, where he and his colleagues would gather to consider curriculum cutbacks in the light of the most recent Budget-memo. Paul sometimes thought that perhaps the three remaining English specialists should simply draw straws to see which one of them would quit, thus effecting a 33 percent savings that would meet the administrative mandates for at least another year.

Paul looked at a vision of himself in the mirror and was filled with self-pity and self-contempt. At fifty-nine years of age he looked ready for retirement. He was balding fast and developing sagging jowls. His face looked tired—exhausted—and he found himself more and more dependent on chemicals to keep himself going.

"I can't do it by myself," he muttered, and reached reluctantly for a small vial on the vanity. He dug out a tiny capsule, looked at it, thought for a moment, then shook out a second. He tossed them to the back of his throat and swallowed them without water.

Almost immediately things began to seem better. Paul drifted back to the window, not to check the weather, for it was always sunny and bright under the Weatherdome, but to glance at the garden. Tommy—bless his heart—had picked the grapefruit and was weeding the artichokes. In the distance, a flash of sunlight off the glass of the monorail reminded him of the time. He punched a series of buttons on his wrist comptrometer and the schedule revealed he had eleven minutes until the next train to school.

Moving more rapidly now, Paul slipped on his tunic and went back to the desk to review his afternoon schedule. It was one that pleased him. After lunch he would check out one of the Board of Education Electro-autos and transit outside the dome to a rural community where he was to be present at the dedication of a new Adjunct Community Learning Center. As English department representative, he had advised in the selection of materials for the resource center and would be teaching several Community Literature Seminars there in coming months.

Then it was back to school, where he was due at the Instructional Media Center at three o'clock to videotape a lecture on algorithmic linguistics for his Public Broadcasting "Science is Literature" series, the tape to be transmitted to Advanced Placement Units all around the hemisphere.

After the lecture he would spend a few minutes meditating by the reflecting pool, then cross the campus to the Student/Faculty Association building, where he and his tutorial students had booked one of the lounges for their weekly proseminar. Although Paul was always invigorated by lecturing thousands via the cable hookups, it was tutoring, by George, that gave him most satisfaction in his teaching. He was good at it, and he loved opening the minds of his students, whether aged six or sixty.

Paul glanced again at his vision in the mirror and felt young, strong, and proud. He appeared ten years younger than his age and felt as if he still had fifty good years of teaching left in him. He snapped his briefolio shut and strode to the bedroom door, eager to greet his family and the world.

Fourteen minutes later, her husband off to work, Maya Benjamin entered the bedroom. "Son of a bitch," she swore under her breath. "After all these years you'd think he could make the goddam bed." She stepped over the pajamas on the floor and swept a stack of Paul's papers off her own briefcase. "Damn drunk," she muttered.

In the bathroom, she spotted two vials on the vanity. One was labeled:

FANTASY INDUCER
For symptomatic relief
of everyday pressures

The other said:

REALITY
RESTORATIVE
For alleviation of
hallucinative depression.

"No wonder he was so bloody happy," Maya said to herself. "I wonder which one he took?"

II

Literacy in the Schools

Introduction

The divisions in this section are a concession to the reality of the present school system with its segmented grade levels, courses, and subjects, and the publishing convention of dividing books into chapters. The thrust of the argument is toward interdisciplinary teaching of literacy, toward schooling that doesn't show "seams" where disciplines meet (and divide), toward schools where students are not graded, classed, or otherwise grouped and clustered (or separated and isolated). Truly interdisciplinary teaching would best be done in a non-graded setting (a non-school, in fact), where teachers with many different skills would meet with children to evolve individualized programs cutting across all subject-matter areas. A book describing that kind of literacy education should, likewise, be seamless, without subject matter or other divisions. It should simply describe the ebb and flow of human experience and the role that language and language learning play in structuring and controlling that experience.

But in the 1980s the conventions of schooling will persist (and publishers still like to see a table of contents with chapters). During the shelf life of this book, it is likely that elementary students will still be assigned in groups to grades, though in a few progressive schools they will be assigned to multi-grade, multi-level classrooms. In the secondary schools students probably will still move from English class to history class to physics to math, though in a few *avant garde* schools they will enter into interdisciplinary classes, mostly English/humanities, but increasingly courses that cut across C. P. Snow's "two cultures" to relate science and the humanities.

This section begins with a discussion of "The Dimensions of English" and sketches out what seem to me the principal roles of English teaching in the school literacy program. I stress expanding English instruction beyond the traditional emphasis on grammar, expository writing, and classical literature, and I show the evolution of a program that consistently relates language to the lives of young people. The two succeeding chapters discuss literacy in the two cultures: "Literacy in the Humanities" and "Reading and Writing in Science." These chapters have been written to show that *any* teacher—be he/she science teacher, historian, or English teacher—can engage in interdisciplinary work, even within a self-contained classroom. Thus, if interdisciplinary studies are slow in growing, the impetus can come from *any* interested teacher. Extended bibliographies of books for young readers are a part of every chapter so that non-specialists—subject teachers, parents, administrators—can find a starting point for interdisciplinary reading programs.

The final chapter moves beyond subject matter and even school boundaries to discuss "Language and Community." It describes practical reading and writing seldom stressed in the academic disciplines, but it also shows the resources available to teachers through the community—any community—which can enrich literacy instruction in the sciences, the humanities, or English. This chapter, too, constitutes my response to proposals for very narrow "survival" English and career education programs. I refuse to isolate such skills in dull, "nuts and bolts" courses and want to show that practical English has a natural, well-integrated place in a comprehensive literacy program.

Thus the various units, courses, programs, and activities I describe in this section might find their way into a conventional school with fifty-minute, subject-divided periods, or they might be part of the ideal, seamless, interdisciplinary school of the future.

English teachers should be advised that some traditional components of "English" will be found in other chapters within this section. "The classics," for example, appear within the context of a discussion of the humanities in Chapter 8. An examination of grammar appears in Chapter 9, "Science Reading and Writing," since grammar and dialect studies are legitimate topics for scientific inquiry and investigation. The history of English seems to fall most naturally under a discussion of the humanities, and, as noted, the English teacher's traditional concern for business and practical English will be found in Chapter 10, "Language and Community." This distribution of topics was not done to be difficult or to be threatening to English teachers; rather, it is intended to reemphasize the point that English studies are naturally interdisciplinary.

7
The Dimensions of English

1. ENGLISH AND THE CURRICULUM

English teachers have always had difficulty describing the aims or goals of their work, much to the frustration of administrators and school boards. In part this problem has been created by the diverse and contradictory expectations placed on English, as I pointed out in Chapter 1. But teachers have complicated the problem for themselves by steadfastly refusing over the years to come to grips with the dimensions of their admittedly unwieldy discipline and to perceive it as some kind of organic whole. Characteristically, English teachers describe their subject in terms of individual components and fragmentary parts—literature, composition, vocabulary, and so on. Thus "literature," described as an aesthetic or enculturating component with no reference to anything but classic books, seems isolated from the real world, from the practical demands that many students will face after graduation. Creative writing, if taught in isolated units, may appear contrary to the mastery of the skills of correctness, just as compartmentalizing spelling by placing words in long lists isolates it from the practical demands of spelling one's theme correctly or writing a note for the milkman.

John Dixon, a British teacher who is a major theorist in English education, provides a focus for our discussion by simply describing what children can be *doing* in English. "An English classroom," he says,

is a place where pupils meet to share experience of some importance, to talk about people and situations in the world as they know it, gathering experience into new wholes and enjoying the satisfaction and power that this gives. But in so doing each individual takes what he can from the shared store of experience and builds it into a world of his own. [1975]

The key word here is "wholes," for in looking at children's experiences as wholes and relating those experiences to language development we can begin to bring some sense to the amorphous discipline of English.

What do children *do* with language? Young people use language as a way of perceiving and coming to know their world, of categorizing and storing their impressions, of thinking (consciously and subconsciously), and of expressing ideas to others (see Chapter 3). They see a car accident, think about it and worry about it, then talk out their feelings with a sympathetic adult. They read a history textbook, memorize the four causes of World War I, and spew it back on an examination for a teacher. They read a comic book, chuckle internally and externally about it, then write an imitation to give to friends. The language cycle—perceive, think, express—goes on all the time, and in the process, the children build wholes; that is, they build an increasingly comprehensive series of views about the world in which they live. They become, in a word, educated.

I hope that this makes it clear why I describe English as the *core* subject in the elementary and secondary school curriculum. The whole of human experience, of the child's experience, does not end with something called language arts or communication skills; it extends into other disciplines and courses—science, math, home economics—and goes beyond the school as well, into the home, the job, the community.

At the same time, English cannot be perceived merely as a ser-

vice subject, offering only those skills that will prepare students
for other courses or for the literacy demands of the real world.
While English looks outward for connections with other subjects,
it must maintain a wholeness and an integrity of its own.

I will label this concept of language study "organic" English. It
suggests, first, that English teachers cease fragmenting the curriculum by dwelling on endless distinctions: creative writing versus
"non-creative" writing, literature versus "non-literature," print
versus non-print media, basic skills versus whatever their opposite
may be (are there *any* skills that are not basic?). Organic English,
in simplest terms, is a language-based curriculum that takes as its
overriding goal providing each student with as many diverse,
growth-producing experiences with language as possible. In
the process, students learn the skills required for accomplishing
specific tasks, whether looking up numbers in a library catalog
or proofreading an examination. Skills are not labeled, identified,
or enumerated *a priori* or listed as a master plan to dictate the
teacher's work. Rather, the basics are identified and taught as the
students proceed in the process of making wholes of their experiences *and* their language.

In describing an organic English program, it is tempting to
follow the current trend and lay down a set of "shoulds" and
"oughts," a clear list of rules that "must" be followed if the literacy
crisis is to be solved. But such a solution is simplistic, and past experience with externally mandated curricula and objectives shows
quite clearly that they fail. Further, it should be evident that
organic English is evolutionary, not static, making it impossible to
establish rigid guidelines anyway.

Rather than setting out some autocratic imperatives (the
"shoulds" and "oughts"), I want to describe possibilities (some
"mights" and "could be's"), showing the potential of organic English. However, this description should not be seen as being pie-in-
the-sky idealism or mere wishful thinking. As the reader will see in
this chapter and the following ones, I will draw heavily on examples of *existing programs*. Thus I will not just be speculating

about English as it *could* be taught in the coming decades, but showing through specific examples what good contemporary teachers are doing *now*. Frequently these people are isolated and working alone; their courses or units may be the only bright spot in an otherwise lackluster program. But the examples I will present show the potential of organic English in the schools. The task of teachers in the 1980s, it seems to me, is to see the isolated pockets grow into organic curricula.

As an organizing principle, I want to refer to the work of G. Robert Carlsen, a specialist in reading for young people, and his exploration of the roles that literature and language play in people's lives (1974). Carlsen has shown that as children grow, their use and enjoyment of language changes and develops. At one stage, for example, books engage principally for their story value—the enchantment of narrative—while at other times literature is important in providing a person with insights into his or her own life or an understanding of the values of the society in which he or she lives. Similarly, the ways in which we employ writing vary as we grow. At some stages we are most interested in writing as a way of understanding the self; at other times, we value writing more for its use in communication with or persuasion of others.

Drawing on Carlsen's work, but adapting it for purposes of this book, I will suggest five stages of growth in language learning and the approximate grade levels at which they seem strongest:

1. *Unconscious Delight*. (Grades K–6) Engagement with language and literature for the sheer pleasure and satisfaction of a good story, the sounds of words, or the enchantment of the unfamiliar.

2. *Vicarious Experience*. (Grades 6–9) Using language to extend the dimensions of one's universe to learn more about the world and the people who inhabit it.

3. *Seeing Oneself*. (Grades 8–10) Reading and writing used to explore personal experience and to see those experiences in the light of others'.

4. *Expanding Consciousness.* (Grade 10 up) Language as a means of learning about human issues, problems, and values and coming to understand the human condition and the perennial questions facing humankind.

5. *Aesthetic Experience.* (Grade 10 up) Enjoyment of language and literature because of conscious appreciation of form, structure, and content.

In identifying grade levels I do not intend to establish a rigid developmental stance or to suggest that these stages neatly pigeon-hole all young people. But this scheme draws on and is consistent with the work of a number of major theorists in psychology and English, Eric Erikson (1963), Jean Piaget (1969), Jerome Bruner (1960), John Dewey (1930), and James Nimmo Britton (1975), to name just a few.

Most important, these developmental stages help us to conceptualize a number of growth patterns that have long been recognized by psychologists, linguists, and rhetoricians:

—from personal and private uses of language to public. Youngest children read and write principally for themselves, to understand their own experiences. As children mature, they increasingly draw upon language to deal with and control issues outside themselves.

—from concrete problems to abstract issues. At the earliest stages in life, young people engage in what Piaget calls concrete reasoning, where they must *see* and *touch* to be able to *comprehend*. As they mature, they increase their powers to use symbols and words to manipulate ideas.

—from spoken language to written forms. The unconscious delight of youngest children in both literature and composing is principally oral. Children listen, talk, chant, and recite first; they read and write later.

In the remainder of this chapter I will describe these stages in some detail, showing the kinds of reading/writing/listening/speaking activities which make up a comprehensive English program.

2. THE ELEMENTARY YEARS

I'd like to make the next journey through life as an elementary school teacher (one equipped with extra measures of patience, noise tolerance, and sense of humor). Elementary kids are among the easiest and most delightful for a teacher to work with. They are inherently curious; they are generally happy; they are entertaining and amusing in their own right. They are also quick of mind and hand and before you can say, "William, put down that . . . ," William has put it to whatever use he (but certainly not its maker) had in mind.

The spontaneity and naturalness of elementary school children extends to language as well. Grade school children don't need to be told that writing is important and a skill that must be mastered, for they are natural storytellers and welcome an opportunity to spin a tale. On the whole, they take to literature as a duck takes to water and have an unconscious (but by no means uncritical) interest in almost anything printed that is read or shown to them. Most elementary children love to talk, and in addition to their exploratory chit-chat, they can manage productive discussion quite comfortably. They spontaneously spring into drama, and if you show them a camera or paint brush, they want to make a picture—to compose—with it.

Thus the grades provide a natural arena for young people to have positive experiences with the basics of English: reading, literature, writing, talking, listening, and media. The comprehensive aim of elementary language arts education should simply be that of supplying as many diverse language experiences as possible. The elementary years are a time for students to enjoy the delight that is inherent in language, a delight that matches their own intuitive assessment of the world in which they've found themselves.

Initial Skill Instruction

Teachers and parents are naturally concerned about the evolution of language skills—particularly the initial skills of reading and writing—in the grades. "Skills are learned through hard work, not through delightful play," I can hear someone argue. Yet as Alfred North Whitehead pointed out in *The Aims of Education* (1929), initial learning is always a kind of romance, of deep interest and even infatuation, where learning takes place at a furious rate. It is terribly important not to diminish the powerful learning mechanisms that children bring to school. After all, the child entering kindergarten has just mastered spoken English as a pre-schooler, without the benefit of formal instruction. The skills of reading and writing are not any more complex. Initial skill instruction has generated an extraordinary amount of debate in educational circles. Teaching reading alone has generated hundreds of books. The great debate continues: Should we teach phonics or not? Can children learn through "look-say" or must they develop skills in breaking words into parts? Even the teaching of a skill like penmanship has its divisions and camps, each claiming supremacy for a particular method.

This book is not the place to review the initial skills debate. Rather, the description of language learning that I supplied in Chapter 3 provides direct support for what might be called a "naturalistic" method, which teaches initial skills, not as separated, isolated items, but within the context of actual language use. For instance, the so-called language experience approach avoids presenting language particles—phonemes, single words, isolated letters—and focuses on letting children learn to write and read by getting the language in their minds down on paper so that it can be read. The idea is described by Roach Van Allen and Dorris M. Lee in an excellent little book, *Learning To Read Through Experience* (1963). Teaching literacy begins by letting children explore their experiences orally, through discussion, show and tell, and so on. Next, through dictation or transcription, children are able to get their words on paper. Finally, the child learns to read by seeing his or her own words in print.

Language experience is an *integrated* approach to literacy learning: What children read, say, and act out becomes the stuff of composition, which, in turn, becomes a part of the literature of the class. Instead of drawing on predetermined vocabulary lists, the teacher allows the child's rapidly expanding experience (and vocabulary) to supply the material for study. The approach does away with exercises and drills by concentrating on language production. Perhaps most important, language experience systematically draws on the child's intuitive learning strategies, rather than forcing him or her to follow a single, adult created mode of learning to read or write.

This approach to initial skill learning also implies a positive answer to parents' traditional question: "Should I teach my child to read or write at home?" While "particle approaches"—techniques based on phonics or alphabet systems or carefully sequenced skills—discourage outside learning because it breaks up "the system," language experience joyfully invites parents to participate in the literacy education of their children. "Read to your children" the advice would go. "Talk to them about their reading. Listen when they tell you stories and, if they want, take down their stories in dictation. When they want to experiment with writing, show them letters and words and help them learn to make letter shapes. (Let them play with a typewriter, too.)" Because language experience is a naturalistic approach, parents can help to educate their children simply by being interested in literacy and helping children become engaged with it in natural ways. No particular training is required, and any reasonably sensitive adult can do it with complete success.

Reading and Literature in the Grades
Reading and literature are the basis of much pleasure in the elementary grades. From pre-school on, children delight in a good story; they are happy being read to; they are excited about learning to read on their own; and they are remarkably diverse in their reading interests. In simplest terms, the role of the elementary teacher becomes one of capitalizing on the intrinsic interest of children in books, using their unconscious delight as a starting

point for what can become a lifetime of pleasurable and functional reading.

The traditional reading group—a circle of children reading a common book, line by line, with books divided by ability levels to meet the alleged needs of the "bluebirds" and the "crows"—has disappeared from the better schools and should be on its way out in most others. The reading group was limited as a teaching method, serving principally to supply the teacher with information on oral reading errors, while inhibiting generations of children about making mistakes. (It has always fascinated me that many good student writers cannot read their own work aloud successfully. This is often a result of the inhibiting influence of the reading circle.) Also disappearing rapidly in the schools is something called the "controlled reader," with a carefully limited vocabulary (words chosen from a researcher's master list), limited concepts (keeping "ideas" within the student's imagined "comprehension level"), and as a consequence, limited interest for children.

By contrast, the best contemporary elementary classrooms have moved in the direction of individualized reading, with children choosing from among the rich variety of children's books available: fables, folk stories, fantasy, poetry, animal stories, realistic stories, nonfiction books, by a range of quality writers from Aesop to E. B. White to Elaine Konigsburg. (As a reminder of the wealth of books available, a list of Newbery Medal winning books—the best of the year in children's literature since 1922—is given.) In the individualized program, children are guided toward books of their own choice, with the teacher serving as overseer of their progress. The focus is on children's response or reaction to what they read, rather than on "comprehension" (a fairly simplistic term to cover a range of ways of deriving meaning from the printed page). In other words, the teacher concentrates his/her attention on the ideas and emotions the child brings to the book, allowing children to test their own rapidly growing set of experiences against those recorded in children's literature.

Parents should extend this reading program at home, helping children find books to read—library books or "store bought" paperbacks and hardcover books—and by reading to their children at a family story hour, at bedtime, or at any other time when an opportunity presents itself. While a few say that being read to is a passive experience, clearly it is an active process, with the listener perceiving, responding, thinking, hearing words, sensing narrative line, responding to rhythm and rhyme. It is no less a valid reading experience than sitting with a book and decoding the words silently.

Talk and Drama

Oral English has probably been the most neglected aspect of the child's language arts instruction. Although children and adults create and receive by far the largest portion of their language orally, the schools have largely ignored instruction in this area to concentrate on print literacy where skill development (and skill deficiency) are more obvious and more easily measured.

Robert Carlsen's concept of unconscious delight with language once again provides the key to integrating oral language work in the elementary grades, for children use spoken language naturally in a number of exciting ways, from their word play and spontaneous rhyme to their struggles to explain their perceptions to apparently dull-witted adults. Elementary teachers, aware of children's natural desire to talk, can provide frequent opportunities for informal discussion that allows children to listen and respond to one another, to present their experiences, to test them out against the real world. "Show 'n tell" as a teaching method is often maligned and satirized as somehow trivial. In fact, variations of show 'n tell are the heart of the oral English program at *any* level: The student synthesizes his or her ideas and shares them with an audience. Show and tell can be as simple and emotional as a kindergartner's describing a new puppy dog to a circle of friends, but it can also be as complex and formal as a nuclear

NEWBERY MEDAL BOOKS

The Story of Mankind, Hendrik Willem van Loon (1922)
The Voyages of Doctor Doolittle, Hugh Lofting (1923)
The Dark Frigate, Charles Hawes (1924)
Tales from Silver Lands, Charles Finger (1925)
Shen of the Sea, Arthur Bowi Chrisman (1926)
Smoky, the Cowhorse, Will James (1927)
Gay-Neck, the Story of a Pigeon, Dhan G. Mukerji (1928)
The Trumpeter of Krakow, Eric P. Kelly (1929)
Hitty, Her First Hundred Years, Rachel Field (1930)
The Cat Who Went to Heaven, Elizabeth Coatsworth (1931)
Waterless Mountain, Laura Adams Armer (1932)
Young Fu of the Upper Yangtze, Elizabeth Foreman Lewis (1933)
Invincible Louisa, Cornelia Meigs (1934)
Dobry, Monica Shannon (1935)
Caddie Woodlawn, Carol Brink (1936)
Roller Skates, Ruth Sawyer (1937)
The White Stag, Kate Seredy (1938)
Thimble Summer, Elizabeth Enright (1939)
Daniel Boone, James Daugherty (1940)
Call It Courage, Armstrong Sperry (1941)
The Matchlock Gun, Walter D. Edmonds (1942)
Adam of the Road, Elizabeth Janet Gray (1943)
Johnny Tremain, Esther Forbes (1944)
Rabbit Hill, Robert Lawson (1945)
Strawberry Girl, Lois Lenski (1946)
Miss Hickory, Carolyn Sherwin Bailey (1947)
The Twenty-One Balloons, William Pène Du Bois (1948)
King of the Wind, Marguerite Henry (1949)
The Door in the Wall, Marguerite De Angeli (1950)

physicist's showing and telling his or her findings in quantum mechanics to an audience of three hundred specialists at a professional meeting.

Oral English extends beyond sharing personal experience, however. Elementary children enjoy creating narratives and building them into longer stories; conversing about plans and possibilities; telling jokes; making up and answering riddles; writing and singing songs; and, of course, reciting poems, limericks, and couplets.

Amos Fortune, Free Man, Elizabeth Yates (1951)
Ginger Pye, Eleanor Estes (1952)
Secret of the Andes, Ann Nolan Clark (1953)
. . . and now Miguel, Joseph Krumgold (1954)
The Wheel on the School, Meindert DeJong (1955)
Carry on, Mr. Bowditch, Jean Lee Latham (1956)
Miracles on Maple Hill, Virginia Sorensen (1957)
Rifles for Watie, Harold Keith (1958)
The Witch of Blackbird Pond, Elizabeth George Speare (1959)
Onion John, Joseph Krumgold (1960)
Island of the Blue Dolphins, Scott O'Dell (1961)
The Bronze Bow, Elizabeth George Speare (1962)
A Wrinkle in Time, Madeleine L'Engle (1963)
It's Like This, Cat, Emily Cheney Neville (1964)
Shadow of a Bull, Maia Wojciechowska (1965)
I, Juan de Pareja, Elizabeth Borten de Trevino (1966)
Up a Road Slowly, Irene Hunt (1967)
From the Mixed-Up Files of Mrs. Basil E. Frankweiller, E. L. Konigsburg (1968)
The High King, Lloyd Alexander (1969)
Sounder, William Armstrong (1970)
Summer of the Swans, Betsy Byars (1971)
Mrs. Frisby and the Rats of NIMH, Robert C. O'Brien (1972)
Julie of the Wolves, Jean George (1973)
The Slave Dancer, Paula Fox (1974)
M. C. Higgins, the Great, Virginia Hamilton (1975)
The Grey King, Susan Cooper (1976)
Roll of Thunder, Hear My Cry, Mildred D. Taylor (1977)
Bridge to Terabithia, Katherine Paterson (1978)
The Westing Game, Ellen Raskin (1979)

When teachers abolish formal reading groups, they create more time for children's talk. Increasingly one sees elementary school classrooms with an open-space design that allows children to move from activity to activity at their own pace, while providing ample opportunity for talk with the teacher, teacher aides, and other students.

From oral language, children move naturally into dramatic activities: They fantasize with their stuffed toys and dolls; they roleplay and pretend with each other and with adults; they spontaneously turn any dull situation into an opportunity for make believe. Drama serves an important function in the child's (and the adult's) life, allowing a person to experiment with his or her identity, to experiment with a range of voices, styles, and language registers. In drama one learns about one's self and one's language while exploring, in a safe way, the possible directions for action and experience. Thus school children will engage, with a minimum of coaching, in pantomime, acting out stories, improvisation, puppetry, costumed skits, and as they grow older, dramas where they memorize words or write their own lines.

Children's drama in the classroom is emphatically not *theater*. This drama is for the benefit of the performer himself or herself, rather than principally for the entertainment of an audience. (However, an audience at an improvised drama may find itself vastly amused and entertained.) Drama also provides a useful bridge between less formal oral English and more structured writing experiences, and a great many teachers find dramatic improvisations a useful starting point for the writing of stories, narratives, even poems, and, of course, plays.

Written Composition
For a great many adults the word "composition" creates a feeling of dread and distaste. But it is very important to note that elementary children do not, initially, share the adult dislike of writing. Children pretend to write notes and letters almost as soon as they have some notion of what the written page represents. They spontaneously work at making their letters to get better at handling the language for themselves. They "write" with their fingers on air and then read to one another what they have "written." In the early years, even such matters as formal correctness seem to be manageable: Young children will talk about a story idea or about how to make a capital "T" with equal enthusiasm.

Unfortunately, in a great many elementary schools the written word becomes used by teachers as a diagnostic tool in language instruction, and, all too quickly, writing becomes associated in the minds of children with mistakes and corrections. Just as teachers have used the reading circle as a way of discovering oral decoding problems, they have also subjected children's writing to analysis for basic skill deficiencies. No one, of course, advocates totally ignoring problems of penmanship, spelling, and usage in the writing of young people (just as a good individualized reading program includes ways of discovering reading problems on a one-to-one basis). But the elementary grades are not the place to turn five- to eleven-year-olds into perfect writers of Standard English. Though junior high teachers regularly complain that children "ought to have mastered the fundamentals" by the time they reach grade seven, in fact, many of the conceptualizations involved in understanding correctness are well beyond the grasp of elementary children and are even difficult for most adults. What is of *fundamental* importance is that elementary children's unconscious delight in writing be extended, supported, and nurtured, so that when they reach the junior high years, they still like to write, even if they occasionally misspell a word or fragment a sentence.

The language experience approach I described earlier gets students to write very early. They quickly move from dictating stories to writing short paragraphs of their own. Show 'n tell presentations can also be written, with the final product posted as part of a bulletin board display. Elementary school children can make short versions of just about every adult form of writing: newspaper stories, short stories, playlets, character sketches, autobiographies, diaries, scripts, and letters. Every elementary school has at least one child who has started out to write a novel, and in schools where the language experience program is in use, almost every child in the school will write, edit, and bind a book of his/her own work. Writing in the grades ranges from factual to astonishingly imaginative, from the real to the fantastic. With elementary children, teaching composition is literally a matter of just saying "let's write," offering a starting point or two, then guiding the children to successful completion.

And that's why I'd like to go back as an elementary teacher, for the grades are the one place where writing is as natural as speaking and play-acting and reading. One hopes that as experience-centered methods of teaching become more prevalent, children's delight with language can be extended upward so that it will be just as pleasurable to teach writing in junior high and senior high as well.

Of course the term "composition" means much more than "writing," and it should be noted that the language experience approach allows children to "compose" their experiences in many forms. Painting and sculpture, for instance, provide nonverbal outlets for children's ideas. So does photography, and young children are quite capable of working creatively with cameras to "write" a photo essay. With the decreasing cost of electronic equipment it seems realistic that in a half decade or so, the schools might equip each child with a cassette tape recorder (just as they may supply hand calculators), not to diminish the importance of the written word but as a tool to enhance learning literacy: notetaking, composing, interviewing, and so on. Elementary children have already shown that they can master the use of videotape equipment to create their own programs, and many teachers have staged classroom drama for the benefit of super 8-millimeter cameras. Multi-media and nonverbal experiences are not the enemy of elementary school English instruction; they ally themselves nicely with children's intrinsic interest in creating ideas in any medium—language, film, tape.

3. JUNIOR HIGHS AND MIDDLE SCHOOLS

Junior high school and middle school teachers have long had an identity crisis: Everybody seems to feel that junior high schools are "important," yet nobody knows quite what to do with them. Junior highs and middle schools often expand or contract to fit space requirements in the school district, so that whether the school covers grades 7–8, 7–9, 8–9, 6–8, or some other combination depends more on population trends than pedagogical concerns. The junior high curriculum is often formless, and the institution seems to function as little more than a holding station for young people going into high school.

Many teachers wind up in these middle-years schools by accident. Few states have certification specifically for junior high schools, so the teachers are either trained for elementary school and are working on the upper end of their K-8 certificate, or they are would-be high school teachers teaching below their level. Thus in some cities, the junior highs resemble overgrown elementary schools; in others they are geared exclusively for high school preparation. As a result, few junior highs and middle schools have been successful at addressing themselves directly to the needs of the students.

The task is unusually difficult. Those young people (roughly ages eleven through fourteen) are extraordinarily complex; they are changing identity on the way from childhood to adulthood and exhibiting a range of behavior that can baffle and frustrate even an experienced teacher. Beginning with the junior high years, young people start to grow up physically with a bang. They are little kids one day and adults the next. The junior high classes are filled with small boys and self-conscious taller girls, sets of pals who resemble Mutt and Jeff, loving couples who look seventeen but reveal by their giggles that they're children, kids who much prefer frogs to members of the opposite sex.

The emotional and psychological changes of early adolescence are just as great, rapid, and puzzling. As Edgar Friedenberg has explained in *The Vanishing Adolescent* (1962), young people of junior high age are in the process of learning to clarify their experience (making abstract judgments about their world) and establishing self-esteem (perceiving and valuing themselves as unique individuals). Jean Piaget called this the stage of "formal operations," in which children of ten, eleven, and twelve develop powers of abstraction that allow them literally to distance themselves from their experience and their "selves."

Of course these changes have important implications for the junior high/middle school years. Instead of seeing children of this age as simply being in transition (it is now fashionable in some educational circles to label them "transescents"), educators must realize that junior high students are at a point that deserves careful observation and development in its own right. Further, the evolution that occurs is done through and with language, as young people use words to learn about and express themselves about the world. In these years of powerful growth, it is useful to consider three languaging/thinking concerns as the focus for the junior high/middle school English program: *extending experience, fantasy and adventure,* and *seeing oneself.*

Extending Experience
One value traditionally attributed to reading is vicarious experience. Through reading one learns of places or events one may never experience firsthand. At perhaps no other time is the impulse to obtain various experiences stronger than it is for junior-high-age students. These young people's reading interests are limitless, ranging from pets and animals to outer space, from oceans and faraway lands to places right around the corner. Some students will delight in bittersweet animal stories like Fred Gipson's *Old Yeller* or the ever-popular *National Velvet* by Enid Bagnold; others will be interested in more adventurous tales—Jack London's *The Call of the Wild,* for example. Many of the boys will be off on a sports reading jag devouring books like *The Guiness Book of Sports Records* or Curtis Bishop's *Fast Break.* (An illustrative bibliography of popular books with young people at this age is given.)

Writing and speaking are also a part of the process of extending experience. The junior high/middle school student uses language both to clarify experience and to connect it with his or her expanding view of the world. Three examples of classroom approaches will help to show how the concept of extending experi-

EXTENDING EXPERIENCE

When the Legends Die, Hal G. Borland
The Good Earth, Pearl S. Buck
The Incredible Journey, Sheila Burnford
Old Yeller, Fred Gipson
Big Red, Jim Kjelgaard
The Call of the Wild, Jack London
The Yearling, Marjorie Rawlings
It's Good to Be Alive, Roy Campanella
Abe Lincoln Grows Up, Carl Sandburg
Travels with Charley, John Steinbeck
Fast Break, Curtis Bishop
National Velvet, Enid Bagnold
Rascal, Sterling North
The Black Athlete, Jack Orr
Bike Tripping, Tom Cuthbertson
Doctor in the Zoo, Bruce Buchenholz
All Things Wise and Wonderful, James Herriot
Grand Canyon, Joseph Wood Krutch
Dolphins, Esse Forrester O'Brien
The Lion of Judah, Charles Gorham
Born Free, Joy Adamson
The Day Lincoln Was Shot, Jim Bishop
Annapurna, Maurice Herzog
Land of the Pharos, Leonard Cottrell
I Marched with Hannibal, Hans Baumann
Calico Bush, Rachel Field
Young Fu of the Upper Yangtze, Elizabeth Foreman Lewis
I, Juan de Pareja, Elizabeth Borten de Trevino
Words from History, Isaac Asimov
The Milky Way: Galaxy Number One, Franklyn M. Branley
Thor: The Last of the Sperm Whales, Robert M. McClung
In Their Own Words, Milton Meltzer
Call Me Charley, Jesse Jackson
Half-breed, Evelyn Sibley Lampman
My Side of the Mountain, Jean George
Here Comes the Strikeout, Leonard Kessler
The Bells of Bleeker Street, Angelo Valenti
The Weasels, Bill Gilbert
The Hunt for the Whooping Cranes, J. J. McCoy

ence provides a logical center for English work in all English areas—reading, writing, listening, and speaking.

J. W. Patrick Creber (1965), a British teacher, has argued that "much adolescent inarticulateness has its roots in a blunted sensibility," that a great many young people today never fully develop the ability to look carefully and objectively at the world around them. This visual inarticulateness may have been induced, in part, by television, because of its selective role in presenting a prepackaged, zoomed-in, instant-replay, high-intensity-color universe to substitute for the living color of day-to-day living. Creber tries to help adolescents "rediscover the familiar." He begins by presenting poems about the everyday world, poems about rocks and trees, plants and animals. He then has the students write with the same kinds of vision and detail. This work of seeing can easily be extended beyond the classroom as students rediscover a block, a neighborhood, or their home town. By heightening their perception, the students extend their language skills.

An American textbook, *Stop, Look, and Write,* by Hart Day Leavitt and David Sohn (1964), also concentrates on perception as it relates to language. The authors present children with photographs and help them move from observations to words. The earliest exercises focus on concentrating, observing detail, and seeing the unusual. The students create titles for photographs, make comparisons, contrast points-of-view, create imaginary dialogs, concentrate on sensory impressions, and finally use a sequential series of photos to create a story. *Stop, Look, and Write* has made its point very effectively: The "basics" of sensory writing are seeing and observing, not merely the manipulation of nouns and colorful adjectives.

In *The Creative Word,* a text series I designed for Random House (1973–74), both reading and writing are combined in experience-based units. In Book I, designed for sixth and seventh graders, Geoffrey Summerfield concentrates on capturing the elementary child's delight in language and language play, while extending his/her range of vision. He begins by having students make lists: *smells I like, things I like to collect, sounds of my neigh-borhood, tastes I like.* In the manner of *Stop, Look, and Write,* he asks students to observe photographs and discover tiny details— on a cluttered desk, in a collection of kitchen utensils, on an elaborately set table. After reading a passage on "Spy Training" from Rudyard Kipling's *Kim* and then writing a composition "with a spy's eye," the students write "poems that nobody writes poems about." A student example:

> Nobody writes a poem about a vein;
> It's a blue, red, and sometimes purple canal of red liquid
> A target for the doctor's archery
> Always taking the same old route,
> A race track for the corpuscles,
> But never reaching the end.

> Mindy Hamway and Tania Gregory

Additional topics in the book include describing sounds, creat-ing new words to describe sounds, "reeling and writhing" riddles, designing new uses for familiar objects and new gadgets to solve familiar problems, and creating symbols. Finally, Summerfield moves students beyond writing about individualized perceptions to string experiences into full-length narratives. Along the way, student readings include poetry on objects by Denise Levertov; a description of the town dump of Whitemud, Saskatchewan, from *Wolf Moon* by Wallace Stegner; passages describing neigh-borhood sounds by Alfred Kazin (New York City) and James Agee (Knoxville); classic riddles; a discussion of contemporary design problems by Victor Papanek; and "I've Got a Name," a short story by Zachary Gold, which explores the relationship so important to adolescents between self-concept and a name.

In the work of Creber, Leavitt and Sohn, and Summerfield, one can see the elements of a comprehensive, integrated, total curricu-lum. While language work is based on the young person's own in-terests, the reading and writing are anything but undisciplined or self-indulgent. The teachers provide a model of what can happen when English instruction takes its direction from the emerging needs of the adolescent, rather than the *a priori* demands of a writing or reading skills list. In exploring the world around them, through language, students naturally become more skilled at the basics of English.

Fantasy and Adventure
Most junior high and middle school teachers know of the considerable interest of eleven- to fifteen-year-olds in fantasy and adventure stories. Adolescents coming of age need to test their concept of self against a range of selves—whether in the real world or in literature. Thus an adolescent boy's interest in factual information about basketball easily spills over into sports fiction stories with thrilling, come-from-behind victories. One's own love affair becomes glamorized through a romantic novel. The enduring popularity of the Hardy Boys/Nancy Drew mysteries provides a classic example, for these books allow young people the vicarious thrill of projecting themselves into the shoes of the teenage sleuths who joust with and conquer the adult world. (Nobody ever asks how Frank, Joe, and Nancy get so much time off from school to run around the country chasing swarthy villains, and nobody really cares.) Adolescents are attracted to other-worldy fantasy as well: the science fiction of Jules Verne or Ray Bradbury or Robert Heinlein, the mythological worlds created by J. R. R. Tolkien and C. S. Lewis, and even the imaginary setting of *Alice's Adventures in Wonderland.*

Junior high kids are often ghouls at heart, and many teachers have been concerned about their students' obvious interest in the macabre, the violent, and the gory. Yet instead of stifling this interest or attributing it solely to the bad influence of television, teachers might well consider how it fits into the developmental scheme of adolescence. To allow students to explore stories of horror and intrigue is not to surrender to popular taste, but to help young people explore these instincts in themselves. One sus-

FANTASY AND ADVENTURE

Shane, Jack Schafer
P. T. 109, Robert Donovan
The Last Nine Days of the Bismarck, C. S. Forester
The Black Pearl, Scott O'Dell
Houdini, Lace Kendall
Hot Rod, Henry Felson
Swiftwater, Paul Annixter
Passport to Romance, Betty Cavana
Hospital Zone, Mary Stolz
Adventures of Sherlock Holmes, Arthur Conan Doyle
Escape to Witch Mountain, Alexander Key
Hidden Trail, Jim Kjelgaard
Adventures of Ulysses, Eustin Bernard
Rocket Ship Galileo, Robert Heinlein
Masks of Time, Robert Silverberg
Dracula, Bram Stoker
Frankenstein, Mary Shelley
The Halloween Tree, Ray Bradbury
Tom Sawyer, Mark Twain
The Pearl, John Steinbeck
Twenty Thousand Leagues Under the Sea, Jules Verne
The War of the Worlds, H. G. Wells
Captains Courageous, Rudyard Kipling
Kidnapped, Robert Louis Stevenson
The Hobbit, J. R. R. Tolkien
Night Flight, Antoine de Saint-Exupéry
Alice's Adventures in Wonderland, Lewis Carroll
Kim, Rudyard Kipling
The Strange Case of Dr. Jekyll and Mr. Hyde, Robert Louis Stevenson
Asimov's Mysteries, Isaac Asimov
The Man Who Was Thursday, G. K. Chesterton
And Then There Were None, Agatha Christie
The Great Train Robbery, Michael Crichton
Bigfoot, Hall G. Evarts
Mutiny on the Bounty, Charles Nordhoff and James Norman Hall
Ivanhoe, Sir Walter Scott
Stories from the Twilight Zone, Rod Serling
Alive, Piers Paul Ried

pects, in fact, that if more junior high kids were allowed to explore their fantasy life through reading and writing, fewer adults would be glued to the tube, acting out their own vicarious experiences through the likes of *Starsky and Hutch, Hawaii Five-O,* and the organized violence of the National Football League. (A reading list of books that successfully meet the reading needs of junior-high-age young people for fantasy is provided.)

Seeing Oneself
At the heart of the junior high years is the establishment of self-esteem. While a strong sense of identity is important at any stage of life, it is absolutely crucial in adolescence, where students establish a "self" that will last them all their lives. Without adequate exploration of that self and its interests and capabilities, without developing a realistic sense that "I'm OK," the teenager will spend the rest of his/her life trying to catch up, struggling to feel secure in a seemingly nonsupportive world. As Edgar Friedenberg has argued, in America we have a tendency to make adolescence vanish, to propel children through the years of becoming as rapidly as possible, pushing them more and more toward adult behavior. While teens and even pre-teens may master most of the external trappings of adulthood, looking, acting, and even talking as if they were older, a great many of them fail to establish a self that is any more than skin deep.

But even Friedenberg fails to emphasize strongly enough the role that *language* plays in the process of personal development. With words students can establish and talk about themselves. In the schools, junior-high-age young people are too often pushed toward the language forms of adulthood (for example, the writing of quasi-academic essays and paragraphs on abstract topics) rather than being encouraged to explore the language of the self.

Without attempting to turn public schools or the English classroom into a psychologist's office, I simply wish to point out that the English classroom is one natural place for linguistic exploration of the self. In English young people can see themselves

SEEING ONESELF

I Never Promised You a Rose Garden, Hannah Green
Diary of a Young Girl, Anne Frank
To Kill a Mockingbird, Harper Lee
Manchild in the Promised Land, Claude Brown
Death Be Not Proud, John Gunther
Karen, Marie Killilea
A Light in the Forest, Conrad Richter
To Be Young, Gifted, and Black, Lorraine Hansberry
Mixed-Marriage Daughter, Hila Coleman
A Single Light, Maia Wojciechowska
Cress Delahanty, Jessamyn West
Huckleberry Finn, Mark Twain
The Old Man and the Sea, Ernest Hemingway
A Member of the Wedding, Carson McCullers
The Catcher in the Rye, J. D. Salinger
Look Homeward, Angel, Thomas Wolfe
Jane Eyre, Charlotte Brontë
The Red Badge of Courage, Stephen Crane
My Ántonia, Willa Cather
Dream of the Blue Sparrow, Victor Barnouw
Then Again, Maybe I Won't, Judy Blume
Julie of the Wolves, Jean Craighead George
I'm Really Dragged But Nothing Gets Me Down, Nat Hentoff
A Day No Pigs Would Die, Robert Newton Peck
I Was a Ninety-eight Pound Duckling, Jean Van Leeuwen
The Car Thief, Theodore Weesner
Daybreak, Joan Baez
Born Female, Carolyn Bird
Soul on Ice, Eldridge Cleaver
Being There, Jerzy Kosinski
The Contender, Robert Lipsyte
Hatter Fox, Marilyn Harris
The Invisible Man, Ralph Ellison
Macho!, Edmund Villasenor
Memoirs of an Ex-Prom Queen, Alix Kates Shulman
Ishi, Last of His Tribe, Theodora Kroeber
Walden, Henry David Thoreau
Good Times/Bad Times, James Kirkwood
The Chosen, Chaim Potok

reflected in the themes and characters of literature. Literature titles appropriate for this age group include both adult and young adult literature: the popular "problems" books like *A Time of Tenderness* (Betty Cavanna) or *Mixed-Marriage Daughter* (Hila Coleman), classic books that focus on seeing oneself such as *Jane Eyre* (Charlotte Brontë) or *The Old Man and the Sea* (Ernest Hemingway), books concerned with ethnic or racial identity like *Macho!* (Edmund Villasenor) or *Hatter Fox* (Marilyn Harris), or even science fiction discussions of coming-of-age and identity such as Ray Bradbury's *Dandelion Wine*. (A list of appropriate books is provided.) In composing they can stabilize a view of themselves, explore their writing voices through writing journals, personal essays, contemplative poetry, even fiction of their own that is concerned with the development of the self.

With this age group in mind, some of my graduate students in a workshop at the University of British Columbia prepared a syllabus for a course called "Personal Explorations" that illustrates the relationship between personal growth and skill in reading and writing. They included such books as Paul Zindel's *The Pigman*, John Steinbeck's *The Red Pony*, James Kirkwood's *Good Times/Bad Times*, S. E. Hinton's *The Outsiders*, Richard Wright's *Black Boy*, and numerous autobiographical accounts of growing up (e.g., Lincoln Steffens' *Autobiography of Lincoln Steffens*, and Yevgeny Yevtuschenko's *A Precocious Autobiography*.)

Weaving the literature of personal experience throughout the course, they began, appropriately, by having the students explore memories, writing in journals to describe memories from early childhood, then moving to current concerns. The students would write short plays, stories, poems, letters, tall tales, modern myths, dialogs, conversations, autobiographies, proverbs, riddles, and scenarios, which in turn could be presented in creative drama and improvisation. They would create filmstrips and tape recordings, exploring a full set of media forms.

Skill Building in the Junior High Years
"Where," it can be asked legitimately, "do the skills for all these projects come from?" How do students learn to read good young adult literature or to write stories, poems, conversations, and dialogs? Other, less patient teachers may state it more directly, "Look, my kids can't put together a decent English sentence and they read at the second grade level. How do you expect them to do the stuff listed here?" Fair as such questions may be, they are loaded. They deserve a cautious, yet direct answer.

First, it must be repeated, the reading and writing failures of this generation of young people have been grossly exaggerated. I have worked with dozens and dozens of so-called non-readers and non-writers who, when placed in a situation where they could read and write on materials of their own selection, perform with skills that nobody knew they had. Nor are my experiences isolated: The professional journals of the past fifteen years have been filled with documented studies of experience-based programs that involve previously unmotivated young people in literacy activities. Young people use language more successfully than most people give them credit for.

Second, it has to be emphasized that the skill deficiencies of young people are, in most cases, not the result of a failure of the schools to teach basic skills, but of overemphasis on skills. In today's schools, children receive so much drill that there is little time left over for actual reading and writing.

The kind of program I have outlined here teaches skills in the most basic of ways: one skill at a time, to one child at a time, as skills are required. It implies that a teacher who sees a child with reading difficulties begins, not by diagnosing the ways in which he or she falls short on standardized tests, but by looking for a good readable book for that child. And when that book has been read (either *by* the student or *to* the student), the teacher looks around for another, perhaps a little more difficult, perhaps on a slightly more mature level. For the student who can barely write a sentence (if, in fact, that is the true limit of his or her achievement), the teacher offers sentence-length compositions—captions, one-liners, jokes or riddles—then gradually increases the length and complexity of the tasks presented. One skill at a time, one child at a time.

Do teachers have time for this sort of individualized work? Can a teacher possibly find time to work with children one at a time, doing the individual planning that this implies? The answer here involves pure and simple doublethink: yes and no.

For practical purposes the answer is *no*, given current teaching conditions in the schools. When junior high teachers must meet with well over 125 children per day, every day, in crowded classrooms, and when they are hampered by forty-minute time periods, they cannot be expected to individualize their teaching completely. Parents and administrators must recognize that if they want skills taught well and successfully to individual students, they must take steps that will, in the long run, reduce class size for teachers of language skills.

On the other hand, the answer is *yes*, teachers can work with children one on one, if we compare what most teachers are doing compared to what they *might* be doing. The number of teachers truly trying to individualize learning for their children is quite small; the vast majority still teach the class as an undifferentiated block most of the time, relying on master lists of skills and making assignments from standardized textbooks and workbooks. If teachers simply stopped (or even cut by one half) the amount of common, whole class reading and drill that goes on in the schools, there would be ample time for them to make contact with individual children, to find out their particular strengths and weaknesses, and to offer them the literacy instruction that they need.

Nor is there a better or more crucial time to do this than the junior high years. As students come of age, they need support from good individual teachers. High schools are larger and less personal, and college is far worse. If students *don't* receive the individualized help they need with language during the junior high/middle school years, it may be too late to do anything about it.

4. SENIOR HIGH SCHOOLS

A great many things happen to young people beginning with the senior high school years, perhaps none more important than the acquisition of mobility through cars. The automobile is the symbol of teenagers' increasing freedom, but it represents the direction of their psychological and linguistic growth as well—stretching out, exploring independently, with less and less control and guidance from the mentor. In the English curriculum, the senior high years ought to be a time for us to turn over the keys to the linguistic car, not for unsupervised hot rodding, but for use, like any tool, to accomplish tasks efficiently. In describing the high school English program, I will touch on four areas of experiental and linguistic growth: *human relationships, expanding consciousness, learning and knowing,* and *aesthetic experience.*

Human Relationships
Just as the junior high years are a time for students to see that their "selves" are secure, high school students (roughly ages thirteen to seventeen) have a deep need to see that self in relation to other people, initially, perhaps, in relation to members of a family, but increasingly to peers and eventually to the entire adult community. In psychological terms, the high schooler is becoming increasingly conscious of other human beings. Thus in English classes, literature and writing that deal with friends and enemies, families, boy-girl relationships and rebellion become important. Among the good books widely read by teens that appeal to these needs are William Golding's *The Lord of the Flies* (the story of the decline into barbarism of a group of children stranded on an island and forced to tend for themselves), John Knowles' *A Separate Peace* (set in a New England preparatory school, it describes

ONESELF AND OTHERS

A *Death in the Family*, James Agee
The Pigman, Paul Zindel
Flowers for Algernon, Daniel Keyes
To Sir, With Love, E. R. Braithwaite
The Human Comedy, William Saroyan
The Outsiders, S. E. Hinton
A *Time for Teenagers*, Betty Cavana
Seventeenth Summer, Maureen Daly
Mrs. Mike, Benedict and Nancy Freeman
Durango Street, Frank Bonham
The Soul Brothers and Sister Lou, Kristin Hunter
Little Women, Louisa May Alcott
Rabbit, Run, John Updike
The Lord of the Flies, William Golding
Cannery Row, John Steinbeck
Of Mice and Men, John Steinbeck
Demian, Hermann Hesse
A *Separate Peace*, John Knowles
The Autobiography of Miss Jane Pittman, Ernest J. Gaines
Tomboy, Hal Ellison
Wuthering Heights, Emily Brontë
Stranger in a Strange Land, Robert Heinlein
Watership Down, Richard Adams
Forever . . . , Judy Blume
I'll Get There. It Better Be Worth the Trip, John Donovan
Mr. and Mrs. BoJo Jones, Ann Head
If I Love You Am I Trapped Forever?, M. E. Kerr
How Green Was My Valley, Richard Llewellyn
House Made of Dawn, N. Scott Momaday
Naomi, Bernice Rabb
Shadow of a Bull, Maia Wojciechowska
It's Not the End of the World, Judy Blume
The Friends, Rosa Guy
The Loneliness of the Long Distance Runner, Alan Sillitoe
Little Big Man, Thomas Berger
A *Bell for Adamo*, John Hersey
The Effect of Gamma Rays on Man-in-the-Moon Marigolds, Paul Zindel
The Heart Is a Lonely Hunter, Carson McCullers
The Hunchback of Notre Dame, Victor Hugo
Romeo and Juliet, William Shakespeare

the pains of adolescent growth during a single summer before World War II), Alan Sillitoe's *The Loneliness of the Long Distance Runner* (dealing with problems of individuality and conformity), and even Shakespeare's *Romeo and Juliet* (which speaks directly to both adolescent and adult concerns). (Other books that deal with human relations, with the self and others, are listed.)

With interest in others comes increased ability to perceive how language enters into human relationships and to develop consciousness of how writing/speaking is received by an audience. Thus as the circle of awareness is extended, writing and other language skills can be extended. Students become capable of serving as critics for each other's writing. Classroom drama can be extended to theater, rather than serving solely for self-expression, and students can be increasingly conscious not only of their response to literature but of ways of sharing and communicating that response to others.

Again I will draw on the work of my students at the University of British Columbia, who developed a course called "Interpersonal Writing and Literature." The course was subtitled "Writing to Somebody with a Face." To emphasize the connection between self and others, teachers had students do a great deal of writing to real people: to parents, brothers and sisters, friends, and adults in the community. Students wrote love letters, thank-yous, excuses, memos, letters to pen pals, and to-whom-it-may-concern notes. The teachers also extended writing into imaginary domains so that the students could write time capsule letters to be opened and read by others in the year 2000, letters to themselves for reading later in life, letters to and from historical characters, and letters found in odd places (in a bottle washed ashore, in a library book). My students also found a wealth of epistolary literature ranging from the classical and difficult novels *Clarissa, Pamela,* and *Humphrey Clinker* to the contemporary: Don Marquis' *archy and mehitabel* letters, James Thurber's humorous exchanges with his publishers, satirical letters and cards in *Mad* magazine, children's letters to political and entertainment figures, and the epistolary stories of an

old *Saturday Evening Post* character, Earthworm Tractor Salesman Alexander Botts.

But forming relationships need hardly be restricted to the letter.
Jerry Reynolds, the English coordinator of the Rochester, Min-
nesota, schools describes a course on the theme of "Alienation"
(1975). Readings for the course include Sylvia Plath's *The Bell Jar*,
John Fowles' *The Collector*, Hannah Green's *I Never Promised
You a Rose Garden*, John Steinbeck's *Of Mice and Men*, and
Nathaniel Hawthorne's *The Scarlet Letter*. Reynolds included
short stories ("Bartleby the Scrivner" by Herman Melville, "Old
Man at the Bridge" by Ernest Hemingway, "Outcasts of Poker
Flat" by Bret Harte, "A Rose for Emily" by William Faulkner),
poetry ("Death of the Hired Man" by Robert Frost, "Eleanor
Rigby" by the Beatles), and drama (*Death of a Salesman* by Arthur Miller, *The Glass Menagerie* by Tennessee Williams, and
Long Day's Journey into Night by Eugene O'Neill). He even drew
on community resources, including student visits to community
activity centers, homes for the elderly, a nursing home, and a mental health center. The students were encouraged to write original
stories on the theme, to plan and present media materials (radio
play, video tape, slide tape), to write analyses of selected literature, or to report on a visit to a community resource.

Expanding Consciousness

Reynolds' use of resources outside the school suggests two directions for the English curriculum: one is the use of community
resources (to be discussed in detail in Chapter 10); the other is the
young person's continuing movement toward a concern for problems of society and morality. Psychologist Lawrence Kohlberg has
done research into the evolution of moral systems in young people, which, he finds, follow growth patterns from intense egocen-
tricity ("be good because you'll be spanked if you aren't") to a full
awareness of one's actions in relation to others (Kant's categorical
imperative and the Christian golden rule: "act as if your behavior
were a model for all humankind") (Mackey, 1975). This growth,
of course, parallels the pattern we have observed in young peo-

ple's language. Students in roughly the tenth grade and beyond, approaching full mental maturity, have the potential to reach Kohlberg's final stages of moral development, where they consider issues in terms of principles rather than solely for their own individual needs. Thus students are interested in urban and suburban problems, politics, human values, minority problems, schooling, the uses of power, reform, dissent, and above all, the future.

The full range of adult literature is open to these young people (a list of widely read books for high school students is given), and their writing naturally deals with an extended range of issues and topics. Drawing on this growth, a great many high schools have moved toward courses that deal with contemporary issues and problems through language and literature.

For example, Arthur Daigon, a professor at the University of Connecticut, has prepared a series of paperback volumes called *The Dig U.S.A. Series,* which shows how these interests can be exploited and extended, though language, in the classroom. In one of the volumes, *Violence U.S.A.* (1975), he presents a series of documents or artifacts from contemporary culture that describe the problem of violence in America. The series title grows from the model of an archaeology "dig," and the students sift through materials to form opinions and, eventually, to write. Subsections include "The Roots of Violence," "Growing Up Violent," "Violence for Fun," "Violence in the Media," "Crime," "Racial and Political Violence." The materials in the dig package include TV ads, photographs, posters, poems, cartoons, news stories, editorials, advertisements, satire, and excerpts from novels, ranging from George Orwell's *1984* to William Golding's *Lord of the Flies.* With the resources of the dig (a package any teacher could prepare just by collecting his/her own materials and organizing them), Daigon stakes out raw materials for an exploration of the social and moral concerns surrounding violence. The teacher can create opportunities for students to explore the problem through writing: creative and expository prose, editorials, letters, essays, and so on.

Students in the high school years and beyond show increasing

ISSUES, PROBLEMS, MORAL CONCERNS

The Jungle, Upton Sinclair
The Ugly American, William Lederer and Eugene Burdick
Rise and Fall of Adolf Hitler, William Shirer
War Beneath the Sea, Frank Bonham
Rendezvous with Rama, Arthur C. Clarke
The Bridges at Toko-Ri, James Michener
Banners at Shenandoah, Bruce Catton
Ring the Judas Bell, James Forman
Hiroshima, John Hersey
The Lilies of the Field, William E. Barrett
Run Silent, Run Deep, Edward C. Beach
The Bridge Over the River Kwai, Pierre Boulle
Operating Manual for Spaceship Earth, R. Buckminster Fuller
The American Way of Death, Jessica Mitford
A Farewell to Arms, Ernest Hemingway
The Great Gatsby, F. Scott Fitzgerald
The Stranger, Albert Camus
Go Tell It on the Mountain, James Baldwin
Dear and Glorious Physician, Taylor Caldwell
Giant, Edna Ferber
The Ox-Bow Incident, Walter Van Tilburg Clark
The African Queen, C. S. Forester
The Snow Goose, Paul Gallico
Black Like Me, John H. Griffin
The Caine Mutiny, Herman Wouk
Gone with the Wind, Margaret Mitchell
The Scarlet Letter, Nathaniel Hawthorne
The Grapes of Wrath, John Steinbeck
Brave New World, Aldous Huxley
Death of a Salesman, Arthur Miller
The Andromeda Strain, Michael Crichton
The Bell Jar, Sylvia Plath
A Night To Remember, Walter Lord
The Female Eunuch, Germaine Greer
All the King's Men, Robert Penn Warren
The Terminal Man, Michael Crichton
The Fantastic Voyage, Isaac Asimov
1984, George Orwell
An American Tragedy, Theodore Dreiser
Notes of a Native Son, James Baldwin
The Pawnbroker, Paddy Chayefsky
St. Joan, George Bernard Shaw
Ethan Frome, Edith Wharton

future-directedness, a concern for the state of the adult world that they are about to enter, which provides interesting opportunities for language work. William Martin of George Mason University and Dan Verner of Robinson High School, Fairfax, Virginia, have developed a problem-centered reading course called "To Cope with the Current," which centers on understanding the present but casts an eye toward the future (1975). Nonfiction includes Alvin Toffler's *Future Shock* and Martin's own book, *To Cope with the Current*. Literature ranges from Nathaniel Hawthorne's "Dr. Heidegger's Experiment" to Robert Frost's "Mending Wall," plus an assortment of films.

In a course with a similar focus, Charmaine Stilinovich (1975) of Lyons Township, Illinois, High School, used contemporary magazines: *Time, Newsweek, U.S. News and World Report, Atlantic, Harpers, The New Yorker, Psychology Today, The New Republic, National Review,* and *The National Observer.* Her course begins with three weeks of small group discussion of issues along with exploratory free writings to strengthen basic writing skills, with writings shared and critiqued in the groups. In the second phase, each student or small group chooses a topic of interest and does in-depth study with an aim of sharing findings with the entire class. Students write personal reaction papers, satire, essays, narratives, and even explore media compositions. Finally, the students move outside the school to visit courtrooms, school board offices, local social services organizations, and so on, to study society firsthand.

I hope it is clear that these courses by Daigon, Verner and Martin, and Stilinovich, though they deal with contemporary issues and moral concerns, are neither trendy nor faddish. They successfully draw on traditional as well as contemporary literature, and they use popular materials—newspapers, magazines, films—as a natural part of the curriculum. Such courses also point a way toward interdisciplinary studies in the humanities, a topic I will take up in the next chapter.

Learning and Knowing

Another area that opens up to the high school student is the use of language as a way of learning, as a way of conducting "research." This is a topic that always generates a great deal of debate among English teachers and parents, for most of us tend to equate research with something called the "term paper," a writing task that most view with some distaste but tend to see as an essential part of student preparation in English, at least for the college bound. Indeed, in the professional journals, dozens and dozens of essays have been written over the years exploring the need (or lack of it) for teaching something called the "research" or "term" paper. In schools where it is taught, it often consumes a major block of time (usually senior year), yet still seems to leave students floundering when they reach college.

Much of the problem, I think, comes from the fact that English teachers have narrowed a very broad topic—learning and conducting research through language—to a single written form: the footnoted term paper. A brief anecdote is required to illustrate my point:

When my son was about six, he went on a frog-collecting jag. Much of mid-Michigan was once a great swamp, and every spring it tends to revert; thus through April and May peepers and baby frogs are everywhere. Steve and one of his pals collected fifty frogs and kept them on the back porch. For two weeks they talked frogs and thought frogs. They acted out little froggie scenes, and he and I even developed a bedtime story hero, Froggie Will, whose exploits with a Frog Adventure Team continued to entertain us for several years. In the midst of the frog collecting, Steve wrote a short poem about frogs, a poem that, unfortunately, I've since lost.

I took the poem to one of my graduate classes and, explaining the circumstances, raised a question, "Will you accept this as a research paper?" It was a loaded, teacher-type question, for I was not prepared to accept their answer, "No." Of course the poem was research, I argued, for it represented a genuine synthesis of knowledge and information, knowledge gained, for the most part, by firsthand observation, and isn't that what research is all about?

The kind of English program that I have been describing is heavily based in research at all levels. Whether the students are simply writing about the natural world (collecting ideas and writing a poem), exploring the world vicariously (reading and writing about faraway places and adventures), learning about themselves (exploring inner worlds and working out the results in a diary or journal entry), or conducting investigations into current issues and problems in society, they are learning how to phrase new knowledge in words. Where many English curricula have failed, it seems to me, is in teaching upper-level high school students the trappings of research writing—notetaking, using the card catalog, writing footnotes in proper form—without a firm grounding in the basics of research into *any* subject: perceiving, reading selectively and responsively, synthesizing information and ideas, writing or speaking about ideas, sensing the reaction of an audience to one's comments.

Further, the conventional approach to term paper writing seldom seems to work. Suzanne Howell, an English teacher in Carbondale, Illinios, writes:

The Research Paper has for years been one of the hallowed conventions of college-bound English classes. I still remember my own experience with this exercise, in the days when students never seemed to question the efficacy of what they were asked to do. We all recognized the Term Paper as the high point of our senior English class. We Chose Our Subject, We Made Our Outline, We Filled Up Note Cards. And so on. As I recall, the topics ranged from eighteenth-century clothing styles to the poetry of Edgar Guest. We worked diligently, because You'll Need This in College. And we felt great satisfaction in the number of pages we produced, at the neatness of our footnotes. This attitude still prevails, as I discovered recently in a conversation with a student from a nearby town. Their research paper had to be at least twenty pages long, she told me. Two footnotes per page. Hard work, exhausting, but We'll Need It in College.

But after teaching English—and Doing the Research Paper—for some years, I had begun to question the legitimacy of this time-honored practice. What was it, exactly, that we were trying to do? Were we accomplishing this goal? And more important, was it worth accomplishing?

[1977]

Howell found that the traditional approach to the term paper prompted plagiarism, encyclopedia cribbing, and cut-and-paste jobs with materials taken from other sources. Thus she began searching for alternatives.

She found one in the national campaign for the presidency and set her students to researching it "for real." The students listened carefully to the presidential debates and wrote commentary on the points that were raised; they analyzed campaign rhetoric; they watched television news and compared the treatment given to the candidates on the three major networks; and in the process they read, observed, synthesized, hypothesized, and generated conclusions. They *researched,* in short. Howell observed that the students' writings were among the best she had ever received, and although the specific topic of the presidential campaigns only comes up at four-year intervals, she found dozens of related spin-off activities that could be conducted at any time, simply engaging the students in investigation of topics of current concern. "Will the students Need This in College?" she asked, in concluding. "Yes— and probably in 'real life,' too."

Good research units, then, can grow from almost any lively contemporary issue or from issues that have long been of concern to mankind. Nor will the research activities be limited to library research. In addition to reading and writing, young people need to see that one can learn through questions and interviews, through experimentation, and through observation and testing. The routes to new knowledge are many, but as I have argued from the opening page of this book, they all involve the use of language as a means of discovery and communication.

Still, the question may be asked, what about the specific demands of college writing? Don't students need to know the rigorous form of the term paper? I have done informal research myself and find that surprisingly few undergraduates actually write something following the conventional model of the term paper, complete with footnotes and bibliographies. ("Too long; too tough to correct," mutters one of my university colleagues when asked about term papers.) Most undergraduate papers call for reading and commenting, writing in formal or semi-formal language, to be sure, but without the bibliographic elements of the formal re search paper. The skills required, again, are perceiving, thinking, and languaging rather than knowledge of a paper form. ("If they can think and write, that's all I need," says another colleague. "I can teach them footnote form in two minutes if they need it, or they can look it up.")

Researching and the research paper, therefore, are not at all outside the range of an English program that concerns itself with adolescent growth and development. Children conduct research at all levels, and they naturally move in the direction of more and more formal kinds of reading and writing as they mature. Teaching college preparatory reading and writing skills can be incorporated comfortably into an organic curriculum, and, to paraphrase Suzanne Howell, it integrates itself just as easily into "real life."

Aesthetic Experience

I suspect that many teachers reading this book may be concerned to see aesthetic experience apparently reserved for the upper levels of the schools. I want to re-emphasize that stages of growth and development are not discrete and that all components are present at all levels. Thus the very youngest children are able to make aesthetic responses to their reading and to look at their own compositions with a degree of objectivity that allows them to say, "This is good. That is bad. Here are some changes that need to be made." The English program must be concerned with developing aesthetic/critical response at all levels. As Louise Rosenblatt, professor emeritus at NYU, has written, "Literature is a performing art" (1968); that is, not only does reading perform for us, we perform on texts, getting better and better at responding to meaning and creating appropriate meanings and responses for ourselves.

Still, at the upper levels of schooling, young people reach an intellectual stage where they are better able to articulate their critical responses. Just as they are capable of speaking and writing about human problems with a degree of abstraction, they talk objectively about literature and writing. Plainly teachers should not attempt to force this formal aesthetic response before students are ready. In dozens of classes I have observed the disastrous effects of trying to make children talk like literary critics, of insisting that high school students come up with analyses and evaluations that were not asked of the teacher until he or she enrolled in college level literature courses. Much of the history of education shows English teachers pushing the classics on children who weren't ready, quantifying and classifying literature into genres and chronological ages rather than *teaching* it, and, in general, impressing accepted interpretations on young people who didn't even know what the work meant. In their quest to make their students appreciate literature, a great many English teachers have killed off any interest the child had in reading in the first place.

But if teachers proceed with caution, it is appropriate at high school for them to begin thinking of the aesthetic qualities of language. In this area, perhaps more than any other, the high schools must break away from the pattern set by college English. In college, people generally select advanced courses because they propose to become specialists in the field. A historical survey of literature, from Jonathan Edwards to Kurt Vonnegut, Jr., may be appropriate for English majors, and so may genre courses that concentrate on literary forms: poetry, drama, and fiction. But the high schools need not imitate the college specialty courses. Even though students are offered courses that concentrate on aesthetic/critical approaches, the literature should be organized around the interests and abilities of the student himself or herself, not by the formal constraints of the disciplines of criticism and rhetoric. Too, even though these kinds of courses will focus principally on literature, it is imperative that the wholeness of English not be lost, that writing not disappear from the curriculum.

To suggest how this integration can be maintained, I want to take the traditional divisions used for literary study—the Historical/Cultural, the Genre, the Thematic—and show how, imaginatively presented, they represent a natural extension of the concepts described in this chapter, rather than a fragmenting of English into reading/writing for experience and reading/writing for aesthetic and critical purposes.

Historical/Cultural Approaches. A seminar on the teaching of English held at Dartmouth College in 1966 launched a strong attack on the historical-chronological approach to literature in the secondary school on the grounds that plodding through literature chronologically takes the life out of it for most young people. Yet the same conference emphasized strongly that a cultural component is a vital part of English education, for all children, not just the college bound:

For the sake of both proficiency and pleasure the student should be able to understand implied as well as surface meanings, to make critical judgments as a basis for choice in his own reading, to recognize the values presented in literature, and to relate them to his own attitudes and values. He should be familiar with the "reservoir" literature that forms a common background for our culture (classical mythology, European folk and fairy tales, Arthurian legends, the Bible, etc.), with a range of selections from English and American literature and with some from other literatures in good translation. So far as possible, he should have some "time sense"—not a detailed, lifeless knowledge of names and dates, but an imaginative sense of the past.   [Squire, 1968]

How can one answer this call for familiarity with the "reservoir" literature without falling prey to pedantry? There is no simple answer, but I'd like to cite some examples of interesting alternatives.

The Scholastic American Literature Program (1977) is a four-volume series designed to fit into the traditional American literature slot in the high school system: junior year. Instead of taking a chronological approach, the series editor, Michael Spring, selected a series of major themes for four books: *Who We Are* (with sub-sections on "The Young," "The Old," and "Men and Women"), *Where We Live* ("City and Country," "Journeys," "A Sense of Place"), *How We Live* ("At Work," "At Home," "At War"), *What We Believe* ("Personal Values," "American Myths and Dreams," "Fantasy and Imagination"). Within each section, materials include fiction and nonfiction as well as drama and poetry. Among the American authors represented in the series are James Thurber, Howard Nemerov, Emily Dickinson, Edgar Allen Poe, Arthur Miller, W. E. B. DuBois, Sinclair Lewis, Carl Sandburg, T. S. Eliot, Mark Twain, Benjamin Franklin, Ralph Waldo Emerson, Henry David Thoreau, Jack London, Walt Whitman, Studs Terkel, Edith Wharton, Amy Lowell, Ray Bradbury, Wallace Stevens, Sherwood Anderson, e. e. cummings, Robert Frost, Bernard Malamud, Langston Hughes, William Carlos Williams, Joyce Carol Oates, F. Scott Fitzgerald, Truman Capote, Nathaniel Hawthorne, Edna St. Vincent Millay, Tennessee Williams, and Jonathan Edwards. This is not a complete catalog of great American authors by any means, but it surely puts students solidly in touch with the reservoir literature, giving them a sense of America's literary past. Further, when placed in context of a discussion of traditional American concerns, the works of someone like Jonathan Edwards make a great deal more sense to students than when they are shown simply as literary artifacts of colonial New England, as is the case in the conventional chronological approach.

Other alternatives to historical/cultural study of literature exist, courses that maintain the integrity of literature without killing off student interest.

—In a course in "Old Testament Literature," Leondus Beach of Dixie Heights High School, Ft. Mitchell, Kentucky (1975), includes such literary topics as epic and biography (Exodus, Moses as an epic hero), short story (Ruth and Esther), poetry (Psalms, Proverbs, Ecclesiastes), allegory (Song of Solomon), dramatic monolog (Job), and prophecy and historical prose (the Prophets).

—Ethnic literature courses have become increasingly popular and important in the schools, and the past decade has seen the growth of courses in black and Chicano literature, the literature of first Americans, and even Eskimo literature. While such courses run the risk of isolating minorities and their literature rather than integrating ethnic literature into the curriculum, they nevertheless have intrinsic appeal, both for minority and majority students.

—Perhaps less immediately "relevant," but equally interesting as an alternative to the survey course, are courses in regional literature. The major cities—Detroit, Chicago, Atlanta, San Francisco—have enough literary tradition to support a course devoted exclusively to the literature of the city. That may not be possible in smaller cities and out in the country, yet even the least populated regions have their good, "local" writers as well as their major figures. Such courses help to connect literature with familiar territory and thus make the historical/cultural side of literature accessible.

A course that seems to pull many strands together is Mary Jo Moran's "Nobel Prize Winning Literature" (1977) taught at St. Francis Academy in Joliet, Illinois. Her core books include *The Solid Mandala* by Patrick White (Australia, 1973), *New Poems* by Pablo Neruda (Chile, 1971), *One Day in the Life of Ivan Denisovich* by Alexander Solzhenitsyn (USSR, 1970), *Snow Country* by Yasunari Kawabata (Japan, 1968), *No Exit* by Jean Paul Sartre (France, 1964), *Siddhartha* by Hermann Hesse (Switzerland, 1946), *Four Plays* by Eugene O'Neill (USA, 1936), *The Magic Mountain* by Thomas Mann (Germany, 1929), *Pygmalion* by G. B. Shaw (Ireland, 1925), and *Growth of the Soil* by Knut Hamsun (Norway, 1920). By stressing common themes rather than chronology or national origin, this kind of course can help give students an aesthetic/cultural sense vastly richer than that imposed by the traditional American, British, and World literature sequences of years past.

The Genre Approach. To approach literature as genre simply means to concentrate on a form of literature—poetry, prose, drama—as the unifying principle of a course. And therein lies the problem with genre courses, for as useful as they may be for literary scholars (for whom questions of definition—what *is* a poem? how does poetry differ from prose?—are crucial), they tend to impose limits on the kind of literature brought into a course when they serve as a central focus. But imaginative genre courses that address important aesthetic questions are possible:

—Mary C. Comers at Southeast High School, Lincoln, Nebraska (1975), takes what could be a deadly course—mythology—and makes it "Myths and Modern Man," incorporating a study of modern "myths" that helps students learn about the function of myth in peoples' lives at any period.

—Phyllis Tashlik begins a science fiction genre course at Satellite Academy in the Bronx (1975) by having students take an anthropological approach to learn about the nature of present-day culture and past and possible future cultures. In defining "culture," she first has her students consider such matters as human survival and the initiation of the young as a matter of survival, discussing how cultures come into existence. After an examination of modern culture—football, McDonalds, rush hour—she explores past cultures, including American Indians, and looks at differing values placed on the family, old age, work, the young, and so on. Finally, through science fiction, she explores with her students some possibilities for future cultures, helping students see how sci-fi writers present cultural values.

In both these courses, Comers and Tashlik avoid being trapped by the genre itself and draw freely on other literary forms to focus the courses on topics and issues rather than simply on literary form.

Topical and Thematic Approaches. Thematic units or courses originally appeared on the English teaching scene in the 1950s, when it was perceived that clustering works about a theme allowed the teacher a great deal of latitude in the kinds of works he/she would teach. Thus a unit on "Courage" or "Frontiers" or "Coming of Age" could be constructed using fiction and nonfiction, poetry and prose, with a range of reading levels. This diversity remains one of the great advantages of organizing English courses and units thematically.

However, the earliest units tended to overemphasize the value of the theme in interpreting literature, rather than helping students interpret literature for themselves. In many thematic studies, then, the students became "theme hunters," studying a poem or story until they found something related to the theme—"Aha, a courageous act!"—then lost interest in the reading since the key had been found.

More recently teachers have recognized that one can maintain the integrity of the work itself and still concentrate on the relation of the work to the lives of the students. For example, examine this thematic course, "Dreams and Nightmares," by Deborah Rosen of Coconut Creek, Florida, High School:

COURSE SEQUENCE: Begin by exploring the reasons for studying the utopian dream and its relevance. Discuss current social problems (education, loss of family structure, pollution) and possible solutions (communal living, social conditioning). After reading excerpts of classical utopias, discuss the philosophical schemes and recurring elements in the utopian vision. Using *Walden II* as a link between the romantic idealism of the utopians and the pessimism of Huxley and Orwell, discuss the reasons for the increase in the nightmare vision of the future. Conclude by reading and discussing *Childhood's End*, a science fiction novel that can be interpreted as utopian or dystopian depending on the student's philosophy of the universe, human nature, and man's ability to change himself. Assignments: Composition topics are unlimited; have students read supplementary material on experimental utopias, classical utopias, current dystopias, current social criticism such as *Future Shock*. Have students set up an experimental utopia on paper; have students participate in the science fiction game to attempt to solve major international crises in moments. [1975]

In stressing the usefulness of the thematic approach, however, I do not want to lose sight of the fact that any course, including the traditional survey, can involve the student as reader and writer. While thematic courses open up possibilities for extending resources, nothing prevents the teacher in any course from concerning himself/herself with the aesthetic/cultural dimension without destroying students' delight in exploring their world through language.

The English Curriculum: Some Expectations

The basic components of the English program I have been describing are outlined in Table 1. It is useful, I think, to see all components of the program together so that growth patterns and relations among stages can be perceived.

It is also useful to describe the kinds of language skills this curriculum can be expected to produce. Parents can legitimately raise the question, "What will young people be able to do with language after twelve years of schooling in English?" From the point of view of English teachers, the question becomes, quite simply, "What can we do for our students?"

Two cautionary notes are required before I offer some answers to those questions:

First, it should be stated emphatically that no curriculum in language will ever prepare (and should not be held accountable for preparing) students to step, "cold turkey," into totally new literacy assignments, reading and writing with perfect success and ease. English cannot and should not attempt to prepare students for the *specific* literacy tasks of, say, Professor X's physics class two years hence or a job as accountant at United General Corporation in eight years. While English *can* prepare self-confident, flexible readers and writers, it cannot possibly ready students for all eventualities. Further, English cannot (and probably should not try to) prepare students for *bad* reading/writing assignments; e.g., a physics examination that merely requires regurgitation of text or lecture notes, a memo-writing assignment that invites bureaucratic prose.

Second, in considering expectations, it is far more productive to think in terms of options, possibilities, and opportunities than to consider "minimums" that must be achieved at all costs. One of the enormous failings of the accountability movement in this country is its obsession with minimum competencies, and we often see disastrous consequences when students (or teachers) fail to measure up. Thus the accounters aim low and achieve little. Even if all children measured up to the minimum, we would still not have anything remotely approaching a truly literate society. When we focus on minimums, too often the *maximums*—the essences of education—are ignored. In writing about expectations for English, then, I will describe not an imperative set of minimums, but opportunity, the maximums that we can realistically hope to accomplish.

In the elementary schools, for instance, it is not unreasonable to suppose that children in the primary grades can read, or have read to them, a book a day, experiencing as many as four or five hundred children's books in the first four years of schooling. In the upper elementary grades, as the books grow longer, the raw numbers of books devoured will decrease, but children can still read and be read to daily. In schools where this happens, a child's reading a hundred or more books each year will not be uncommon.

Elementary children should write every day as well—not just penmanship or alphabet practice—but short compositions: stories, notes, letters, diary entries, and personal observations. The teachers need not grade or mark all the writing (and should not even if they have the time). While some children's writing should be developed and revised for display under the guidance of the teacher, much daily writing can simply be shared among the children, with no direct intervention by the teacher.

Although little *formal* instruction in oral English is required for children of this age, the elementary curriculum should provide

Table 1. A Model Curriculum for English

	UNITS/TOPICS/COURSES	READING	COMPOSITION
ELEMENTARY YEARS	A full range of experiences make up the "curriculum" of the school. Subjects for language work range from field trips to personal experiences to school subjects.	Wide reading and use of print and non-print media. Free reading, picture books, being read to, listening to recorded literature. Informal book talks with teachers or librarians.	Equally free writing, storytelling, sharing show and tell. Playing language games. Giving dictation. Improvised drama, charades, pantomime.
JUNIOR HIGH/ MIDDLE SCHOOLS A. *Vicarious Experience*	Topics: *The World Around Us, Sounds and Sights, Fire and Ice, Snakes, Hunting, Our Town, Sports Animals, Faraway Places, Travel, Truth Is Stranger Than Fiction.*	Fiction and nonfiction dealing with the natural world, with an emphasis on the exciting and adventuresome, as well as things close to home.	Sensory writing, writing about observations, haiku poetry, personal narratives, keeping diaries.
B. *Fantasy Adventure*	*High Adventure, Romance, Survival, The Supernatural, Unknown Worlds, Detectives, Science Fiction, Ghouls and Goblins.*	Much action-packed fiction. Sci fi, detectives, mystery, adventure, horror, Hardy Boys stories, Nancy Drew, Alfred Hitchcock.	Writing of the same—tales of adventure, mystery, horror, intrigue. Improvised and scripted drama of horror, adventure, romance. Roleplaying: "If I were. . . ."
C. *Seeing Oneself*	*Who Am I?, Coming of Age, Loneliness, Dreams and Visions, Autobiographies, Personal Puzzles and Problems.*	All genres: poetry, prose, essays, films, and video dealing with identity. Especially stories by and about young people.	Personal and introspective writing: journals, diaries, personal narratives, contemplative poetry, personal poetry, values clarifying roleplay.
SENIOR HIGH SCHOOL A. *Human Relationships*	*Conflicts, Family Relationships, Rebellion, Friends and Enemies, Youth and Age, Making Connections with Others.*	Increasing use of adult as well as young adult literature. Literary discussion focuses on characters and their interaction. While some books describe peer problems	Introspective writing, with an increased emphasis on sharing thoughts in public. Dramatic improvisations on human problems. Conscious effort to im-

emphasis shifts toward adult relationships.

B. Expanding Consciousness	Cities in Decay, Man and Nature, Politics, Minorities, Schooling, Death and Dying, Hero/Anti-Hero, Might and Right, Future Shock, Utopian Visions, Prophecy.	At this point the full range of literature—juvenile and adult—is available to students. Many opportunities exist for the teacher to move beyond "pure" literature into magazines, newspapers, and the like.	While private and personal writing remain important, students can move into a full range of public discourse, including creative essays, formal letters, discuss on, debate, analysis.
C. Learning and Knowing	Issues, problems, moral concerns. Plus increasing connections with exploring and knowing in other disciplines; e.g., chemistry, anthropology, physics.	The full resources of the library should be made available. In addition, students can learn to "read" and gain information through media, interviews, research, and experimentation.	"Research" can be written in many forms: essay, term paper, poem, story, drama. The full range should be explored.
D. Aesthetic Experience		As appropriate to the subject, including contemporary and classic fiction and nonfiction, media resources, magazines and journal articles, elementary critical articles. Discussion begins with exploration of the text and the reader's responses, then moves toward informal critical analysis. The connections between personal response and objective criticism are explored in depth.	The focus of composition will naturally tend to emphasize the analytical and critical—writing about literature. However, the thrust toward personal, introspective, and creative writing can and should continue, lest the program become strictly 'academic.' Further, the students' own writing is appropriately subject to more formal critical analysis. Drama in English will increasingly focus on presentation, of student writing as well as literature, through readers' theatre, plays, etc.
History/Culture	Civil War Literature, The Literature of the Twenties, The American Revolution, Ethnic Literature, Literature of East and West.		
Genre	Folklore, Mythology, Science Fiction, The Lyric, Contemporary Poetry, Classic Plays, The Western, The Spy Novel, Television Novels.		
Theme	Existentialism, Politics in Literature, Frontiers, Courage, The Young Person in Literature, American Myths and Dreams.		

daily opportunities for talk: in pairs, in small groups, for the whole class. Dramatic activities can grow naturally from reading, writing, and oral work, and dramatic play and improvisation ought to take place almost as often as writing.

In the secondary schools—junior and senior high—the English work is, unfortunately, likely to be concentrated in a single class period of fifty minutes or so, which severely limits possibilities and tends to isolate English from other subjects. Nevertheless, language *use* should still dominate the English program. While I am somewhat reluctant to suggest numbers for fear that they will be taken as minimums, it doesn't seem at all unrealistic to expect the English program to have secondary students reading eight to ten books per semester, fifteen to twenty per year, and perhaps four times as many shorter pieces: poems, articles, stories, essays, etc. Similarly, since writing for increasingly larger audiences is a natural outgrowth of the maturation process, secondary students might polish ten to fifteen papers a term for analysis and discussion, and perhaps write two to three times that many informal, non-graded pieces: journal entries, notes, and drafts.

Oral language skills grow to full maturity at the secondary level. If teachers simply eschew the lecture method, students will be involved regularly in productive spoken English activities: discussing, debating, problem-solving, reviewing, critiquing, and brainstorming. As young people mature, they seem less and less inclined to participate in improvised and creative drama, yet dramatic activities—particularly reader's theater—should still continue to occur regularly at the upper levels.

To many beleaguered English/language arts teachers, these may seem impossibly high expectations. Yet it should be remembered that students are in secondary English classes 250 minutes per week, forty weeks per year. Elementary teachers have a full six- to seven-hour day with their students, and thus have available a substantial amount of time for language work. I submit that if the schools were to curtail the drill, lecture, and pseudo-discussion that presently predominate, there would be plenty of time for students to meet these expectations.

As a result of this curriculum, we can expect that students (and thus, subsequently, adults) will:

—retain and develop their sense of pleasure and delight in language, seeing reading as a natural part of their lives and finding satisfaction rather than fear in writing.

—use language as a mode of learning and sharing knowledge successfully.

—feel a sense of individuality through their language, demonstrated through evolution of a strong personal voice in speech and writing and in the ability to respond to spoken and written language in unique and thoughtful ways.

—use oral and written language successfully with a wide range of audiences representing the entire spectrum of mature discourse.

—use language to evaluate and discriminate among experiences, making assessment through reading and writing independently of the value judgments of others.

—employ language to solve problems, to explore and research questions, and to write and speak articulately about the answers.

—clarify and develop their own sense of human values through literature and writing.

—develop a sense of their cultural backgrounds through the "reservoir" of literature and see connections between that background and their own culture and values.

—know how to assess unfamiliar language situations and bring existing language skills to bear on them.

—master the surface conventions of English, as necessary for the students' own aims and purposes.

These are great expectations, not small ones. However, nothing less will ensure a truly literate society.

5. A NOTE ON COLLEGE ENGLISH

The teaching of English in colleges and universities is not a major topic in this book, but the role of colleges in the basics crisis is so important that two points of articulation must be pointed out. First, the natural extension of English work at the college level is toward increased emphasis on the historical, cultural, and aesthetic study of literature and language, as it always has been. College students of literature and language are fully capable of abstract analysis and criticism, and, moreover, they often enjoy it. At the same time, a great many college instructors, in their own delight over teaching the discipline, forget that their courses are populated by nineteen- to twenty-one-year-olds who have human needs and concerns that can be met through language. That college students will pursue a traditional chronological study of literature with apparent willingness does not mean this is the best of all possible approaches to historical/cultural study. All things considered, many high school teachers have done a much better job of exploring alternative approaches to language and literature than their counterparts at the university, where the curriculum is often static and locked into tradition.

Second, teachers at all levels must be concerned about college freshman English. The students who have read at the levels and written with the frequency described in the previous section will not have serious problems in freshman English. The trouble with freshmen is not so much that they lack skills, but that they simply haven't read very much or written very much, and thus they are at sea when they reach college. While the colleges have every right to point out the deficiencies of entering students, I think university people would be better advised to concentrate on educating—one at a time—the students who enter their classes. There will always be students coming to college poorly prepared (a decreasing number, one hopes), and there will always be students who come fully prepared to do new work. The question is, what will happen to them both? Will both be plugged into a conventional freshman course with its reliance on a grammar handbook, or will they find their individual needs being met by diverse courses? Will freshman English provide little more than a service function to other academic departments, or does it have a *raison d'être* of its own? Certainly the way colleges have responded to the literacy crisis does not create an exemplary model for the schools. One has to hope that instead of carping back and forth, teachers at both levels will do their best to improve the quality of reading and writing in America.

8
Literacy in the Humanities

1. THE HUMANITIES AND ENGLISH

The word "humanities" conjures up a good many different impressions. For some, it is a reminder of an eight-o'clock class in college that featured an endless slide show of Great Art, interrupted from time to time by the playing of a Great Symphony, all to be tested by multiple choice at midterm. For others, it creates images of people called the Greeks and Romans, who did whatever they did better than we do, and who were successful in conquering the known universe through military might at the same time. For some it evokes memories of a tweedy teacher in high school or college who droned on about this or that artistic or literary masterpiece, only dimly aware of the century he or she was living in.

For many, it carries connotations of something called Culture, creating mixed feelings that Culture is something possessed principally by Snobs, but if one doesn't have it one feels Uncultured—a Philistine—somehow left out of the picture. The extent to which this image persists and bothers people is revealed by a book called *Catching Up* (1978). Written by a college professor, Charles Veley, the book is an attempt to put all of the humanities in a capsule form of 277 pages. Veley explains,

We feel the need to catch up on what's important, but we don't know where. It would be nice if local colleges had a course in Today's Essentials. Then we could get the best of all those courses we had to skip because we were too busy with math requirements. But colleges, unfortunately, don't operate that way. In the academic world, there's no such thing as a General Practitioner. For alternatives, the Britannica and the Great Books are both too big, and neither will tell you what you can afford to leave out.

There is an alternative, he explains. One doesn't actually have to *read* the great works, "unless one wants to get really immersed in a subject" and learn it firsthand.

For the comparisons and analogies that we all like to make in our everyday talk, a knowledge of a few basic things in each field, from art to opera will be enough.

That people "feel the need to catch up" is a damning indictment of what schools do to people, but the irony seems lost on Veley. Having offered what might be called a Cocktail Party Theory of Education—let's learn the facts that will help us drop a few allusions in our day-to-day talk—he proceeds to explain, in breezy style, what you should know and what you can forget. The "names you should know" in ancient times include most of the major Greek and Roman artists, politicians, and mythological beings. (At cocktail parties the Known World apparently ends just east of Athens.)

As the reader approaches our own times, he/she is told:

Two novelists one *ought* to know are JANE AUSTEN (1775–1817) and expatriate American HENRY JAMES (1843–1916). Why? To know civilized sensitivity and irony.

Of course, "to know" in this case does not mean actually *reading* the books; it merely means knowing that James and Austen represent "civilized irony," whatever that is. Among writers Veley tells us we can safely ignore are Herman Melville ("*Moby Dick* is one of the great American novels that nobody reads"), Ralph Waldo Emerson, Henry David Thoreau, Charles Dickens ("Nowadays his books aren't talked about outside the academic world, where they have time for him"), and Alfred, Lord Tennyson, whom he dismisses as "the poetic equivalent to TCHAIKOVSKY." (So much for you if you happen to like Tchaikovsky.)

After running through the twentieth century in twenty-five pages, Veley concludes the book with a section called "How To Talk Like a Critic," including a list of foreign phrases (*noblesse oblige, quid pro quo*), some critical jargon (*artistic control, slick pandering, technical facility*), and a few "safe" opinions (in ballet, the orchestra can probably be criticized accurately since the pay scale for pit orchestras attracts only second fiddlers.)

It is tempting to think that Veley wrote the book as a joke for our amusement. But whether it is a joke or not, *Catching Up* is an attack on humanities education. As a joke, it shows how the typical offerings of humanities courses in schools and colleges can be satirized for their shallowness, pretentiousness, and presumptuousness. If the book is read and used seriously, then it shows how badly humanities studies have misled their students into believing that *they* must be shallow, pretentious, and presumptuous. In either case, Veley's ridicule of humanities teachers supports another popular view: that of the humanist as one who is idealistic and impractical, with plenty of time on his hands to pursue the trivial. If the humanist were any good at anything, he'd probably be teaching science or working for General Motors.

In many respects, this stereotype has been earned by humanities teachers. For instance, a book on *Basic Concepts in the Humanities,* edited by Maria Wagner and Jeanette Ainsworth (1977), a self-instructional manual designed to accompany the authors' humanities course, shows some curious parallels to the Veley book. Describing a painting, *Earth Green,* by Mark Rothko, the book asks:

How would you describe the colors? If you merely said red, light blue, or green, you would be only partially correct. The distinctive quality of Rothko's color is to use varying tonalities to produce the feeling of flickering light. Part of the effect of color involves the manner of application so as to produce varying tonal quality.

What the student learns here is that his or her intuitive responses to a work of art are inadequate or "only partially correct." So the students scribble down in notebooks what they're supposed to see ("varying tonalities to produce the feeling of flickering light") along with the conclusion, bound to turn up on the final, that "manipulation of tone or light is an important aspect of color to recognize and perceive."

Interestingly, this section concludes with a segment that, like Veley's book, would teach "Being a Critic of the Arts." The writer explains:

> In the act of description, the critic reveals his perceptual awareness and hopes the reader will also become aware of some of the points he is making.

The implications are clear: The critic occupies his pre-eminence because he sees varying tonalities where the yokels only see red, light blue, and green. The critic hopes to share this knowledge, but no matter how hard he tries, the reader is only likely to "become aware of *some* of the points he is making" [italics added]. I suspect that most good critics would deny that they are serving this kind of educational function and suggest that the humanities teacher is probably describing her own view of herself and her students, not the relationship of critic and reader. Nevertheless, the student is, in effect, being told to model himself after the critic/teacher: "Learn to talk the way I do about art and you'll be above the rest of the folks (and get an A on the final, too)." Not only is this attitude damaging to arts appreciation, it is deadly for literacy as well, promoting superficial language manipulation at the expense of perception and honest communication.

Most damaging, perhaps, is the attitude toward the student that is implied in this course, which is supposedly about human-ness. Describing a research writing project, the authors of *Basic Concepts* state:

> . . . *credit cannot be given for any term paper which has not been completed in the prescribed manner,* i.e., by submission of the various preliminary assignments, *one at a time, on time.* Each exercise will be checked,

recorded, and returned with comments for your guidance. What does all this mean? It means simply that you cannot put off this part of your composition requirements until a week or two before the due date; you must follow the rules, that is, submit to periodic check-ups in order to avoid a good deal of pain—and grief—in the end.

If Plato or St. Augustine or Michelangelo or Beethoven had been forced to work in this way, they never would have accomplished a thing. Even medieval apprenticeships where one learned "the basics" of brushwork from the master before being allowed to do touch-up work on the fresco were hardly this patronizing. One of the lessons people can learn from the humanities is that the human spirit is one of inquiry and experimentation. This research assignment dwells on precisely the opposite qualities—subservience and routine—all the while attempting to indoctrinate students into the "right" way of perceiving human accomplishment. No wonder people wind up with ambivalent feelings about the humanities, the arts, and themselves and thus turn to a Charles Veley for help or amusement.

Of course not all humanities programs are like this one, and many humanities teachers take a far different view of their work and their students. (I will describe some more positive examples further on in this chapter.) Nevertheless, the picture of humanities education presented by *Basic Concepts in the Humanities* is all too familiar to a great many people who are veterans of HUMS 101.

Humanities and the Individual

The study of the humanities, then, must be far more than a smattering of names, dates, great works, and the basics of arts and history. It must, in the schools, include the individual student—man or woman, boy or girl. For an operating definition of the humanities, I want to return to the Greeks and a simple motto that has been chiseled over the door of half the high schools in this country: "Know thyself." The Upanishads of India say, "By knowing the Self, through hearing, reflection, and meditation, one comes to know all things." By learning about one's self, whether through contemplation or study, a person comes to know the larger universe of mankind as well. As a student—age six or sixty—answers the question, "Who am I?" he or she is simultaneously answering the question, "What is mankind?" Humanities courses have often failed because they have perceived culture as something "out there," created by others—Greeks and Romans, painters and musicians—rather than as a body of works created by individual men and women as expressions of their own attempts to know the self and, in the process, to define the collective self of mankind. What the English teacher brings to the humanities is the "literacy connection," for the exploring of oneself as well as understanding humankind is language based.

An Aztec poem reminds us of the role of language in the process of knowing and describing one's self:

> Who am I?
> As a bird I fly about,
> I sing of flowers;
> I compose songs
> Butterflies of songs
> Let them burst forth from my soul!
> Let my heart be delighted with them!

Not all the songs we sing are songs of delight; a great many deal with human conditions of pain and suffering. Nevertheless, like Walt Whitman, we sing songs of ourselves. We experience the world; we explore the self; we communicate with others about that self. In composing, mankind has chosen many different forms and media: carving on cave walls to record events; telling myths and legends to explain the unknown; writing poetry and stories; creating paintings, photographs, symphonies, pop songs, films, and sculpture. Each is a "language" that connects one self with many others, inviting others to respond to and to share in the experience.

Benjamin DeMott of Amherst College has described English as a humanistic study this way:

English is about my distinctness and the distinctness of other human beings. Its function, like that of some books called great, is to provide an
arena in which the separate man, the single ego, can strive at once to
know the world through art, to know what if anything he uniquely is,
and what some brothers are. The instruments employed are the imagination, the intellect, and the texts or events that rouse the former to life.

[Squire, 1968]

In contrast to the HUMS 101 approach, DeMott, the Upanishads,
the Greeks, and the Aztec poet (and most of the humanists and
artists in history) call, not for indoctrination or enculturation, but
for understanding how one fits into the community of mankind.
And, lest this sound hopelessly vague, let me add that this concept
of humanities calls for *dimensioned* education, that is, education
that is firmly based in the day-to-day experiences of the student.
The study of the humanities through reading and writing begins at
home.

Backyard Humanities

In *Underfoot: An Everyday Guide to Exploring the American
Past,* David Weitzman (1976) writes:

Much of our history comes not from the distance of once upon a time but
from the memories of those closest to us with whom we have lived our
lives. Search as we might in the historybook lives of others we don't
know, and have never known, sooner or later we will return to find that
the answers to who we are and where we've been are nearby, and many
of them are underfoot.

Further, each person is himself or herself an historian—historian
"everyman":

The historian "everyman" belongs to an old, honorable tradition whose
participants extend far into the past and continue into the present day—
the tellers of tales; the elders; puppeteers, dancers and actors who initiated the young; the folksingers, clan leaders, teachers, grandmothers,
habitués of the general store down at the fork, . . . ten-year-old girls
who keep diaries, and ninety-five-year-olds . . . who recall a story of
long-ago childhood.

It is obvious from the list above that literacy is intertwined with history. Historian everyman is a singer, storyteller, diary keeper, teacher, and talker—both historian and language user.

Weitzman's book is concerned with informal historical techniques, and although designed primarily for adults, many of his suggested historical explorations seem quite appropriate for young people in history/English classes.

For instance, he suggests collecting oral history reminiscences from "elders," who, for our purposes, might range from an elementary child's mom and dad, born in the early 1950s (who can never recall living without TV), to grandparents and great-grandparents, born at the turn of the century, who can even remember tales told by *their* parents and grandparents about nineteenth-century events. Interview topics suggested by Weitzman include:

school days
earliest childhood memories
voyages and journeys
old country family history
a farm girl's chores
the life of a soldier
opening up a first shop or business
early automobiles, trains, and boats
first radio program remembered
favorite actors and actresses, movies and plays from childhood
Saturday evening around the fire
favorite early television programs
food and cooking
clothes and fashions
toys fondly remembered
new inventions
apprenticeship and jobs
books and authors of a lifetime
phonograph records and dancing
concerts

He would also have the historian review photographs, visit cemeteries, study family artifacts (bottles, antiques, coverlets), etc. And as a school project, this kind of historical work would naturally lead to written narratives, reports, memoirs, and biographies.

The popularity of Alex Haley's *Roots* as both a book and television phenomenon generated a clutch of find-your-own-roots books that could be genuinely helpful to historian everyman. A Consumer Guide publication, *Tracing Your Roots* (1977), provides practical advice on tracing ancestors through albums, diaries, marriage certificates, public records, military files, immigration records, and an examination of the evolution of family names. Such firsthand historical research teaches a considerable amount of history and humanities in the process.

A great many readers of this book will recall having seen the *Foxfire* publications at a local bookstore, all of them written by students. *Foxfire* originated in 1966 as a student magazine in Rabun Gap, Georgia, under the direction of an English teacher, Eliot Wigginton. He sent students out to recapture the rural culture of their ancestors and taught them how to publish their own magazine. A collected edition of the essays, published as *The Foxfire Book*, sold over a million copies.

The young authors of *Foxfire* researched arts, crafts, folklore, and local history; they collected stories, jokes, and tall tales. The articles ranged from techniques for grinding corn and ways of keeping deer out of the corn to making pack saddles, bricks, and coonskin caps. Students learned how to locate a storyteller, conduct an interview, transcribe notes, write and revise a story, take photographs, design a page, lay out a page for publication, and even how to raise money to support the magazine.

The *Foxfire* concept of cultural history need not be limited to *rural* areas. Deborah Insel, a Boston teacher, had her students try a similar kind of project in an urban setting (1975). She made contact with a number of senior citizens in South Boston and arranged for students to interview them on such topics as family life, housing and neighborhoods, schooling, work, leisure time, religious life, and important persons. Outside speakers gave the students help on learning historical research techniques, and the project led directly to the writing of a bicentennial book, *A Social History of South Boston from 1900 to the Present*.

Foxfire spawned many imitators, and in the past few years student-written cultural history magazines have sprung up all over the country (e.g., *Salt,* a downeast publication; and *Bittersweet,* published by a group of Missouri students). However, lest we throw the baby into the printing press, it is important to emphasize that *formal* publication is not a prerequisite for a project. Students can research and report on a wide range of topics without starting an expensive magazine. Research might lead to something as simple as a bulletin board display or a series of posters. Students can edit tape recordings into an informal documentary radio show, arrange for an in-class panel or interview with a local character, or turn their research into a media project. For some students, even fiction writing or the writing of poetry based on interviews can provide a useful outlet for their findings. Books on local history, written by students and hand bound following traditional procedures, can be placed in the school or community library or a local museum.

Nor do the projects necessarily have to be limited to the pattern of interviewing *living* informants. Marjorie McClelland, who teaches English at Rockland High School, Rockland, Massachusetts, had her students do informal historical research into the life of Maria Louise Poole, a writer who had lived in Rockland from 1841 to 1898 (1974). Her students began their search with a dictionary of American authors to learn some basic biographical facts. They combed the microfilm files of the town newspaper for references and found resources in a volume on the history of the city. The city librarian located a collection of Maria Louise Poole's novels, and students found the site where Poole was buried and located the house where she was born, along with some photographs of the house as it had appeared in the nineteenth century.

From these materials the students prepared a slide tape (a sequence of 35-millimeter color slides accompanied by a taped commentary). Nineteenth-century objects and artifacts were photographed or re-photographed and some of the students borrowed period costumes to stage photos of what Maria Poole must have looked like as a schoolgirl. Finally, the students actually read a number of Miss Poole's books and wove quotations into the slide presentation.

Cultural information can also be brought into the classroom directly so that students need not stray outside the school walls for their work. In *Museum People* (1977), Peggy Thompson describes some of the interests and skills of the staff of the Smithsonian Institution: a restoration carpenter, a freeze drier of animals, a herpetologist (snake stuffer), a model maker, a restorer of musical instruments. While not every town has such experts available, most communities are close enough to a museum (or a university, where such people also hang out) to arrange for a series of visits and lectures, leading, ultimately, to writing projects and perhaps even to the construction of an in-school museum of historical artifacts, complete with written explanations.

"Backyard humanities" is a beginning, but many of these techniques apply to the study of other cultures as well. For example, Geoffrey Summerfield (1968) describes a unit by two British teachers who brought in resource materials, both literary and historical, and had the students re-create a family living in Peking in 1400 A.D.:

We created three generations of the Tzu family: Grandfather Tzu had a passion for breeding crickets and for making firecrackers; Father was a fisherman who employed picturesque and voracious cormorants for landing his catch; and the two children, boy and girl, were very slightly older than our pupils.

In addition to studying Chinese art, culture, cuisine, and warfare, the teachers introduced literature in this simulated culture so students could read, and subsequently write "Chinese poems about Chinese experiences":

Our methods were really very simple. First of all we read poems to them on the themes of war, nightmare, exile and friendship. We then wrote some out on large sheets of paper so that they could see what they looked like; these we added to the Chinese bowls and spoons, table mats, paintings (in reproduction), and the drawings of household gods with which we filled the room, so as to "saturate" the children in visual and tactile experiences of things Chinese. Some of the poems which we read were presented as coming from the hand of Grandfather Tzu. We then suggested that they might care to write poems either singly or in pairs on the various aspects of Chinese life that had excited them, and that they need not worry unduly about rhyme. When these had been written, we wrote them out, again on large sheets of paper, so that within a fortnight the room was full of poems by the children themselves. The slower, more hesitant children were allowed time to rethink and refurbish their poems, being spurred on by the successes of their peers. Finally, we duplicated most of the poems and produced a small booklet, decorated marginally with Chinese motifs of birds and dragons and bamboo, for example, which some of the children then painted, decorated, and elaborated as they wished.

Humanities and history teachers will recognize this Chinese project as a variation of what is variously called the "inductive" or "project" or "post-holding" approach to the study of a culture. (It is also a library-based variation of *Foxfire*.) The project emphasizes learning through discovery, through examination of primary and secondary sources, and especially, through raising questions about a culture and seeking answers by exploring history books, paintings, music, sculpture, artifacts, biographies, transcripts, and so on. It teaches facts by the bushel, but places them within the context of cultural understanding rather than simply listing them on the page. It is an approach that can be used for almost any culture at any period of time—from the history of Greece and Rome or the examination of European roots of four hundred years ago to the popular culture forms of the 1960s.

Most of these activities—including examination of nonverbal artifacts or works of art—involve language work. Thus the English teacher—working alone or as part of an interdisciplinary team—can organize small group discussions, panels, and debates; help students raise questions and find answers about history; establish roleplaying and simulation activities to generate the "feel" of distant cultures; provide reading resources; and offer outlets through writing poems, stories, reports, monographs, displays, newsletters, magazines, plays, media presentations, and essays. It matters little whether humanities projects are initiated by the English teacher, by other teachers, or by teams. Literacy instruction provides both a center and a set of procedures for learning to know oneself by knowing others, through language.

Reading Resources for the Humanities

The number of books, monographs, magazines, and articles available to the teacher of English/humanities is inexhaustible, for "the humanities" covers just about every human concern and thus includes just about everything ever set in print or carved on a cave wall. The choices are so many, in fact, that in this section, I will merely offer a sampler of some of the best and most representative materials.

Children's Literature. To begin the survey, one has merely to look at some of the books that are generally called children's classics. Every child is introduced at one time or another to the Mother Goose rhymes, which have historical roots in England and France, but which also have an American history that dates to colonial times. Mother Goose is literally older than the country, and her poems, which have been published in thousands of editions, are a natural part of the cultural heritage of every child.

When teachers speak of the "cultural heritage," they frequently link it to another phrase: "to expose," which implies that the indoctrination into one's culture will be unpleasant or possibly harmful, like exposure to the measles or X rays. It need not be, of course. As children's books show, classics are classics because they naturally and consistently delight the human spirit.

I think, then, that children "ought" to be "exposed" to their classics, not because they must, but because the books are too good to be missed. In addition to Mother Goose, every child ought to have an opportunity to read or hear some of the folk tales collected by the German Brothers Grimm (including such tales as "Hansel and Gretel" and "Rumpelstiltskin") and those of

Frenchman Charles Perrault ("Puss in Boots," "Cinderella," and an early version of Mother Goose). Any list of "must" books for children will vary according to the compiler. My own includes such titles as Lewis Carroll's *Alice in Wonderland,* Clement Moore's " 'Twas the Night Before Christmas," A. A. Milne's *Winnie the Pooh* books, E. B. White's *Charlotte's Web,* Randall Jarrell's *Animal Story,* and Maurice Sendak's delightful fantasy of misbehavior, *Where the Wild Things Are.*

Children also have a good deal of curiosity about historical events, and both historical fiction and biography/autobiography meet this reading need. Fiction may be structured about specific events in history as are Nathaniel Benchley's *Sam the Minuteman* or Esther Forbes' *Johnny Tremain,* but equally interesting are "period pieces" like the Laura Ingalls Wilder *Little House on the Prairie* series, which is concerned much more with portraying a culture and period than with reconstructing historical events. Biography and autobiography, of course, touch on every historical period from the Revolution on.

Finally, children's literature offers the English/humanities teacher an opportunity to introduce multicultural concerns through the children's tales, fables, legends, and stories set in different countries. Virginia Haviland has written a *Favorite Fairy Tales* series, which includes books of collected tales from such countries as Czechoslovakia, Denmark, Scotland, and Japan. Padraic Colum has written of his native country in *The King of Ireland's Son* as has Natalie Carlson in *The Talking Cat and Other Stories of French Canada.* Interesting for parents, teachers, and children is that so many tales turn up in slightly different forms in so many different countries. Thus children can begin to see some common concerns of humanity as they note similarities between say, German, Japanese, and Indian folk tales.

It is important in presenting these kinds of historical and multicultural books for children that teachers resist the temptation to engage in formal teaching. Rather, they should rely on the stories themselves to carry the weight of information. By negative ex-

BOOKS FOR CHILDREN

Children's Classics

Mother Goose
Grimms' *Fairy Tales*
Tales of the Arabian Nights
Fairy Tales, Charles Perrault
Fairy Tales, Hans Christian Andersen
Alice in Wonderland, Lewis Carroll
A Book of Nonsense, Edward Lear
"'Twas the Night Before Christmas," Clement Moore
Peter Rabbit, Beatrix Potter
Just So Stories and *The Jungle Books*, Rudyard Kipling
Winnie the Pooh and *The House at Pooh Corner*, A. A. Milne
The Adventures of Pinocchio, Carlo Lorenzini
The Wind in the Willows, Kenneth Grahame
Mary Poppins, Pamela Travers
Peter Pan, James Barrie
Black Beauty, Anna Sewell
Bambi, Felix Galten
Charlotte's Web, E. B. White
Lassie Come Home, Eric Knight
The Bat-Poet and *Animal Story*, Randall Jarrell
Where the Wild Things Are, Maurice Sendak

Historical Fiction for Children

Sam the Minuteman, Nathaniel Benchley
The Drinking Gourd, Ferdinand Monjo
The Courage of Sarah Noble, Alice Dalgliesh
The Matchlock Gun, Walter Edmonds
The Fair American, Elizabeth Coatsworth
Little House on the Prairie, Laura Ingalls Wilder

ample, some historical accounts of the life of George Washington written in the nineteenth century tried to glorify our first President, raising him to near sainthood for his honesty when caught, hatchet-handed, cutting down a cherry tree. Children do not need the intervention of either author or teacher to draw morals or lessons from their reading. A good book is capable of enculturating on its own.

Men of Iron, Howard Pyle
The Wonderful Winter, Marchette Chute
Calico Bush, Rachel Field
Johnny Tremain, Esther Forbes

Biography and Autobiography

Ringling Brothers, Molly Cone
The Boy Who Drew Sheep (Giotto), Anne Rockwell
Edgar Allan Poe, Philip Stern
George Washington Carver, Peter Towne
John Adams, Joyce Blackburn
Three for Revolution (Patrick Henry, Thomas Jefferson, and George Washington), Burke Davis
How the Wright Brothers Invented the Airplane, Robert Quackenbush
The Story of Benedict Arnold, Clifford L. Aldermann

Children's Books with a Multicultural Focus

The Talking Cat and Other Stories of French Canada, Natalie Savage Carlson
Chinese Myths and Fantasies, Cyril Birch
Tales of a Chinese Grandmother, Frances Carpenter
The Treasure of Li-Po, Alice Ritchie
Favorite Fairy Tales Told in Czechoslovakia; Favorite Fairy Tales Told in Denmark; Favorite Fairy Tales Told in Scotland; Favorite Fairy Tales Told in Japan, Virginia Haviland
The King of Ireland's Son, Padraic Colum
The Blind Men and the Elephant (India), Lillian Quigley
Russian Tales and Legends, Charles Downing
Swiss-Alpine Folktales, Fritz Muller-Guggenbuhl
The Dancing Kettle and Other Japanese Folktales, Yoshiko Uchida

Books for Secondary Schools. Reading resources for older readers in the junior high schools and beyond include materials written specifically for young adult readers as well as adult books that young people enjoy. My bibliography of representative titles lists some classics of American, British, and world literature, for example Mark Twain's autobiographical *Life Along the Mississippi,* Anton Chekhov's *The Cherry Orchard,* Nathaniel Haw-

BOOKS FOR JUNIOR AND SENIOR HIGH READERS

American History and Culture

The Most Dangerous Man in America: Scenes from the Life of Benjamin Franklin,
    Catherine Drinker Bowen
The House of the Seven Gables and *The Scarlet Letter,* Nathaniel Hawthorne
A Folksinger's History of the Revolution, Oscar Brand
Roots, Alex Haley
Drums Along the Mohawk, Walter D. Edmonds
The Last of the Mohicans, James Fenimore Cooper
The Witchcraft of Salem Village, Shirley Jackson
The Oregon Trail, Francis Parkman
Banners at Shenandoah and *A Stillness at Appomattox,* Bruce Catton
To Be a Slave, Julius Lester
The Red Badge of Courage, Stephen Crane
Jubilee, Margaret Walker
Billy Budd, Herman Melville
Notes of a Native Son, James Baldwin
America, Alistair Cooke
Life Along the Mississippi, Mark Twain
Custer in '76, Walter Camp
My Ántonia, Willa Cather
Boots and Saddles, or Life in Dakota with General Custer, Elizabeth Custer
The Man Who Loved Cat Dancing, Marilyn Durham
The Negro Cowboys, Philip Durham and Everett L. Jones
To the Last Man, Zane Grey
Centennial and *Chesapeake,* James Michener
Riders of the Pony Express, Ralph Moody
The Naming of America, Alan Wolk
The Life of Audubon, Clyde Fister
Daniel Boone: The Opening of the Wilderness, John Mason Brown
Young Thomas Edison, Sterling North
Abe Lincoln Grows Up, Carl Sandburg

World History and Culture

The Ascent of Man, Jacob Bronowski
The Bible
Agamemnon and *Prometheus Bound,* Aeschylus
The Iliad and *The Odyssey,* Homer
Medea, Euripides
Antigone and *Oedipus Rex,* Sophocles

The Tomb of Tutankhamen, Howard Carter
The Siege and Fall of Troy, Robert Graves
Gods, Graves and Scholars, C. W. Ceram
Mythology and The Greek Way, Edith Hamilton
Reading the Past: The Story of Deciphering Ancient Languages, Leonard Cottrell
The Bronze Bow, Elizabeth George Speare
Don Quixote, Miguel de Cervantes
The Cherry Orchard, Anton Chekhov
The Three Musketeers, Alexandre Dumas
Madame Bovary, Gustave Flaubert
A Doll's House, Henrik Ibsen
The Rubaiyat, Omar Khayyam
Candide, Voltaire
The poetry and drama of William Shakespeare
Aku-Aku, Thor Hyerdahl
The Mound Builders, Robert Silverberg
The Source, James Michener
Things Fall Apart, Chinua Achebe
Exodus, Leon Uris
Galileo and the Magic Numbers, Sidney Rosen

Contemporary Values and Problems

Operating Manual for Spaceship Earth, R. Buckminster Fuller
Lord of the Flies, William Golding
A Farewell to Arms, Ernest Hemingway
One Flew Over the Cuckoo's Nest, Ken Kesey
The Fixer, Bernard Malamud
The Human Zoo, Desmond Morris
The Grapes of Wrath, John Steinbeck
Slaughterhouse Five, Kurt Vonnegut, Jr.
Demian, Hermann Hesse
The Days of War, Frederick Forsyth
All Quiet on the Western Front, Erich Maria Remarque
The Siege of Leningrad, Harrison E. Salisbury
August 1914, Alexander Solzhenitsyn
Dr. Zhivago, Boris Pasternak
The Guns of August, Barbara Tuchman
The Caine Mutiny, Herman Wouk
The Stranger, Albert Camus
Looking Backward, Edward Bellamy

thorne's *The House of the Seven Gables* and *The Scarlet Letter,* Alexandre Dumas' *The Three Musketeers,* Henrik Ibsen's *A Doll's House,* the drama and poetry of William Shakespeare. However, it is important to stress that the classics, written originally for adults of a different time period, are difficult for many young people, removed from contemporary experience by time and language. Thus, though teachers seem generally agreed that students "ought" to be introduced to Shakespeare in the schools, the fact is that The Bard is simply too difficult for a great many secondary school students to read. Attempts to translate his works into everyday language or to simplify them for the sake of enculturation simply destroy interest in literacy and the humanities. Similarly, while some students may be able to enjoy the Greek dramatists—Aeschylus, Euripides, Sophocles—for the values they present or, in some cases, for sheer violence and bloodlust, reading those writers is beyond the reach of a majority of students. (It should be added that a much greater percentage of students can enjoy seeing Shakespeare and the Greek dramatists on stage. Similarly, many students enjoy hearing recordings or readings of classic books that may be beyond their reading interest. To present the works in this way should *not* be regarded in the same vein as the teaching of a simplified edition of Shakespeare.)

Reading materials in the humanities must then be presented as the teacher would any reading—offering books because they describe experiences of interest in language students can comprehend. If English/humanities teachers will follow that relatively simple guideline, they will discover that an extraordinary amount of good, classic literature will be taught in the process.

Multiethnic Literature. Of particular interest in recent years has been including multiethnic and multicultural literature in English/humanities courses. Minority groups—blacks, American Indians, Oriental- and Jewish-Americans—have protested that the literature taught in American public schools is primarily about middle-class Americans, whose ancestry, if it is even mentioned, is

Anglo-American or European-American. At least in literature, the American melting pot seems to melt everybody into WASPs.

The initial response of textbook publishers to these demands was literally to paint some faces in children's readers brown and black and to change a few names from Ralph and Mary to Miguel and Ramona. A second stage was, more properly, to begin including representative multiethnic literature in textbooks, though in many cases, the appearance of ethnic literature is simply tokenism. In some secondary schools, teachers in elective programs began to introduce occasional courses in ethnic literature, for the most part about blacks and Indians, but occasionally about other minorities as well. While such courses seem important to help remedy the imbalance, they do not appear to have been altogether satisfactory. For one thing, in many schools, only minority students enrolled in minority literature courses; that is, the blacks took "Black Literature," the Indians signed up for "First American Literature," and as a consequence, the WASPs continued to read literature primarily about the white experience. Further, at least one study (Page, 1977) discovered that a course in black literature designed to raise white consciousness had a contrary effect of actually increasing hostility toward blacks. It seems as arbitrary, and possibly as harmful, to devote courses *exclusively* to minority literature as it has been to ignore minorities altogether.

Humanities/English courses offer a third alternative, one that teachers probably should have developed from the start: including ethnic literature in *all* courses on its own terms as a description of human experience worth reading. The ethnic consciousness movement has helped teachers discover the resources, books that, in many cases, have been available to teachers for years but because of a combination of bias and ignorance have been neglected by the schools. (A sampling of these is given.) Thus Richard Wright's *Black Boy* stands on its own as a superbly written account of coming of age, worth reading for its insights into childhood, in general, as well as the childhood of a black boy growing up in the South. Virginia Irving Armstrong's *I Have Spoken: American His-*

MULTICULTURAL LITERATURE

American Indian

"I Will Fight No More Forever": Chief Joseph and the Nez Percé War, Merrill D. Beal
Little Big Man, Thomas Berger
Chief, Frank Bonham
The American Heritage Book of Indians, William Brandon, ed.
Bury My Heart at Wounded Knee, Dee Brown
Custer Died for Your Sins, Vine Deloria, Jr.
Crazy Horse: Great Warrior of the Sioux, Shannon Garst
Hatter Fox, Marilyn Harris
Soul Catcher, Frank Herbert
The Way to Rainy Mountain, N. Scott Momaday
Sing Down the Moon, Scott O'Dell
Indian Oratory, W. C. Vanderwerth
I Have Spoken: American History Through the Voices of the Indians, Virginia Irving Armstrong

Black Americans

Sounder, William Armstrong
Manchild in the Promised Land, Claude Brown
Shirley Chisholm, Shirley Chisholm
Soul on Ice, Eldridge Cleaver
The Water Is Wide, Pat Conroy
Invisible Man, Ralph Ellison
The Autobiography of Miss Jane Pittman, Ernest J. Gaines
Nigger, Dick Gregory
To Be Young, Gifted, and Black, Lorraine Hansberry
The Soul Brothers and Sister Lou, Kristin Hunter

tory Through the Voices of the Indians discovers the same sort of eloquence in Indians that a *Foxfire* project found in rural Americans. Edmund Villasenor's *Macho!* is fiction that makes just plain good reading, in addition to providing insights into a Mexican-American experience. Other minorities have skilled spokesmen, including William Saroyan (Armenian), Piri Thomas (Puerto Rican), James T. Farrell (Irish), and Saul Bellow (Jewish).

Black History: Lost, Stolen, or Strayed, Otto Lindenmeyer
The Cool World, Warren Miller
I Know Why the Caged Bird Sings, Maya Angelou

Chicano

Viva Chicano, Frank Bonham
Chicano Girl, Hila Coleman
Child of Fire, Scott O'Dell
Chavez: Man of the Migrants, Jean Madern Pitrone
La Raza: The Mexican Americans, Stan Steiner
Chicana, Richard Vasquez
Pocho, Jose Antonio Villarreal
Macho! Edmund Villasenor

Other Minorities

A Girl from Puerto Rico, Hila Coleman
The Quiet Americans (Japanese), Bill Hosokawa
Mount Allegro (Italian), Jerre Mangione
Down These Mean Streets (Puerto Rican), Piri Thomas
My Name Is Aram and *The Human Comedy* (Armenian), William Saroyan
So Big (Dutch), Edna Ferber
The Free Man (German), Conrad Richter
Maggie: A Girl of the Streets (Irish), Stephen Crane
Studs Lonigan (Irish), James T. Farrell
Marty (Italian), Paddy Chayefsky
The Victim (Jewish), Saul Bellow
The Man with the Golden Arm (Polish), Nelson Algren
Mama's Bank Account (Norwegian), Kathryn Forbes
Obscure Destinies (Czech), Willa Cather

Non-Literary Resources. Finally, teachers of English/humanities need to be aware of the non-book reading resources that are available to them, beginning with the daily newspaper. I have often shown teachers how they can construct an entire curriculum based on little more than the Sunday *New York Times,* with its near-universal interest in news, travel, anthropology, books, the fine arts, music, sports, gardening, history, hobbies, and world issues.

Even a daily paper is a gold mine of reading material, not just for current events but for the entire humanities curriculum.

Popular magazines also provide an inexpensive resource that has generally high interest and good readability. For instance, there are a number of magazines that focus on the history of the American West: *Pioneer West, Frontier Times, True West, Real West, True Frontier, Western Frontier,* and *Old West,* with articles ranging from the history of the shootout at the OK corral to a listing of Indian treaties broken by U.S. soldiers. For fifty cents on up, an interested reader can also study *Sea Combat,* the history of aeronautics, *Coins, Antiques, Model Railroading* (with extraordinary attention to historical accuracy and detail), and the *Good Old Days* (a pop history magazine). *History Today* is an excellent review of contemporary issues and problems, and most of us know the cross-cultural richness of *National Geographic* from hours spent waiting in dentists' and doctors' offices. (A list of popular magazines in the humanities is provided.)

Most bookstores also carry magazines and monographs on state history. In Michigan, for instance, choices include a cookbook of traditional Michigan recipes, the history of Fort Michilimackinac (which guards the entrance to Lake Michigan), a kind of "bird watcher's" guide to the national origins of the Great Lakes' shipping fleet, a bicyclists' guide to historical sites in several counties, and the saga of *The Wreck of the Edmund Fitzgerald*, about an ore carrier lost in Lake Superior in the early 1970s, which was also the subject of a top forty record.

Arts and crafts have become big business in this country, and books and libraries have a number of monographs, magazines, and books on such topics as glassblowing, blacksmithing, needlepoint, quilt making, graphic design, and printing. Most of these hobbies have historical roots that are worth examining. (I know of one English teacher who has conducted a mini-unit on the poetry embroidered into colonial samplers.)

Classroom materials can also be supplemented with publications available from the U.S. Government Printing Office, most of them cheap, all of them printed at your and my expense, dealing with topics from sheep breeding to principles of oral history research. County historical archives and museums will frequently be open to students, as will some local records at city hall. Newspapers will generally allow students limited access to their files, and the microfilm file at most libraries contains a treasure trove of historical and cultural information. Finally, English/humanities courses should draw freely on non-print resources: filmstrips, art slides, photographs, recorded literature, short and feature-length films, oral history tape recordings, radio and television programs.

2. APPROACHES TO HUMANITIES / ENGLISH

The question is not *whether* reading and writing are concerns of the humanities, but *how* they are to be controlled and managed. At first glance, the print and non-print resources may seem overwhelming, and the teacher may want to return to the relative safety of the textbook, where material is prepackaged and selected. But in fact, teaching a multiple materials approach is

TOPICS FOR ENGLISH/HUMANITIES STUDIES

Chronological Approach

The Origins of Man and Culture
Vanished People and Lost
  Civilizations
Union to Disunion (1776–1860)
Civil War Literature
Military History of the United States
History of the Natural Sciences
Changing Conceptualizations of the
  Universe
After Darwin
Victorian England
The Literature and Art of the French
  Revolution
The Decades:
  The Gay Nineties
  The Roaring Twenties
  The Fabulous Fifties

Geographic/Ethnocentric Approach

Greek Culture
The Literature and Art of Rome
Canadian Studies
Latin American Culture
African Literature in Translation

American Minorities
Ethnic Communities and Their Roots
Hindu Literature
The Arts of the American Southwest
Great Cities: Art and Ideas
Ancient Egypt
Black Literature
Oriental-American Culture
Ancient Chinese Inventions and Art
American Radical Thought

Development by Types and Genres

Folklore
Myths and Legends of Many Lands
Romantic Literature
Realism and Naturalism
The Bible in Literature and Art
Religious Dimensions in Literature
Nobel Prize Literature
Speeches Heard 'Round the World
The Celluloid Muse
Existentialism
The Western
Private Eyes in Film, Television, and
  Literature

largely a matter of planning and organizing—focusing study so that it doesn't drift aimlessly—and then selecting a manageable supply of materials.

In the elementary grades (where I have argued reading ought principally to be aimed at satisfying children's curiosity and enhancing their delight with language), "organizing" is largely a matter of finding appropriate books clustered about a topic— Egypt, colonial America, hobbies—bringing them into the classroom, and providing time for children either to read or to be read to. But in the junior high years and beyond, young people are quite capable of more organized, systematic inquiry. Although in-

Thematic Approach	Issues and Problems
Major Themes in English Literature	Issues in American Civilization
City and Country	Myths of Modern Man
Science and the Humanities	The American Dream
The Life of Inquiry	War and Peace
Man's Place in the Natural World	Language and Culture
Sin	Religion and Culture
Guilt and Retribution	Science and Pseudo-Science
Childhood and Coming of Age	Persuasion and Social Responsibility
Crime and Criminals	Pollution: Causes and Cures
The Family	Computers in/and Society
Aging	American Utopianism
Liberty and License	American Radical Thought
Universal Constants	The "Isms"
Death and Taxes	Ethnicity and Nation Building
People in Crisis	Technology, Weapons, and World
Hero/Anti-Hero	Politics
The Law	Laws for Outer Space
Decision Making	The Press and Democratic Societies
Rebellion	Politics and Inequality
Frontiers	Coping with Change
Dreams and Visions	Fiction and Social Reform
Identity and Community	Work and Leisure
	Mind Control
	What Shall We Do Next?

dividualized study should play an important part in the curriculum, teachers generally organize material into courses or units, if only to systematize the search for materials.

Some interesting course topics for schools, gleaned from both high school and college catalogs, are given below. The courses fall into five major, but not necessarily exclusive, categories: *Chronological, Geographic/Ethnocentric, Type and Genres, Themes,* and *Issues and Problems.*

The Chronological Approach. The traditional survey begins at the beginning and studies growth and development of a field to its present state. In the humanities, surveys have a habit of becoming too large to be managed and thus degenerate into rather sterile, period-by-period comparisons of literature, art, music, and ideas, frequently team taught by faculty specialists on a rotating basis. However, when tightly focused on a particular era or topic, a chronological or period course can provide a convenient and interesting way of clustering materials. For example, courses like "The Origins of Man and Culture," "History of the Natural Sciences," and "The Gay Nineties" all allow a teacher opportunity to introduce a controlled variety of materials. Similarly, instead of attempting to describe all of American history in a grand survey, a teacher might concentrate on a single aspect—say, military history—bringing in war literature, art and music of war periods, popular culture artifacts or facsimilies from wars, and so on to provide focus and in-depth study.

The Geographic/Ethnocentric Approach. This approach takes national or ethnic backgrounds as a starting point. I have already written of the dangers inherent in isolating minority literature courses. Still, minority culture courses—"Black Literature," "Oriental-American Literature"—are popular in the schools, and, until multicultural literature is better integrated in English/humanities programs, they also serve the useful purpose of introducing new cultural materials into the school.

Other neglected cultures deserve attention as well. A course or unit in Canadian studies, for example, seems a natural addition to any North American school curriculum, and Latin American Culture seems not only an interesting area for young people to pursue, but one that will enhance their understanding of the relationships among inhabitants of the American continents. Similarly, the geographic/ethnocentric approach offers a way into the study of ancient cultures, not simply the traditional Greek and Roman, but others as well: Egyptian, Hindu, Ancient Chinese.

Development by Types and Genres. A types or genres unit allows the teacher to select and concentrate materials, making them manageable. Such courses can range from ancient history, "Myths and Legends of Many Lands," to popular genres: "The

Western," or "Private Eyes in Film, Television, and Literature." Further, mixed genre courses—"Film and Television," "Literature and Film," "Art and Music," "Philosophy and Literature"—can help to break down disciplinary barriers, though they also run the risk of engaging one in pointless debate over the superiority of particular forms and disciplines.

Thematic Approach. My own preferences lie with courses and units organized along thematic lines. The teacher is less limited by artificial boundaries—geographic origin, time period, form, or genre—and is thus able to bring in literature and art of any form and from any period. He or she selects a topic that recurs in many works of art, say, the theme of Coming of Age or Rebellion or The Family. In some cases, a theme can be very broad, as in a unit called "Universal Constants," which is, in effect, a search for recurring themes in the humanities. A theme like Frontiers could either be restricted, say, focusing on the American West, or very broad, searching for "frontiers" ranging from Alexander the Great's frontiers *en route* to conquering the known world to the frontiers of outer space. Thematic courses have the potential of becoming too broad or vague—"Love" and "Death" hold that possibility—or becoming merely taxonomic: "Ah, ha, the *Love* motif!" But they are also useful in helping the teacher organize the search for materials.

Study of Issues and Problems. Broadest in focus, yet possibly holding the greatest potential for school programs, are courses that center on specific human issues and problems. Frequently the students themselves can be involved in selecting topics for study, identifying problems, and deciding on key questions. Further, issue-centered courses have the value of making a connection with the real world, of relating centuries of human thought and expression to current concerns.

At the same time, if badly taught, issues courses can reduce the glorious art and literature of the ages to mere "tools" in a "problem solving" approach. Thus an issues course needs to walk a tightrope, using the central idea as a way of focusing materials and discussion, without concentrating so closely on the here-and-now that the achievements of the past become trivialized.

The topics listed give some idea of the breadth of problem units, which include surveys ("Issues in American Civilization"), language ("Language and Culture," "Myths of Modern Man"), practical problems ("Pollution: Causes and Cures," "Technology and World Politics"), social issues ("The Press in Democratic Society," "Politics and Inequality"), cross-disciplinary studies ("Science and Pseudo-Science," "Natural Resources and Modern Society"), and futurism ("American Utopianism," "Laws for Outer Space," "What Shall We Do Next?")

The Dimensions of the Humanities

Courses in the humanities are a little difficult to identify clearly because they are taught in many different units and departments in schools and colleges. Thus a humanities course in college may turn up labeled *English, History, Social Science, Psychology, Art, Music, Interdisciplinary Studies,* or, in some cases, *Linguistics.* In the schools, the options are somewhat fewer, but in some cases classification is equally confusing. For example, those who teach about the past have, for many years, engaged in a debate over whether to call their subject *History* or *Social Studies,* and this division represents a genuine difference in ways of presenting ideas and materials.

A humanities/English program can be taught under almost any heading, with different emphasis depending on the teacher's specialties. A history or music teacher need not be a specialist in English to assign more reading and writing in his/her courses; the teacher needs merely to bring knowledge of the field to the class and channel it through reading/writing. Similarly, though the English teacher obviously must have at least rudimentary understanding of the arts and history in order to teach humanities, he/she need not feel handicapped by lack of a specialized degree outside the English discipline. The task of the English teacher is to help students probe and understand language as it is used in the humanities, not necessarily to teach history or art. Literacy can be taught anywhere it is needed, though it is obvious that interdepartmental and interdisciplinary cooperation makes teaching both the subject and the language easier.

With that preamble, I want to present a series of units, courses, and interdisciplinary sequences in the humanities—all of them in use in today's schools—which indicate some of the possibilities open to the English/humanities teachers.

Change: A Social Studies/English Program. One of the best developed sequences of humanities courses I have seen was created by a team of teachers for the Learning Institute of North Carolina. The report, *Change: A Handbook for the Teaching of Social Studies and English,* edited by Sylvia Wilkinson and Ed Campbell (1971), provides a sequence of units that has been tested all over North Carolina. The program, planned for use in secondary schools, is designed to be taught in parallel units by English and social studies or history teachers, but as the editors note, it is ideal for interdisciplinary team teaching, either for a single pair of teachers or for several teams that would share a common resource area.

The broad topic of Change is broken into four major areas of exploration: *Change on the American Scene, The Student, Comparative Governments,* and *The Arts.* These are subdivided further into thematic or issue-centered units in English and social studies.

The Change Program

I. CHANGE ON THE
   AMERICAN SCENE

Human Rights
Social Studies	Part I.	Man and His Culture
	Part II.	Minorities
	Part III.	Struggle for Human Rights
English	Part IV.	The Negro and Literature

Weapons
Social Studies	Part I.	War and Peace
English	Part II.	War and Human Values

Technology
  Social Studies   Part I. Labor, Industry, and
                      Technology
  English   Part II. The Future Novel

II. THE STUDENT
  Social Studies   Part I. Schools vs. Learning
  English   Part II. Me and Holden Caulfield

III. COMPARATIVE GOVERNMENTS
  Social Studies   Part I. A Comparative Study
                  Part II. Power and the Southern
                      Demagogue
                  Part III. Power and the Modern
                      World

IV. THE ARTS
  English   Part I. Poetry and Song
                  Part II. Evolution of a Story
                      (creative writing)
                  Part III. Film

There are some obvious gaps and inconsistencies in this program. For example, it is unfortunate that there is no English component in the Comparative Governments section, since governance is an obvious and integral part of many literary works. Similarly, isolating The Arts as a separate section seems a mistake because it seems to set "Poetry and Song" apart from real world concerns. Further, omitting a social studies unit in The Arts implies that literature and the arts are somehow beyond or removed from history. ("How the Arts Shape and Are Shaped by History" would be an interesting topic to insert into Unit IV.) Nevertheless, as an established interdisciplinary sequence, *Changes* is impressive.

Equally impressive is the use of multiple resources in both the social studies and English units. For example, in the opening social studies units on change, the students read, write, view films, study art and music, and meet in small groups to prepare presentations on six cultures: Eskimo, Maori, Semang, Hopi and Pueblo, and Dobù. In the English unit on "War and Peace" they view films ranging from the documentary, *Decision To Drop the Bomb,* to a short art film on the *Toys* of war. They study Pablo Picasso's *Guernica* and listen to music that includes Benjamin Britten's "War Requiem" and Pete Seeger's "Where Have All the Flowers Gone?" Readings include John Knowles' *A Separate Peace,* Plato's *Republic,* Thomas More's *Utopia,* Richard Hughes' *The Fox in the Attic,* Erich Remarque's *All Quiet on the Western Front,* Barbara Tuchman's *The Guns of August,* Dwight Eisenhower's *Crusade in Europe,* and Anne Frank's *Diary of a Young Girl.*

Change provides a framework rather than a blueprint. It can be used in a variety of schools under many different organizational plans. Most important, it helps to demonstrate for humanities/English teachers how interdisciplinary studies can be structured, even in schools where cross-corridor cooperation is made difficult by conflicting bell schedules or administrative unwillingness to set up team teaching situations.

Humanities Through English. As part of the Random House *Creative Word* program (1973, 1974), Patrick Courts and I prepared an English unit exploring the ways in which social and historical forces help to shape human values. In "How Do People Become What They Are?" we asked the students to explore their own values, using literature as a starting point.

We opened the unit with a series of comments on child rearing from Aristotle, the biblical Proverbs ("Train up a child in the way he will go, and when he is old, he will not depart from it"), Ralph Waldo Emerson, Francis Bacon, and Mark Twain ("A cat that has set on a hot stove lid won't do it again; but it won't set on a cold one neither").

After a Reed Whittemore poem describing children making mudpies and considering adulthood "with wild surmise," we presented students with a variety of fiction and nonfiction: Janet Frame describing children who pass over some "forbidden" adult barriers; Margaret Mead writing from an anthropological point of view about the climatic conditions that shape the values of the Eskimo; Carolyn Bird describing what it's like to be "born female"; Walt Kelley's cartoon character, Pogo the Possum, warning, "Do not wind up your child and set him to watch the T.V. unguarded"; Carl Sandburg asking "What Shall He Tell That Son?" and John Aldridge writing about "the country of the young," describing the present generation as spoiled and self-indulgent.

Along with these materials we offered ideas for discussion and writing: describing how one's values change from second grade to seventh grade to high school, telling stories from childhood, dredging up memories through a family photo album, studying how our own electronic environment shapes us, interviewing older people in the *Foxfire* manner, and collecting and evaluating adult wisdom.

In teaching the unit now, I would add some materials from a book in The Scholastic American Literature Program, *What We Believe* (1977), which I also had a hand in preparing. Among the prose selections in the book are Jonathan Edwards' "Resolutions" and Ben Franklin's autobiographical discussion of self-improvement, Dick Gregory's narrative from *Nigger* about encountering—and not helping—a fellow human being, W. E. B. DuBois' discussion of the "craziness" of being black in a white world, and Ernest Hemingway's "Indian Camp," a story that, among other things, describes the initiation of a young boy into the mysteries of birth and death. Poetry in *What We Believe* includes Walt Whitman's "Song of Myself," William Carlos Williams' "The Gift," Stephen Crane's "A Man Said to the Universe," Emily Dickinson's "I'm Nobody," and Denise Levertov's "Stepping Westward."

Among the writing activities I suggested for that unit were making a log of the beliefs and values one encounters in a single day, comparing values in newspaper and television news, and examining how values are communicated through painting, sculpture, music, and photography.

While these units are principally "English," with a focus on literature and composition, their thrust is toward the humanities and interdisciplinary studies and the quest to know and understand oneself through language.

Historical Jackdaws. Coming from the history side of the humanities is the *jackdaw*, a teaching device of British origin. Jackdaws teach history by placing historical documents in the hands of students. For example, a jackdaw on "Shakespeare's Theatre" by Howard Loxton (distributed in the United States by Grossman Publications, New York City) includes a dozen facsimile documents on the Elizabethan theater, among them:

A proclamation "al maner Interludes" dated 1559 concerning the licensing and censorship of dramas.

Portions of Robert Greene's "A Groatsworth of Wit Bought with a Millian of Repentance," a critical attack on Shakespeare himself, "an upstart Crowe."

The Revels Booke, Anno: 1605, containing a record of plays being presented in London, including Shakespeare's.

Pages from the First Folio collected edition of 1623.

A contract for building the Festival Theatre, dated 1599, a theater that was modeled after the Globe.

Plans for the reconstruction of an Elizabethan theater in our own time.

The property and costume registers of the Admiral's Company, a theatrical troupe, dated 1598.

The packet is also accompanied by a series of sheets adding supplementary information on the Globe and its times, along with some suggested discussion questions.

Generations of school children have learned this kind of material by struggling through prose introductions to Shakespearean plays. The "hands on" approach to the historical backgrounds is far superior to a discussion of explanatory text. The documents invite browsing and study; they excite curiosity; they certainly give the students a feeling for the times and the problems surrounding Elizabethan theatrical productions.

The jackdaw concept can be applied in many areas of English/humanities. Other titles in the Grossman series focus on American and British history (*The American Revolution, Clipper Ships and the Cutty Sark, The Battle of Britain*), biography (*Winston Churchill, Gordon of Khartoum, The Rise of Napoleon*), science and industry (*James Watt and Steam Power, Darwin and Evolution, Harvey and the Circulation of the Blood*), and literary backgrounds (*Shelley, Lewis Carroll, Charles Dickens*). These last are especially useful to English teachers in offering an alternative to the textbook review of the life of an author. The Dickens jackdaw, for example, includes a facsimile cover of *The Pickwick Papers*, a sketch of Dickens by George Cruikshank, a newspaper review of The Great Boz Ball in celebration of one of Dickens' illustrators (where, among other things, 43,000 stewed and pickled oysters were consumed), and several printed pages from *Hard Times* with Dickens' notes for revision.

Teachers need not be limited to commercially prepared jackdaws, of course. Teachers can use the jackdaw approach to present poems, stories, letters, and short plays along with the author's background. A packet with fifteen to twenty items—literary and historical—can form the basis of several days' work and discussion. Larger packs, containing upwards of a hundred items, can serve as the resource core for sustained units of several weeks or more. Jackdaws are especially useful if the school has a less-than-adequate library or a restrictive budget, since, for the most part, only single copies of works are required.

A variation on the jackdaw approach is represented by *Eyewitness* (1975), an audio cassette program. It consists of taped interviews with a number of persons who have witnessed major events in American history: two elderly black women who were slaves, an Indian who was at the battle of the Little Big Horn, two survivors of the San Francisco earthquake, a veteran of the Alaska Gold Rush, and Herbert Morrison, the reporter who broadcast the crash of the *Hindenburg* in 1937. Activities for English classes described in the instructor's manual include creating diaries of the people interviewed, drafting movie scenarios based on the eyewitness accounts, discussing the events portrayed, and putting oneself in the place of one of the key people interviewed. The program notes also suggest having students interview their own family members about recollections of some of the events that have been recorded.

Historical/Cultural Studies of the English Language. A detailed examination of the history of English is probably best reserved for college-level students, who have the linguistic sophistication to understand the significance of phenomena like Grimm's Law and the Great Vowel Shift, which dramatically altered the nature of English. Nevertheless, younger students can engage profitably in a number of explorations into the origins of the language. For example, in *The Nature of Language* (1973), William Reynolds presents a junior-high level survey of possible origins of human speech in prehistory, helping students understand how and why man first began to use speech and then to use drawn symbols—the precursors of writing—to record events. I. J. Gelb's classic *A Study of Writing* (1965) is principally useful as a resource for teachers, but it includes many illustrations of early writing systems that could be included in a teacher-created jackdaw to help students study the evolution of our own alphabetic writing system. This book might be supplemented with the use of *How Djadja-Em-Ankh Saved the Day*, a facsimile scroll of an ancient Egyptian hieroglyphic tale, translated, with discussion, by Lisle Manniche (1976).

Kenneth Katzner's *The Languages of the World* (1975) provides another set of primary materials for students to examine over two hundred different languages—including Dutch, Estonian, Turkish, Chinese, Sioux, Pidgin English, and Hawaiian—each illustrated with short passages from the literature of that language. The interconnections between languages are made apparent in a nicely illustrated book for students, *Words Come in Families* by Edward Horowitz (1977), which shows the historical origins of words (e.g., the Greek *logos,* "speech") and their English families (*epi-*

logue, logarithm, eulogy, syllogism, monologue, logic, psychology, biology, dialogue).

A useful text on the evolution of American English is J. N. Hook's *The Story of American English* (1972). Hook describes early Indian languages and shows the infusion of Indian words into English. He discusses early colonial writings in English, noting the evolution of American spelling, and reviews the struggle for supremacy of American over British English. He also reviews some of the principal word sources in English, borrowings from Dutch, French, Spanish, and concludes with an excellent discussion of the dialects of American English.

Exploring Popular Culture. Popular culture is the art—books, magazines, paintings, films—enjoyed by large numbers of people at any time in history. It concerns itself with manners and morals, fads and fancies, and the artifacts produced by a culture, from Tin Lizzies and Edsels to nineteenth-century barns and futuristic twentieth-century architecture. As a field of study, popular culture has received mixed reviews within the academy. Some have ridiculed it as the pursuit of the trivial. They point, for example, to "serious" studies like one presented at the Convention of the Modern Language Association on Ronald McDonald—the clown featured in McDonald's hamburger ads—as folk hero and cultural icon. Others assume that "masscult"—the literature and art of the masses—is by definition of low quality and thus unworthy of serious consideration. They support their argument by showing the incredible array of pop and pulp—second-rate music, third-rate magazines, and fifth-rate television programs—which the public ardently supports.

At the same time, it is important to recall that William Shakespeare was part of the popular culture of his time, as were Benjamin Franklin, Charles Dickens, Walt Whitman, Harriet Beecher Stowe, Ernest Hemingway, and in our own time, Saul Bellow, John Updike, Sylvia Plath, Margaret Mead, James Baldwin, and Allen Ginsberg. Popular tastes are not always bad, and although one can worry that Americans would rather watch football than the opera, it is worth noting that the Chicago Symphony sells out the house more often than the Chicago Bears.

Further, it is important to recognize that popular culture is in every sense a humanity, reflecting our human interests and concerns and telling us what we are as a people. Susan Judy, an English professor at Central Michigan University, has argued:

The study of popular culture enriches students' understanding of America and Americans. The fiction and poetry, magazines and newspapers, radio and television programs, movies and plays that Americans like provide insight into their tastes, values and beliefs. Through the study of popular culture students can begin to answer the questions: What is peculiar or unique about Americans? How have Americans changed and developed throughout their history? What traits and beliefs have endured? How have we come to be what we are today? What traditions seem strongest in America? How do I reflect those traditions? In what ways am I different?

[1977]

In studying popular culture she suggests such activities as examining the popular culture of principal eras—the Revolution, the Civil War, Prohibition, the Kennedy presidency; re-creating art forms from American eras (dime novels, minstrel shows, radio plays); comparing popular and elitist poems from a particular period; studying the best-seller lists as a reflection of popular interests and beliefs; examining the evolution of musical forms from symphonies to jazz; studying the history of the movies; reviewing the images of minorities in advertisements; and examining the patterns of taste exhibited in the Academy Awards.

In *Teaching the Decades: A Humanities Approach to American Civilization* (1975), Brooke Workman has presented material for three parallel courses in American humanities for the twenties, thirties, and forties. In each course, he begins by asking students to think about their own values in the context of American culture: "Why is it that you are one of the few nations with cheerleaders? Why do you dress the way you do? . . . Are we born with a love of football?" The students consider some of the major beliefs that Americans have come to hold central: practicality and efficiency, progress, material wealth, freedom, patriotism, democracy, the rights of the individual. He then plunges into a decade by decade examination of popular culture.

For the decade of the twenties, for example, he presents a review of history through prominent names and cultural phenomena: Douglas Fairbanks, H. L. Mencken, Sinclair Lewis, KKK, Paul Whiteman, "normalcy," bathtub gin, Miss America, and Mah Jongg, to name a few. The students divide into committees to create a handbook of events and names, year by year, for the decade and to locate artifacts from the era for class examination. They read the best sellers of the day (which, for the twenties, included Sinclair Lewis' *Main Street,* F. Scott Fitzgerald's *The Great Gatsby,* Horatio Alger's *Ragged Dick,* and Ernest Hemingway's "Soldier's Home"). They look at the decade's radio, films, architecture, painting, popular theater, and dance. Finally, each student prepares a project, an in-depth research project that may lead to a report, an 8-millimeter film, a slide tape, photography display, or even musical composition.

Workman seems to have achieved a central aim of humanities instruction: integration of history and art, language and literature. The investigation of the decades flows smoothly from one discipline into another, from one art form to another, without concern for academic distinctions. In this sense, *Teaching the Decades* provides a model for all humanities courses whether focusing on chronology, geography, ethnicity, themes, or issues.

The Media Revolution, Reading and Writing, and the Humanities

Although television is more than fifty years old, it is principally within the past two decades that the effects have been investigated—and worried about—by the public and by educators. The statistics that we've all heard are frightening. We know that children are likely to spend more time in front of the tube than talking to their parents, as much time watching shows like *Kartoon Kar-*

nival and *Mob Story* as they spend in school, and considerably more time watching TV than reading and writing. Advancements in electronics have brought down the price of transistor radios, stereo sets, and cassette recorders to put popular music and its accompanying culture within easy reach of young people. The combined media exposure and subsequent influence of a group like the Beatles in the sixties makes the Bobby Soxer impact of a Sinatra in the pre-electronic forties look small. In *The School Book* (1973), Neil Postman and Charles Weingartner argue persuasively that by ignoring the media revolution teachers have helped to create "the reading problem." The schools place too much emphasis on print, they claim, making it the principal or sole means of communication, when in fact the young people are better equipped to handle media forms. Reading becomes a problem not because kids are dumb (or even because they can't read), but because the schools fail to recognize how print and non-print media function in their out-of-school lives. Postman and Weingartner point out that:

Electronic media now play a more important role than print media as a source of aesthetic satisfaction to the young. . . .

Electronic media now carry the burden for the dissemination of information in the culture. . . .

The major political influences in our society, especially on the young, are exerted through electronic media. . . .

As youth becomes more oriented toward electronic media and away from print, the reading problem will become more acute.

I agree strongly with the first three statements but must enter some reservations about the fourth. The reading problem need *not* become any worse. It is likely to become more serious only if teachers continue to teach reading badly, by forcing students to learn through drill and workbooks rather than through actual reading, responding, and synthesizing. Further, if teachers continue to use reading as the only or principal method of presenting information, ignoring the electronic media out of fear or dislike or an attempt to make the schools a bastion for print, conflict is inevitable.

As a matter of fact, there is very little reason to suppose that teachers need to defend print against the visual and electronic media. When Marshall McLuhan argued that "print is dead," he was widely quoted and frequently misunderstood. McLuhan was not announcing the death of literacy; rather he was arguing that the linear modes of thought promoted by print were being replaced by "all-at-once" thinking fostered by television. As most rhetoricians recognize, those modes of thought can be reflected in print as well as in the electronic media.

Books themselves are anything but dead as a popular culture form. In the excitement over the post-World War II television explosion, it is seldom noticed that we have seen a bookstore revolution as well. Thirty years ago the local bookstore (if there was a local bookstore) carried a limited number of hardbound books, which were sold principally to people who wanted to buy gifts, or to the few who could afford to buy best sellers rather than waiting to borrow them from the library. Paperback books (mostly detective thrillers of low quality) were relegated to a small rack—not at the bookstore, but at the pharmacy. As paperbacks have become more respectable we have seen the evolution of what are appropriately called "community newscenters" in almost every town. These carry an astonishing array of titles: paperback books, magazines, newspapers, and so on.

The newscenters promote literacy as well. They advertise on TV asking, "Have you read a good book lately?" They describe themselves as your "neighborhood bookstore" and urge you to stop in to browse. The paperback bookstores have broken several patterns that have been established by schools and/or libraries:

First, the bookstores recognize that reading is a voluntary act. They promote reading, not because "it's good for you," but because, like TV, it can be entertaining and interesting.

Second, they make the materials of literacy accessible. Having learned a lesson from supermarket managers, the bookstore managers know how to display the product to encourage impulse browsing and buying. (Compare the face-up displays of books at the store to the spine-only filing system of libraries.)

Third, they respond to the expressed interests of the readers/buyers. Bookstores nowadays don't tell you what you "ought" to be reading. Rather they find out what people want to read and promote it. After *Star Wars* and *Close Encounters of the Third Kind* swept the country, the bookstores set up displays of outer space materials. When *Roots* appeared, they produced titles on family genealogy and cultural history. Each summer they put out maps and travel guides, and in the autumn, the football books show up in the front window. Both teachers and librarians can learn a good deal by studying how the bookstores offer their wares.

All things considered, then, print is here to stay, and teachers should welcome the electronic revolution rather than trying to fight it. Despite the dreadful display of junk on TV, television also produces and promotes on a regular basis good, solid, informative, and artistic programs. *Teachers' Guides to Television* and *Prime Time Television* regularly review and highlight forthcoming shows and suggest the kinds of classes for which they are appropriate. These guides even include bibliographies of related books prepared by the American Library Association for the use of teachers. Teachers I know who have used the guides suggest that instead of destroying literacy, good TV programs incite interest in reading-related materials.

Of course, students (like adults) are not interested in watching only the quality programs on TV. Public Broadcasting languishes when placed in competition with a rowdy detective or family crisis show on the commercial networks. Perhaps the most important function an English/humanities teacher can serve, then, is to help young people gain a critical awareness of what they are watching. Students can examine plot patterns and character stereotypes, review the function of advertising, discuss the roles of children or women or minorities on TV, and look for hidden appeals and subtle expressions of values. Just as they can be expected to examine literature as an aesthetic experience, young people can, as they mature, be invited to discuss TV critically.

This kind of examination should not be placed in isolated courses. In many schools the response to new media has been to create new courses—"Television and You," "TV, Film, and Literature"—designed to teach appreciation of the media. While at first glance such courses would seem to prepare students to understand the media, they often have the effect of isolation. The media course becomes insular, unnecessarily concerned with production details, and the connection with other forms of communication is neglected.

TV belongs in English and history and art and music and science classes. It has plenty of good and interesting things to say about each, and television demonstrably helps teachers enrich and improve their courses. Television and the humanities can assume a symbiotic, rather than adversary, relationship.

Most important, perhaps, is to note that television does not simply provide entertainment to adults and young people. People watch it because it seems to meet particular human needs. In *Towards a Visual Culture* (1969), Caleb Gattegno observes, "Adolescent viewers are seeking. They are seeking themselves as people who can function independently in the areas of strength, of love, and of intellect. . . ." Young viewers, he continues, don't know quite what they are seeking or why they are seeking it. They can't always formulate the questions, much less recognize good and bad answers to the questions. The questions adolescents ask are those of the humanities. If television is isolated or ignored by the schools, it will provide "answers"—mostly shallow ones— whether or not teachers and parents want it to. If it is incorporated, naturally and comfortably, into English/humanities it can be "a humanity," no less than art, sculpture, music, or literature.

9
Science Reading and Writing

1. INTEGRATING SCIENCE AND ENGLISH

My purpose in this chapter is to talk about English, not methods of teaching science, but I want to argue that reading and writing are central to science, and that both English and science teachers need to attend to it. Jean Stafford writes:

> Whether we are drowning Japanese beetles in turpentine, or gathering seashells by the seashore, or drinking up a storm at a cocktail party, we are at work as writers. We are eavesdropping and spying and asking questions and storing away the answers like pack rats.

She might have added that we are at work as *scientists* as well: perceiving, classifying, synthesizing, hypothesizing, verifying. A good scientist of any age will employ language, not just to label specimens or phenomena, but to understand them, and he or she will use language creatively, expressively, yet tentatively to offer hypotheses to the outside world and to seek confirmation or refutation. The use of language cannot be separated from scientific inquiry.

One of my own least pleasant encounters with science reading and writing came in an advanced course in college chemistry. I had gone to college with my best grades and board scores in math and science and with some thoughts of going into medicine. So I signed up for Physical Chemistry as a recommended elective for future physicians and found myself in trouble. The design of the course seemed simple enough. We read about the experiments of some of the early giants in physics and chemistry: Boyle, Pasteur, Gibbs, Helmholtz. We were then to re-create some of their experiments in the laboratory, thereby learning firsthand some of their crucial discoveries.

Unfortunately, my basic skills as a chemistry lab technician were not great, and frequently my results deviated rather significantly from those of the masters. I can recall, for example, doing one experiment where my data seemed to indicate that instead of being constructed of tiny atomic particles, our world is made up of fundamental units that are the size of golf balls, weighing a quarter of a pound apiece. Our experimental work was then to be written up in a logbook. We were to review possible sources of error in the experiment and thus be able to explain why our experimental results had gone awry. It mattered less that I had created a universe of golf balls than that I could explain the inept manipulations of test tube, pipette, or balance beam that had led to the error. My lab reports were frequently more in the domain of creative writing than exposition: I became quite adept at conjuring up breezes, freezes, power surges, equipment inaccuracies, and other laboratory phenomena that would allow me to justify the monstrosity of my errors.

As it turned out, that was the last science course I took. I had been leaning toward the humanities in my studies anyway, and shortly after I took Physical Chemistry, I cancelled my medical school application, took vows of poverty, and decided to enter the ranks of English teachers (who, in those days, were pulling in a whopping $4,900 per year in salary).

Since then, I've wondered from time to time what became of me as a scientist. As an elementary school child I had been fascinated by natural science, and I can still recall poring over a book with a red cover called *The Boy Scientist*. (It included an intriguing drawing showing how one's girlfriend, were she a thousand times larger than you, would exert enough gravitational force to pull you to her like a magnet.) In high school I did my best work in general science, biology, physics, and chemistry, and I wrote my English research paper (the one where you learn the ins and outs of footnote form) on the International Geophysical Year, a cooperative effort of world scientists to probe nature's secrets.

High school science had been interesting and pleasurable. But in college, the chemistry courses were much more concerned with mastery of the basic knowledge of the discipline and with our preparation to become professional scientists. Though I cannot blame my own failure on my chemistry profs, the basic mastery approach of college courses fell short for me. It does seem to me that my college chemistry professors were guilty—albeit unconsciously—of creating a situation where one could become superficially competent in chemistry without ever becoming deeply involved in the discipline. In a sense, the courses were taught like history: One read of the evolution of chemistry from the discovery by Boyle of a relationship between gas volume and temperature, to the milli-second creation of a new, unstable atomic element by teams of chemists and physicists. My basic literacy skills were enough that I could read the textbook and understand the problems at the end of the chapter, and I could work a slide rule well enough to come up with answers. I learned the labels for atomic and subatomic particles; I could tell you where elements fit on the periodic table; and if you drew a diagram of an organic compound, I could figure out a name for it.

But my literacy in chemistry never grew any deeper than decoding and encoding, naming and describing. Further, most of my chemistry texts fostered that kind of higher illiteracy by presenting science as fixed and objective and scientists as dispassionate, neutral observers of natural phenomena. Thus I can recall being shocked and angry to learn senior year that Boyle's Law (on which I had spent a month as a freshman calculating $V = T/P$ equations) was, in fact, not very accurate at all, because Boyle had visualized ideal gases and not taken into account the actual volume of the atomic particles themselves. (I don't think Boyle's equipment was precise enough to detect smaller particles. It's too bad he didn't have my golf balls to work with.) Further, as I plowed through the *Journal of the American Chemical Society,* a formidably objective publication, I was only dimly aware that the articles represented not ultimate truth, but arguments, some of them quite personal, advocating one approach or view or attitude over another.

Some of the problems that I encountered as a science student have been solved—theoretically at least—by a new emphasis on the discovery method, so that students in many schools learn through experience. New science programs are structured around key concepts—say, the *cell* in biology or *quantum theory* in chemistry—in contrast to the taxonomic approach that I experienced, where a biology course is arranged around categorization of genera and families and chemistry around the names and rank order of atomic elements. Such approaches, I think, will go a long way toward helping students become true biologists and chemists rather than mere biology and chemistry readers, as I was.

In many respects, science reading is (or should be) quite like reading a poem: One brings past experiences to bear on the words on the page, then synthesizes material with an existing vision of the universe. And science writing, even when couched in impersonal, abstract language, grows from and is an expression of personal experience, and as such is not dissimilar to a short story or personal letter. In short, language rather nicely allows us to bridge C. P. Snow's "two cultures"—the humanities and science—seeing them united in human experience and language, rather than struggling against each other in a world perceived simplistically as either a material world or a world of values.

Science in an English Classroom

At the risk of becoming too anecdotal, I want to begin this discussion by describing at some length a teaching experience of mine in an East Lansing, Michigan, middle school, working with seventh graders. I taught with Rhoda Maxwell, Chair of the English Department, and a number of the principles that we worked out in our teaching are fundamental to the entire chapter. We wanted to test several premises about science reading and writing:

1. *Science reading is a natural part of English.* Too often, it seemed to us, English teachers cut themselves off from student interests by focusing exclusively on what they consider "literature." Good books about science belong and can be used successfully in English classes.

2. *English teachers need not know a great deal about science to teach science reading and writing.* The English teacher is not a scientist and in many cases has minimal experience in science. But if the English teacher concentrates on what he or she knows best— English—students can still learn a lot of science.

We didn't have an opportunity to test the converse, but I think it probably pertains: *The science teacher need not know a great deal about English to teach science reading and writing.* Simply becoming aware of the possibilities for language use in a science class may be enough for the non-English teacher to help students become more literate.

3. *Students can write about science in creative ways.* Scientific expression need not be cold and strictly objective; nor do creative writing forms need to be limited to the English classroom.

4. *Students can write research without turning into encyclopedia-cribbers.* Although students will not conduct much truly original research, they nevertheless can read widely enough that their findings will represent their own internalized view of the world, rather than simply being a recording (or more bluntly, plagiarizing) of someone else's work.

Our project was to have each student write an original science book over a five-week period of time. We launched the project by distributing a list of book titles from the Roma Gans' *Let's Read and Find Out* series, a set of science books for young readers, which has an unusually inviting set of titles, including: *How a*

Seed Grows; Roots Are Food Finders; Bats in the Dark; Cock-roaches: Here, There, and Everywhere; Ducks Don't Get Wet; The Eel's Strange Journey; Ladybug, Ladybug, Fly Away Home; A Drop of Blood; The Skeleton Inside You; and *What Happens to a Hamburger.* Topics selected by our students varied from auto mechanics to nature. A few students selected titles directly from the Gans series and wrote their own version of the book. Most moved off in new directions. *Dinosaurs* was an area of high interest for our students; so was *horses.* Other topics included *ants, computers, the internal combustion engine, outer space,* and *sharks* (thanks to the popularity of *Jaws* at the time).

To "teach" science reading, we simply helped the students formulate a series of questions to guide them in their reading and research. We wanted them to relate their new knowledge to an already existing base, so we asked, "What do you already know about your subject?" The students found that they knew a surprising amount already. "What *don't* you know?" was the next question. "What do you want to find out?" "What do you think readers of your book will want to know?" This second series of questions helped the students prepare a list of ten or so crucial questions that they wanted to answer in their books: "Which sharks are man-eaters?" "How do ants know where they are going?" "What do we know about life on Mars?"

Then with these lists in hand, the students went off to the library. We didn't say much in advance about how to use the library. Rather, we stationed ourselves near the card catalog, and when students had specific topics to research, we offered help as needed. Getting seventh graders to stick to the task while they are in the library can be a mind-boggling experience, but, again, the guide questions helped. "Which question are you on?" helped more than a suggestion that they get to work. Questions also gave short-term goals, and if students found information, they knew where they were in terms of finishing their reading.

Before the students began to write, we explored some of the possible forms their books could take. Students seem to think of "reports" they have done in the lower grades as models for writing. The problem is that most of their own report writing suffers from the copied-from-encyclopedia syndrome, partly because reports tend to emphasize transmittal of information rather than exploration of a topic. We explained that ideas and information could be shared in many different discourse forms. "Suppose you were writing about sharks," we suggested. "You might write a *report* giving information to your reader, but why not try writing a *short story* that contains the information that you want?" In this way, we encouraged the students to stretch beyond the limits of expository forms.

Then our students wrote: drafting essays, stories, poems, and games; sharing these with each other and with us; moving to a second draft; and finally preparing polished, proofread copy.

We emphasized that the books ought to be graphically interesting with illustrations, charts, photographs from magazines, and interesting covers. We provided a lesson in simple bookbinding, showing ways of making book covers, from decorating a commercial report cover to making a simple cloth-bound book. We brought in a supply of felt-tip pens, stencils, and some dry transfer lettering (a commercial art product used to make headlines) and let the students work on making their books look real.

The books came in on the due date in gaudy array, all sizes and shapes, from a 2″ by 3″ minibook on tropical fish to a sunburst-shaped book on solar energy. The students had also accepted our invitation to share their knowledge in a variety of forms. For example, Bill started his book on ants with a science fiction story into which he wove "the facts about ants":

One day a scientist was studying how to make ants grow in size to be pets, like dogs and cats. He had almost perfected the formula, but when the ants grew, their abdomens popped.
Here are some of the things the scientist learned about ants. . . .

David had looked into the habits of birds and decided to present his information as the "Dear Eggy Scrapbook," with "translations" from bird language of an advice column for birds:

Dear Eggy,
I am one week old and would like to ask for some help. My mother will
float real low in the water, then suddenly zoom into the water. I always
think an alligator has her, but she always comes back up safe and sound.
Sincerely,

Baby Grebe

Dear Baby Grebe,
Your mother is simply diving for food which you need to live. Grebes are
expert divers and swimmers and get much of their food that way.
Sincerely,

Eggy

Among the books our students wrote were *Twins: How Does It
Happen, and Why?; Outer Space: What Is It?; Ponds and
Streams; The Coral Reef; All About Dogs; The Moon;* and a
forty-three-pager by our class high achiever on *Concepts of Space.*

One of the books that most intrigued me (and kept the class intrigued during the writing) was called *Runaway to Africa.* Laura's
plot centered on teenaged Mark, who had family problems that
were reminiscent of a good many adolescent novels: His parents
were separated, and although Mark wanted to live with his father,
his father was too busy and the boy wound up with his mother,
with whom he was in conflict. So he ran away . . . to Africa.

Once she had moved the character to the African continent,
Laura plunged into the real purpose of the story, to describe African animals, but Mark's personal problems continued to crop up
in the story:

He could hear the screech of two fighting monkeys and somehow that
made Mark feel more at home than ever. He liked it here, not having to
worry about homework, being sent to the principal's office for not agreeing with the teacher, and most of all, not being yelled at.

The direction of this story fascinated me, so I asked her teacher about Laura's background. Was she from a troubled family? Did she run amok in school very often? In fact, Laura's home life seemed quite secure, and she had never been sent to the principal's office in her life. Nevertheless, her writing was, in effect, a double fantasy, on the one hand, exploring her emerging adolescent concern for human relationships, on the other, writing a good adventure set in a faraway place. (See Chapter 7 for a discussion of those twin adolescent concerns.)

Not all the students were as articulate and imaginative as Laura, but we were impressed by the effort and imagination that the students used in presenting their ideas to their readers.

The project confirmed a number of hypotheses about literacy in science and English. Most important, perhaps, is that this kind of project began to open up a wide range of new reading/writing projects. What about a springtime investigation into the wildlife of a marsh behind the school? What about an exploration of urban ecology? Could students visit some local manufacturing companies or small shops to study science in action, say, assembling an auto or making yeast-raised donuts? What about a trip to the natural history museum to study nineteenth-century farming devices? Could students write introductory science books for younger children? The possibilities seem both inviting and endless.

Reading in Science/English

The claim that students "can't read the text" is one the echoes around the halls of science and presents a serious problem for teachers of both science and English. That young people can't read (or perhaps more likely, do *not* read) their science books seems to me in no small measure a result of the quality of the texts themselves. School science books seem especially pedestrian when contrasted with the vibrant trade books that are available. Further, as one of my colleagues in science has remarked, there are very few concepts in science textbooks that are not covered—in more detail and more interesting language—in a good paperback or library nonfiction book written with a younger reader in mind. The thrust of this section, then, is toward literacy programs based on non-text materials. The pressures on teachers to adopt textbooks is not at issue here; it may well be that many science teachers, especially at the secondary level, either feel they must adopt a textbook, or have found a textbook they like to teach. Nevertheless, I will argue that the science literacy program ought to begin, not with a textbook, but with some of the materials described on the following pages.

For instance, I have already alluded to the Roma Gans' *Let's Read and Find Out* series as a model of quality books for young readers. In such books as *Mushrooms and Molds; Birds Eat and Eat and Eat; Green Grass and White Milk; My Visit to the Dinosaurs; Twist, Wiggle and Squirm: A Book about Earthworms; Watch Honeybees with Me;* and *Straight Hair, Curly Hair,* one finds the entire natural world opened up for exploration. Further, the books are well written in prose that eschews the dullness and formality of many texts.

Another series written for young readers that impresses me is published by MacDonald/Raintree of Milwaukee and Toronto. Science and technology books for pre-school and early readers include *Springs, Sound, Sand, The Wheel, Gears, Water, Time, The Lever, Strength, Electricity, Speed, Oil,* and *Heat.* Another portion of the series puts concepts into their real world context: *In the Jungle, On the Farm, At the Zoo, At the Fair, In the Park, At the Circus, In the Garden.*

A number of prominent adult authors have also written for young children. Roy Chapman Andrews has written *All About Dinosaurs;* the prolific Isaac Asimov has done dozens of books; Newbery winner Jean Craighead George has written the poetic *Spring Comes to the Ocean.* (A selected list of good science books is given.)

Equally rich are the books for juvenile or young adult readers. Thousands of new titles for adolescent readers are published each year, and a great many are on science topics: sea shells, bones, microscopes, horses, glowing bugs, marsupials, ecology, the future, the human body, love and sex, disease, outer space, solar energy, wind power, and so on. Also of interest are books that introduce young readers to the science disciplines: Hal Helman's *Biology in the World of the Future,* Irving Adler's *The New Mathematics* and *The Tools of Science: From Yardstick to Cyclotron,* Irwin Freeman's *About the Worlds of Chemistry,* and William Crouse's *Understanding Science.*

A great many of the books for young adult readers encourage experimentation by providing simple activities in "kitchen science" that allow students to explore and understand the universe using household equipment and supplies: spoons, flashlight batteries, baking soda, and so forth. Thus young people experiment with snow (Phyllis Busch, *A Walk in the Snow*); discover animal life (Marshal Case, *Look What I Found! The Young Conservationist's Guide to Care and Feeding of Wildlife*); experiment with air, water, and heat (Rocco V. Feravolo, *Easy Physics Projects*); and even learn about science through lemons (Harris A. Stone, *The Chemistry of a Lemon*). The Boston Children's Museum has published a book called *Recyclopedia* that shows young people how to build such gizmos as a water clock, water microscope, balance board, a rubber-band spring scale, a slide projector in a shoebox, a pinhole camera out of recycled boxes, bags, tin cans, cardboard, and coat hangers. UNESCO's *Source Book for Science Teaching* provides a resource guide to experiments as well as supplies and materials.

At the adult reading level equally interesting books are available and deserve a place in science or English classes. A quick scanning of the science section at a paperback bookstore will produce a reading list with such authors and titles as: *The Creation of the Universe* by David E. Fisher; *Unacceptable Risk,* a discussion of nuclear leakage by McKinley C. Olson; Isaac Asimov's *Please Explain,* with answers to science questions ("How will the earth end?" "How were oceans formed?"); *How To Be a Survivor,* a

ILLUSTRATIVE SCIENCE READING RESOURCES

Books for Children

All About Dinosaurs, Roy Chapman Andrews
How Babies Are Made, Andrew Andry and Steven Schepp
ABC's of the Ocean, Isaac Asimov
What Made You Ill? Jean Bendick
After the Sun Goes Down, Glenn Blough
Eggs and What Happens to Them, Margaret Cosgrove
60 Million Years of Horses, Lois and Louis Darling
Paws, Hoofs, and Flippers, Olive Earle
Spring Comes to the Ocean, Jean Craighead George
The Chicken and the Egg, Iela and Enzo Mari
The Birth of Sunset's Kittens, Carla Stevens
A Book of Mars for You, Franklyn M. Branley
The Changing Earth, Hy Ruchlis
A Drop of Blood, Paul Shavers

Books for Young Adults

Bone for Bone, Margaret Cosgrove
Kangaroos and Other Animals with Pockets, Louis Darling
The Weasels, Bill Gilbert
High Meadow, Eleanor Heady and Harold Heady
The Living Community, Carl S. Hirsch
The Human Story: Facts on Birth, Growth, and Reproduction, Sadie Hofstein
Love and Sex in Plain Language, Eric W. Johnson
The Hunt for the Whooping Crane, J. J. McCoy
The Body, Alan E. Nourse
Animal Camouflage, Dorothy Shuttlesworth
Television Works Like This, Jean Bendick and Robert Bendick

Adult Reading for Young People

Promise or Peril? The Role of Technology in Society, Robert A. Liston
Silent Spring, Rachel Carson
The Creation of the Universe, David E. Fisher
The Poison That Fell from the Sky, John G. Fuller
Unacceptable Risk, McKinley C. Olson
The Nutrino; Please Explain; Science Past and Future; The Human Brain; and *The
     Genetic Code*, Isaac Asimov
How To Be a Survivor, Paul R. Ehrlich
The Immense Journey, Loren Eiseley
Geology; Zoology; Rocks and Minerals; Pond Life; Botany; Stars; Reptiles; and
     Trees, Golden Nature Guides
Black Holes, John G. Taylor
Profiles of the Future, Arthur C. Clarke
The Great Chain of Life, Joseph Wood Krutch
The Making of the Earth, Haroun Tazieff
Waves, Wind, and Weather, Nathaniel Bowditch

Truck, John Jerome
Future Facts, Stephen Rosen
Hunger on Planet Earth, Jules Archer
Subdue the Earth, Ralph Franklin Walworth

Experiment Books

A Walk in the Snow, Phyllis Busch
Look What I Found! The Young Conservationist's Guide to Care and Feeding of Wildlife, Marshal Case
Easy Physics Projects: Air, Water, and Heat, Rocco V. Feravolo
Eric Plants a Garden, Jean Hudlow
The Chemistry of a Lemon, Harris A. Stone
The Adventures of Three Colors, Annette Tison and Talus Taylor
Recyclopedia, Robin Simons
Go Fly a Kite, Ray Brock
Source Book for Science Teaching, UNESCO
Ideas for Science Fair Projects, Ronald Benry et al.
New Ideas for Science Fair Projects, Roger Sawyer and Robert A. Farmer
The Scientific American Book of Science Projects for the Amateur Scientist, C. L. Strong
Science for the Airplane Passenger, Elizabeth A. Wood

Introductory Books in the Disciplines

The Language of Life: An Introduction to the Science of Genetics, George and Muriel Beadle
Biology in the World of the Future, Hal Helman
The New Mathematics; The Tools of Science: From Yardstick to Cyclotron; The Words of Physics, Irving Adler and Ruth Adler
Realm of Measure; Realm of Number; Words of Science, Isaac Asimov
Biography of an Atom, Jacob Bronowski and Millicent E. Selsam
Understanding Science, William H. Crouse
The First Book of Electricity, Sam Epstein and Beryl Epstein
Wonders of Ancient Chinese Science, Robert Silverberg
The New Golden Book of Astronomy, Rose Wyler and Gerald Ames

Science Related Magazines

American Horseman	*Jogger*
Gymnastics	*UFO Magazine*
Cosmos	*Motor Trend*
Consumer Reports	*National Geographic World*
Audubon	*Road and Track*
Analog: Science Fiction/Fact	*Flying*
Popular Science	*Popular Mechanics*
Science Digest	*Earth Science*
Sky and Telescope	*Scientific American*
The Conservationist	*Wildlife*
Dog World	

book on the future of the planet, by Paul R. Ehrlich; Loren Eiseley's beautifully written *The Immense Journey;* a number of Golden Guides on geology, zoology, rocks and minerals, pond life, botany, stars, reptiles, trees; the Roger Tory Peterson guides to bird and animal life; *Black Holes* by John G. Taylor; *Profiles of the Future* by Arthur C. Clarke; *The Great Chain of Life* by Joseph Wood Krutch; and *It's Going To Sting Me: A Coward's Guide to the Great Outdoors* by Ronald Root.

Magazines also provide reading materials for students at all levels. *Ranger Rick's Nature Magazine* and *National Geographic World* are aimed at younger readers, and the various in-school newspapers and magazines published by Scholastic and other commercial houses regularly include science features. Commercial magazines can be used as well, and both science and English teachers should make use of such science-related magazines as *American Horseman, Dog World, UFO Magazine, Consumer Reports, Motor Trend, Hi-Fi Buyer's Review, Flying, Popular Science, Science Digest, Wildlife, Sky and Telescope,* and, of course, *Scientific American.* Obviously, many students who are not book oriented are nevertheless interested in the content of magazines and capable of reading them. Thus it's not unusual to see a remedial reader, who tests out on the school's exams at a second grade level, poring over something like *Road and Track,* with technical language that knocks the top off most readability scales.

One example of an existing high school program will show the potential for interdisciplinary reading. Jim Wilsford, the principal of Dreher High School in Columbia, South Carolina, wanted reading materials in all classrooms. He announced that a portion of the school textbook budget would be available to teachers of any subject who wanted to develop an in-class library. With a little nudging, teachers began to submit supplementary paperback reading lists, and pretty soon the flow of materials began. Students in the shop classes constructed brightly colored book cases. Now an astonishing number of rooms at Dreher—including the science labs—are stocked with quality paperback reading materials. Wilsford also involved librarians by having them help teachers develop simple checkout systems and by having in-class library circulation count as part of the school library total. (Naturally, book circulation totals at Dreher soared.) Establishing an across-the-school reading program can be one of the first stages in developing interdisciplinary programs. English teachers and librarians can help science teachers locate reading resources for their rooms; the science teachers can return the favor by helping the English teachers and librarians select appropriate science reading materials for their readers.

Of course, the materials I have described here are exclusively nonfiction. Elsewhere in this chapter I will show another literacy connection between science and English through discussion of imaginative literature—especially science fiction. In the meantime, the selected list of science reading materials presents what I hope will seem an enticing sampler of the possibilities in science reading.

2. SCIENCE AND THE HUMANISTIC CLASSROOM

One of the most exciting books on education that I have encountered in recent years is called *Loving and Beyond: Science Teaching for the Humanistic Classroom* (1976). Concerned about the reduction of science to mere textbook mastery, the authors, Joe Abruscato of the University of Vermont and Jack Hassard of Georgia State University, have developed plans for an inquiry-based science program. Science, they say, is a "verb," in that it is concerned with *doing,* not just remembering. They argue that science is not just the learning of an abstract body of truth; it involves exploring, groping, hypothesizing. Further, science is (or can and should be) a humanistic concern. Good science education must be concerned with human values and the humanistic use of knowledge as well. Their basic premises include:

1. Science is a *human experience*. It involves humans looking out at their world.
2. Science usually involves a *cooperative effort*. The scientist, high in the ivory tower, is an inaccurate view of the scientific role.
3. The basic processes of science, such as discovering, valuing, and exploring are applicable to *many of the human social problems* people face, problems that include advancement of social change and the improvement of interpersonal relations.
4. Certain products of science as transmitted through knowledge can be used to *alleviate human suffering* resulting from poverty, disease, and illiteracy.
5. The essence of humanism, as we see it, is that each human being should be encouraged to *utilize his or her full human potential,* as well as intellectual and social potential. Science as a human endeavor provides us with valuable capabilities for investigation and a responsibility to use those capabilities for the benefit of others.

The similarities between these attitudes toward science and contemporary ideas about the teaching of English are striking. English, too, is a "verb," in that processes of discovering *through language* are as important as the final language product. The connection between Abruscato and Hassard's work and our interests here should thus be apparent: Just as language is bound up with all phases of humanities study, it is a central part of the process of learning science, too.

"Webbing": An Inquiry Approach
Loving and Beyond is based on what educators call the "inquiry method." Instead of directly mastering a set of prescribed facts, children learn how to raise questions and seek solutions following the scientific method. In the long run, inquiry teaching covers the traditional base of facts—for one cannot solve fundamental questions without a knowledge of facts—but, more important, it provides students with a questioning attitude and a set of procedures for seeking answers to their questions, which make the children *scientists* rather than rote learners.

One of the authors' techniques for developing questions is called "webbing". Two samples of "webs" done by elementary

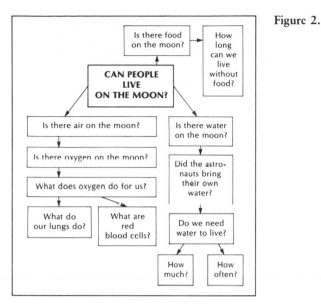

Figure 2.

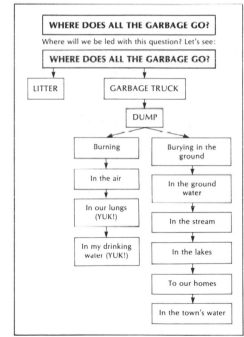

Figure 3.

children are presented in Figures 2 and 3. The teacher starts with a central question, "Can people live on the moon?" or, more earthy, "Where does all the garbage go?" and simply asks the students to explore the web of additional questions. A web can carry a topic into unexpected territory: Thus the children's questions about life on the moon lead to an oblique—but crucial—discussion of how red blood cells function. The point is to follow the web of interrelated questions as far as necessary to be certain the problem is well defined. From the fully developed web, an individual, small group, or entire class can launch an investigation.

I have employed webbing with students of several levels—including college—with good results, but have added the "literary connection," by including language resources in the web. For my own classes I use the form in Figure 4, a web consisting of four levels. A topic or central question is placed at the center of the web: "Magnetism," "Can people live on the moon?" "What are we going to do for energy in the twenty-first century?" Level two calls for a listing of key issues and questions that grow from the initial topic: "What are the commercial applications of magnets?" "Can we develop adequate life support systems for moon life?" "Can coal be converted to other energy forms economically?" Of course students are not limited or forced to fill in all the blanks in the diagram; they can raise as many or as few questions as appropriate. The diagram is a visual aid, not a limiting form.

Level three moves into resources: Where can you find out answers? I stress three principal kinds of resources, each of which involves language:

1. *Human resources.* Every school and community includes a number of people who can answer questions that children and young people raise. Thus, for our hypothetical topic of magnets, students might want to visit an automobile graveyard to question the operator of an electromagnetic crane; they might go off to a branch of the U. S. Weather Service to interview a meteorologist about compasses and the earth's magnetic flow; they might contact a university physics professor to seek answers to questions; or

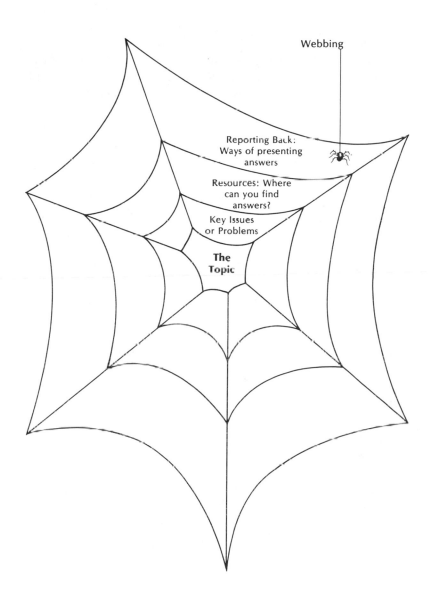

Webbing

Reporting Back: Ways of presenting answers

Resources: Where can you find answers?

Key Issues or Problems

The Topic

Figure 4.

they might visit an electronics firm to learn about how magnetism is used in electronic gadgets. Experts around the school can be questioned, too, from the physics teacher to that kid in second-period history who won a science fair award in electricity last year.

For each interview, some kind of notetaking and record keeping will be required. Students will need to plan and write out questions in advance and to keep track of replies. In preparation, the science or English teacher will need to talk a bit about how to ask a good question, how to keep the interview to the point, and how to keep a legible set of notes. Many of those techniques, however, will be self-evident to young people who are planning a real interview. Alternatively, an interview might be tape recorded and transcribed and edited later, in which case different English skills come into play. Of course, the project should not be used simply as an excuse to sneak in written assignments. Language should be introduced as an essential tool in scientific inquiry, not as an adjunct.

2. *Experimental sources.* The heart of scientific inquiry is experimentation—"lab" work—which, depending on the class (English or science) and the age of the students, may range from tightly controlled experiments in a laboratory to informal kitchen chemistry with household gadgets and makeshift apparatus. Experimentation usually involves literacy through reading. Students will consult project books of the sort described earlier, read up on experimental techniques, and record results. On our topic of magnetism, the classic *UNESCO Source Book for Science Teaching* lists dozens of projects and experiments: exploring the poles of a magnet; making a simple compass from a pin, a piece of paper, and a cork; making a "dip circle"; discovering the natural magnetism of substances; mapping lines of force; making a magnetic coil; inducing current with a magnet; making an electromagnet from a bolt; creating a telegraph key; building a door buzzer; and making a generator and electric motor.

3. *Reading resources.* Finally, students can explore a great

many questions directly through reading rather than experimentation, an avenue that is probably more appealing to the English teacher. For the magnetism topic, the teacher might provide a reference library including such books as Ira M. Freeman's *All About Electricity*, Sam and Beryl Epstein's *The First Book of Electricity*, Harvey Weiss' *Motors and Engines and How They Work.* The elementary school teacher can even find children's fiction that relates to the topic; in this case, a book for young readers is *Mickey's Magnet* by Franklyn Branley and Eleanor K. Vaughn (the book comes complete with a magnet). In addition, back issues of many of the science magazines previously described will include articles related directly and indirectly to the topic.

The final (outer) ring of the web involves reporting back, the traditional move from laboratory to audience, from learning to sharing. Many young people have become locked into the format of "the school report," and as a result, look only to the encyclopedia as a model. To encourage students to explore new forms, I offer some of the following options to the traditional report:

—Write an introduction to a book on the topic, condensing your knowledge and presenting it in a comprehensible form to the reader.

—Write a book (or a chapter of a book) for children about it.

—Translate your knowledge into a short story, using it either as background data for the tale or as an important part of the plot itself. For example, write a story of the computer theft of cash from a bank. How does the thief do it? How does the detective figure out whodunnit and howhedunnit?

—Be the thing itself. Write from its point of view.

—Write a letter to a friend, beginning, "I just learned the most interesting thing about _____ (your topic) _____."

—Write a poem or a series of poems about it.

—Project your knowledge into the future: What will the area be like in the year 2000? 2050? 3000?

—Put yourself in a time machine and travel backward. As an on-the-scene reporter, describe what was happening in the subject area fifty, one hundred, or one thousand years ago.

—Write a popular magazine article about it.

—Develop the outline for a TV special or documentary on it.

—Tape a radio broadcast about it.

—Write an interview between yourself and an important person in the field. (Or tape record or improvise your interview with another person acting the part of the interviewer.)

—Write a legislative proposal for development of a needed project in this area.

—Put on an improvisation or skit that will illustrate your ideas.

—Write a letter to the editor of a paper about it.

—Write a letter to a prominent person connected publicly with it.

—Write an advice column for people having trouble with it.

—Make a short super 8-millimeter film about it.

—Write a practical applications column showing how to use it in everyday life.

—Plan a panel discussion on it.

—Stage a debate on some of the issues surrounding it.

Of course, not all of these assignments are appropriate for all students or all topics, but they help to suggest that reporting back involves shaping one's message to the interests and needs of an audience. Students can present ideas about science through discussion, formal speech, media presentation, creative drama, expository writing, and creative writing. Science teachers can safely operate from within their domain as experts in science in advising projects; they need not find themselves teaching poetry writing where they aren't comfortable or worrying about whether or not they are teaching short story writing properly. The science teacher is the expert in good questions about experimental techniques and science resources. If he or she simply concentrates on helping students negotiate the web of inquiry, the work will shine through in their writing.

Nor need English teachers feel that if they offer science writing options, they will be deluged with incomprehensible jargon or technological data that will leave them at a loss in their own classes. The purpose of reporting back is *communicating,* and this is the English teacher's domain. If the content of a science paper is not comprehensible to the teacher (and to other students), then quite clearly, the project has failed. Without having to know a thing about nuclear physics or magnetism, the English teacher can guide students in reporting back successfully by helping to raise rhetorical questions: "Did you keep your initial questions in mind?" "Do you need to define some terms here?" "Whom do you visualize as your readers?" "Can we phrase this another way?" "Did you think of beginning with a story or anecdote?" Best of all, the English teacher can say, "I never knew that. How interesting. You explained it well."

Language Study as Science

For the genesis of ideas in this section I am indebted to two of my graduate students, Kim Coggins and Ron Emaus. Kim is in law school and would like to teach legal writing; Ron is a Ph.D. candidate in biochemistry. Both enrolled in one of my summer workshops with a common interest: helping students learn to write better. They studied the kind of English/science schism that traditionally has been a problem in the schools and combined efforts on a paper, "Let the Students Do It: Analysis and Synthesis in Education" (1976), in which they proposed science/English instruction through a "laboratory" staffed by teachers from both disciplines. In the lab students would choose topics, and, rather like the webbing sequence described earlier, would probe questions under the direction of the appropriate literacy and science experts.

Coggins and Emaus proposed that learning to write be treated as a scientific process of exploration. That is, in the lab the students would not only write about science topics, they would treat the effectiveness of their writing as a scientific experiment. Thus before presenting a paper or project to an audience, the students would take preliminary audience surveys. How much does the audience know about the topic? What does it need to know? What writing form would be most useful in presenting information? What terms need to be defined? After presenting the paper, the students would be equally concerned with effect and evaluation: Did the paper reach its audience? Were the readers persuaded? Was the necessary information retained by readers? Such questions might also be raised at a draft stage with "test" audiences as well.

Of course, classical rhetoricians have been concerned with these kinds of questions for thousands of years and have thus developed the "science" of rhetoric, a body of knowledge about the structure and structuring of discourse that helps writers and speakers function effectively. How much more valuable, it seems to me, to have students discover rhetoric for themselves by taking a scientific attitude toward their own language. Though the Coggins/Emaus interdisciplinary lab is probably not an immediately practical idea in most schools, where disciplinary boundaries are still strong, their proposal provides a useful model for English or science teachers working alone or for team-taught and interdisciplinary projects.

Yet, there are some dangers inherent in using the scientific method to assess one's writing. One implicit assumption in a scientific/rhetorical approach is that if the discourse "works," it is "good." Such an attitude has, in the past, led to political rhetoric that concentrates more on effect than message, on pleasing an audience at all costs rather than uttering truth, and to television commercials that sell sex, the good life, and just plain good feelings instead of talking truthfully about the contents of detergent and cereal boxes.

But humanists have no monopoly on questions that deal with moral issues. Scientists must wrestle with the moral responsibility for applications of their discoveries, just as English teachers have worried over sophistry that might make "the worse appear the better cause." As a part of a language/science course, then, the teacher must raise the problem of rhetorical success and its possible effect on the content of discourse. As part of such a unit, students might well make a scientific study of television content, political speeches, and other public uses of language to create and form their own values.

Treating language as an object for scientific study has long been the occupation of linguists as well, and it offers some intriguing possibilities for exploration in English classes, in science classes, or both:

Dialect Study. A considerable amount of very *un*scientific mythology about dialects exists. It is widely believed, for example, that there is one "right" dialect, which all "good" speakers manage. It is frequently asserted that minority or foreign dialects are less effective and less good than the Standard English. And, of course, most of us know in our hearts that dialects and accents are something other people have, not us.

Linguistic study has established a quite different set of facts: Standard English, for example, is not some sort of preordained, pure dialect at all, but is spoken by people who, for reasons of wealth, breeding, or position, have that intangible quality called "prestige." Non-standard dialects are *not* demonstrably inferior. In fact, although they mark the class origins of the speaker, they work quite well for most purposes of communication and certainly do not limit one's thinking. And, of course, each of us speaks a dialect—has an accent, as it were—speech habits that identify our language as different from that of other people.

Examining dialects scientifically could go a long way toward helping dispel some of these myths, and, in addition, it is a fascinating area of study for young people. Textbooks such as Roger Shuy's *Discovering American Dialects* (1967) and William Reynolds' *Dialects in America* (1973) have been used in many English classrooms to help students understand where dialects come from, how they differ, what they do and do not say about speakers.

The raw data for dialect analysis might also come from tapes or sound recordings. *Americans Speaking* (1967), compiled and edited by dialectologist Raven McDavid, is a recorded sampler of major dialect forms in the United States. But oral history projects also suggest themselves here: Armed with cassette recorders, students might collect samples of the dialects in their community. Given Americans' geographic mobility, it is likely that nearly all major dialects can be found in speakers who live within a few miles of school. Tapes can be analyzed by students to learn how intonation patterns, vocabulary, and even syntax differ from one dialect to another. In many schools, students have even compiled dialect dictionaries based on differences to be found within the school itself.

Grammar Study. Like dialects, "grammar" is surrounded by a great many myths. For most people, grammar means "good English," which, in turn, means standard middle-class American English. But grammar to an English teacher or linguist means something quite different from proper English; it refers to the study of the ways in which English sentences are put together, a topic that goes well beyond debates over the use of *who* and *whom, may I* or *can I.* The study of grammar as science is an intriguing possibility; as students examine the language, they will come to understand it more fully and comprehensively.

For instance, a Chicago English teacher, Rita Hansen, has long had her high school students make tape recordings of the speech of their one-, two-, and three-year-old brothers and sisters. The students bring in the tapes and, functioning as linguists, they try to discover the regularities—the grammar—in young children's speech. They discover, in the process, that children tend to use object and action words (nouns and verbs) before they use linking words (prepositions, articles, etc.). Students thus discover some of the ways in which the language-learning mechanisms of children bring them into the community of adults.

Mark Lester has written a good little textbook called *Constructing an English Grammar* (1973), which introduces students to the study of English syntax by doing a simulation of a computer language program. The computer, Tobor ("robot" spelled

backward), is taught to speak by being presented sentence-genera-
tion rules. Students are given the not-so-easy task of developing
rules that would allow a computer to generate English sentences
rather than nonsense. In developing rules to teach the computer,
the students also discover the nature of language itself.

Lexical Studies. "Lexicography" is defined by Webster as "the
art, process, or occupation of making a lexicon or dictionary."
Actually, dictionary making is a great deal more science than art.
It involves collecting thousands of examples of a word in actual
use (citations), from which definitions are extracted by a scientific
process of experimenting with descriptions (generalizations) that
will describe satisfactorily all known occurrences and *only* those
occurrences. (If you think that is easy, try coming up with a definition to fit "run" in the following citations: "I will *run* to the
store." "I have a *run* in my stocking." "Hank Aaron passed Babe
Ruth's home *run* record." "I've had a *run* of good luck.") Lexicography offers a natural topic for exploration in English/science,
one that helps students understand scientific methodology while
learning more about the nature of words and definitions. Students
can create slang dictionaries, dictionaries of colloquialisms, collections of new words, bilingual dictionaries, and so on to learn the
processes of language science.

At one point in distant history, the word "philology"—from the
Greek *logos,* "to speak"—referred to all of learning, showing the
centrality of language to all knowledge. In our own time, it has
been restricted to mean the field of word analysis and study. Philo-
logical studies dominated the English curriculum in the nineteenth
century; students did detailed analyses of language references, historical origins of words, and literary language. In a more practical
and more interesting domain, however, philology belongs in Eng-
lish/science studies in some of the following forms:

—*The study of names.* Students can study the origins of their own
names, first and last, tracking down their own linguistic roots.
Equally interesting are studies of place names—streets, neigh-

borhoods and communities, towns, geographical locations, and so on.

—*The history of words.* Students can look for the origins of technical terms (*television, laser, microscope*), everyday words (*house, school, wall*), word families (*horse, horsepower, horseplay, horse opera, horselaugh, horseradish, horseshoe crab*), and taboo words (words that shock or offend).

—*The meaning of meaning.* General semantics is the study of how words acquire meaning and how that abstracting process creates problems in human communication. In a general semantics unit students can scientifically study words as abstractions, connotative and denotative meanings, buzzwords, soothing words, and slanting and biasing through word selection.

Linguistics and Science Fiction. I will write about science fiction at length in the next section, but in the context of a discussion of language sciences, it is useful to mention the work of Beverly Friend, former SF editor of the *Chicago Daily News*. She has documented the wealth of linguistic material presented in science fiction (1973). SF writers have dealt imaginatively with intergalactic communication. In *VOR,* James Blish employs the color spectrum as a means of communication, an idea that has since resurfaced, with musical tones added, in the seventies film, *Close Encounters of the Third Kind.* In *The Black Cloud,* Fred Hoyle has earthlings transmit a corpus of five hundred words into outer space to explain earth culture to creatures out there. In *Dune,* Frank Herbert gives the Bene Gesserit trainees the power of reading and controlling minds through voice intonation. In *1984* George Orwell explores the possible ways in which language choice can be used for mind control. The implications for English/science discussions are clear: Are these languages science fact or science fiction? Could they work? Can we find current examples of language use to substantiate or refute these as possibilities? What do these fictional languages tell us about our own "real world" language?

Science and Literature

Throughout this chapter I have deliberately separated fiction and nonfiction to help draw attention to the wealth of scientific nonfiction available to teachers of English and science. But I have done so at the risk of appearing to isolate "literature" from "non-literature" and reinforcing the stereotype that literature (and English teachers) deal with an unreal world while nonfiction (and scientists) deal with objective and practical truth.

In fact, it is in discussions of science through literature that we can perhaps come closest to bridging the two cultures. What seems most important is that literature courses not simply treat science as a curiosity or naïvely assume that science somehow can be known or studied through the words of imaginative literature.

English teachers have discovered the appeal of SF, and so have their students. There are plenty of good, teachable science fiction materials available ranging from the technically sophisticated work of Arthur Clarke in *A Rendezvous with Rama* and the high fantasy of Ursula LeGuin in *Earthsea* to the historical curiosities of H. G. Wells in *War of the Worlds* to the technical curiosities of the *Star Wars Blueprints* and the *Star Fleet Medical Manual* (see list). Virtually any theme one might want to treat in an English class has been explored in science fiction—love, peace, war, human (and alien) rights, education—and a great wealth of technological and scientific data is stored away in the writings of sci fi authors. (A fascinating reference text, the *Visual Encyclopedia of Science Fiction,* edited by Brian Ash, indexes crucial themes and technological developments for major science fiction works. One could use it easily as a guide to course construction.)

Science fiction courses are popular at all levels of the junior and senior high school. Yet at the same time, many of these courses seem quite limited in structure, relying principally on the sheer magnetism of SF to engage students. Books are presented at random, one "hot" book after another, and the only unifying theme or issue of the course becomes the pseudo-literary questions,

"What is science fiction? Is it a valid literary form?" As a result, SF becomes locked into a single (probably quite interesting) course and the rest of the curriculum proceeds merrily along without much regard for science or science fiction.

I'm convinced that SF is good stuff and ought to be read in English (and science) classes. But I am also convinced that concern for and recognition of science ought to be infused throughout the English curriculum (just as the concerns of literacy should be central in science classes). I will present, then, some literature-based courses that imply the kind of interdisciplinary literature/science program I have in mind.

Topics in English. An excellent guide for teachers at the upper elementary/junior high school level is Geoffrey Summerfield's *Topics in English* (1965), describing a "project approach" to English for the intermediate years. I have been impressed with Summerfield's interdisciplinary interests, particularly his ability to incorporate science work naturally into English. Of the forty or so thematic topics presented, over half deal with the natural world, for example: Predators, Fire and Flame, Snakes and Reptiles, Motorcycles, The Antarctic, Storms, Sky-Journeys, Fish and Whale, The Sea, Pestilence and Famine, and Caves. (Examples of non-science topics include: Christmas, Home and Parents, Our Town, and War.) In each unit, he provides a reading list for children, a separate list for reading aloud by the teacher, and ideas for individual and small group projects.

The unit on Predators, for example, begins with recognition that adolescents are not only interested in predators in nature; they sense predatory instincts in their own emotions and behavior. "It is through the exercise of the imagination," Summerfield asserts, "that they can come to experience themselves the tensions of feeling, of sympathy and revulsion, that the predator-victim relationship creates."

His reading list for Predators includes poetry and prose like William Stafford's "Travelling Through the Dark," Robert Frost's "Design," Ruth Pittner's "The Bat," "The Ravens" (a medieval

A SELECTED BIBLIOGRAPHY OF SCIENCE FICTION

The Illustrated Man; The Martian Chronicles; Fahrenheit 451, Ray Bradbury
Foundation; Earth Is Room Enough; Fantastic Voyage, Isaac Asimov
A Rendezvous with Rama; Childhood's End; 2001: A Space Odyssey,
 Arthur C. Clarke
The Andromeda Strain; The Terminal Man, Michael Crichton
Out of the Silent Planet; Prisoners of Space, Lester Del Rey
Dune; Dune Messiah; Children of Dune, Frank Herbert
The Left Hand of Darkness and *The Earthsea Trilogy*, Ursula LeGuin
Stranger in a Strange Land and *The Red Planet*, Robert Heinlein
The Time Machine; The Invisible Man; and *The War of the Worlds*, H. G. Wells
Cities in Flight, James Blish
The Planet of the Apes, Pierre Boulle
Enchantress from the Sky, Sylvia Engdahl
Alas, Babylon, Pat Frank
Dragonflight, Anne McCaffrey
The Synthetic Man; More Than Human, Theodore Sturgeon
Star Trek Intergalactic Puzzles
Star Fleet Medical Reference Manual
Star Trek Blueprints
Star Trek Concordance
Star Wars Blueprints
Trek or Treat, Terry Flanigan and Eleanor Ehrhardt
Beneath the Planet of the Apes, Michael Avallone
Carson of Venus, Escape on Venus; The Lost Continent, Edgar Rice Burroughs
Into Deepest Space and *The Westminster Disaster*, Fred Hoyle and Geoffrey Hoyle
The Tale of the Big Computer, Olaf Johannesson
Cat's Cradle; Player Piano; The Sirens of Titan, Kurt Vonnegut, Jr.
A Clockwork Orange, Anthony Burgess
Android at Arms; The Beast Master; Intergalactic Derelict, André Norton
Marooned in Orbit, Arthur W. Ballow

Fiction with a Science Theme

The Last Eagle, Ben East
The Monkey Wrench Gang, Edward Abbey
Dancers in the Scalp House, William Eastlake
A Heart to the Hawks, Dan Moser
Far Tortuga, Peter Matthiessen
The Year of the Whale, Victor B. Scheffer
Harpoon Gunner, Bruce Walton
The Peregrine Falcon, Robert Murphy

lyric), Robinson Jeffers' "Hurt Hawks," John Wheelwright's "The Huntsman," Jim Corbett's *Man-eaters of Kumaon* and *The Man-Eating Leopard of Rudrapayag,* Arthur Williamson's *Tarka the Otter,* Arthur Grimble's *A Pattern of Islands,* and Geoffrey Chaucer's "The Nun's Priest's Tale." As Summerfield notes, the literature leads students to consider the theme of "nature red in tooth and claw," but it also invites discussion of such topics as design in nature, the human role of intervening in natural cycles, and death of both man and animals.

Summerfield's projects are, to my mind, so inviting that they bear reprinting *in toto:*

1. Observe a cat on the prowl for birds. Make a record of his behavior; was he an impulsive kitten or an experienced cat? How did he display his cunning? Was he easily deterred? Patient? How did the birds react?
2. Write a piece of free verse to express vividly the movements of cat and birds: pay particular attention to rhythms.
3. Observe a fly in a spider's web and write a careful account of the spider's actions.
4. Make a study of the talons and beaks of owls, hawks, and eagles and of their wings and flight. Write a short monograph on the subject with illustrations.
5. Write an account of the qualities of Jim Corbett [author of *Man-eaters of Kumaon*] that helped him to succeed in his difficult task.
6. Write an explanation of the way in which birds and animals convey warnings to each other when in danger.
7. Write a story about the nocturnal adventures of a fox or a cat.
8. What do people mean when they use the word "cruelty"? Ask them—say, a dozen pupils and some members of the staff—and then write an account of their answers, together with your own comments.
9. Late at night, you hear a scuffling sound at the bottom of the garden. It is very dark, but you venture out to see what is going on. Write an account of what you find.
10. Find half a dozen people who are afraid of spiders or mice or bats. Make a note of their reasons, and add your own observations: are some reasons more sensible than others? Are some of them "old wives' tales?"

11. Is the a rat-catcher, or a "rodent operative" in your town? If so, try find out what his duties are and how he performs them.
12. Ima you are a mouse: write a description of your worst enemies:
13. Ha u been "hunted"? Write an account of any such experience.

Is ience or English? The breadth of the reading and diversity topics make the question irrelevant. The claims of both disc are satisfied, for students have the opportunity to learn sc bservation and experimentation as well as to write ob r imaginatively about their observations.

Renewal Through Nature. At the high school level, aw's course, "Human Renewal Through Nature," St. Catherine's School, Richmond, Virginia, offers the dth of aims, materials, and concerns (1976). The course ary exploration of how man has turned to nature as a order, meaning and enlightenment." Her course readings Vordsworth's "Tintern Abbey," Annie Dillard's *Pilgrim Creek,* Thoreau's *Walden,* Emerson's "Nature," the po mily Dickinson and Robert Frost, and Hemingway's "The Hearted River." She brings in paintings of the Hudson hool and music by Vivaldi, Beethoven, and Debussy to course a humanities thrust.

dition to keeping a journal of their perceptions and obser s, the students discuss the works of the principal authors in of their view of the relationship between man and nature the use of nature as a source of solitude. Like Geoffrey Sum rfield, Phyllis Shaw has her students move beyond the basic list readings into projects, some of which include:

Photographic essay and commentary, possibly with music, expressing the results of a personal encounter with nature.
The American Indian view of the human relationship to nature.
How a painter, musician, or other artist suggests the essence of an encounter with nature.
A comparison of the Transcendentalist and Taoist views of man and nature.
Exploration of the purpose and meaning of organizations like the Sierra Club, Appalachian Trail Club, Wilderness Society.

Interviews with people who have chosen to live the "simple li,,
A study of architecture which emphasizes harmony with the na
ronment.   al envi-

   Science, Literature, Morality, and Humanism. Mark
(1976), a teacher in Radnor, Pennsylvania, has proper
sequence of science-related English courses that provides a a
disciplinary focus on science and human values. In Springer
however, the courses might constitute an entire component
school curriculum or be offered as units across the span of s
years. He notes that "science" has taken on two meanings:
strictest sense, it refers to experimentation and research;
broadly, it has come to refer to a set of applications—inclu
moral applications—of science in the world. He argues that
second concern is the realm of interdisciplinary studies,
among the courses he recommends are the following:

Science and New Art Forms. This course traces the artistic effec
duced by such technological advances as the printing press, th   at Tm.
and the synthesizer, to name but a few.

Science and Man in Literature. A course like this follows through litera
history, the philosophical, artistic, and moral changes that have occurre
as a result of scientific discoveries. How have the theories and findings o
Copernicus, Galileo, or Einstein, for example, altered man's artistic and
literary conceptions of himself?

Science as Archetype. Here students try to discern the role that science has
played as the archetypal "unknown," from the days of alchemy to the
present. Why have magic and science always been so feared?

The Scientist as Hero. Similar in focus to the preceding course, this one
investigates works in which the scientist is portrayed as the archetypal
hero figure battling the forces of the unknown.

Literature of Scientific Morality. In this course students read books that
comment directly on the moral role and nature of science. Mary Shelley's
Frankenstein comes directly to mind in this respect, as does Stevenson's
Dr. Jekyll and Mr. Hyde.

Science Fiction—Essays on Morality. This course focuses on the moral
messages often contained in popular science fiction works. Ray Bradbury's stories, together with those of Heinlein, Vonnegut, Huxley, and
Wells, among others, are appropriate.

Science Fiction—Science Fact. Again using popular science fiction stories from the past and present, students learn how the artistic imagination is akin to, and often sparks, the scientific imagination; how science fiction often becomes science fact. The books of Jules Verne are ideal in a course of this kind.

Springer's minicurriculum is by no means complete, and as he remarks, the courses described here are just a sampler of the kinds of science/English courses which are possible. Too, these are simple titles and descriptions; the actual course readings and activities would need to be developed in detail. Nevertheless, the English department or an English/science interest group interested in launching a new set of courses could do far worse than simply to adopt and develop as units or entire courses the topics described here.

Science Reading / Writing for Academia

This final section is in response to what I anticipate as a "Yes, but . . ." reaction to many of the teaching ideas that have been presented in this chapter. The reaction runs something like this: "Yes, these science/English projects sound engaging, and I'd like my child or my students to try them; but there is an academic world out there, and in both high school and college, students will be asked to write papers, not poems, to read essays and textbooks, not science fiction fantasies."

I would agree with the implicit assumption that a science reading/writing program fails if it does not prepare students to deal with the real demands of academic (and presumably post-academic) assignments. At the same time, it is important to note that most students—a vast majority—will never be required to write or read anything remotely resembling the prose that scientists produce for one another. Reading the professional journals and writing articles for them are by and large restricted to the upper levels of the university, to M.A.- and Ph.D.-level work.

What students *are* asked to read and write in high school and college science courses is popular in tone, written for non-specialists. While chemistry and biology textbooks present knowledge in relatively concise, humorless fashion, they are still written for people who know very little about the subject. In this respect, they have much more in common with an article in, say, *Science Digest*, than with an exchange among fellows in the *Journal of the American Chemical Society*. Similarly, in writing examination papers, both high school and college students write material that is essentially informal and introductory in tone and content: "In your own words, explain photosynthesis." "Describe and illustrate the nitrogen cycle."

The point is that much of what students read and write in science courses is general and informal. The purpose is to explain common knowledge clearly, not to raise knowledge to new heights.

What then should the schools do to prepare students for these situations?

The first step, it seems to me, is to provide a good twelve-year education that includes a strong science literacy component. If students experience the kinds of reading/writing projects I have described here at regular intervals from the elementary years on, the specifics of academic education will partly take care of themselves.

Second, is to offer (for those students who need it) a look at the specific reading/writing used in academic science courses and in the scientific world, in general, so that students can go into new situations knowing the kinds of demands that will be placed on them. For this kind of instruction, teachers can borrow from the idea of the English/science lab and let the students explore and discover the forms for themselves. Teachers can supply students with copies of science textbooks, popular magazines, college papers, and professional journals and raise a few, basic questions: "What are the common elements here?" "What does good science writing have in common with all good writing?" "How do science writers present new information to non-specialists? to specialists?" Students can examine everything from stylistic mannerisms to mechanical conventions—tables of contents, charts and graphs, discursive footnotes—to learn how good science papers are put together.

As the students practice writing academic forms, scientific questions should be applied to the paper: "Did it work?" "Could your readers pass a test on the subject after reading your paper?" "Are the terms explained clearly?" "Are there any information gaps?" Older students can examine the objective style of formal report writing and can review examination questions to deduce the kind of information being requested. Such knowledge will give students a sense of the dimensions of scientific writing, and coupled with broad, interdisciplinary instruction in literacy will do a far superior job of preparation than the traditional term paper unit.

10
Language and Community

1. READING AND WRITING "FOR REAL"

It's no secret that parents, students, and many educators perceive a great dichotomy between *schooling* and *living*, between what happens to students in the schools and what happens to people when they enter the "real world." Business people are quick to claim that employees lack fundamental skills in all areas of work. Every high school teacher knows that each year he or she can expect the return of many of last year's graduates to explain how their high school training left them feeling inept and inadequate in dealing with the demands of college life. And in no area of the curriculum are the complaints more vocal than they are for literacy instruction. The teaching of reading and writing, it is regularly claimed, just doesn't measure up when people move on to their life activities.

In this chapter I want to examine the broad relationship between school and community and between the clichéd "learning for living" and "learning for earning a living." In doing so, I also want to examine some of the myths and misconceptions that surround literacy instruction.

For example, it is commonly believed that the schools should prepare students with "job level entry skills," which means, in effect, that the student can step smoothly from school into a job. Yet we might well want to question whether it should be the task of the school system to concern itself directly with the literacy demands of business, industry, and college *at all*. Career preparation in the schools often becomes studying for careers that a student never enters or that disappear altogether in ten or twenty years. When this happens, the school/life gap is actually broadened, even though the schools honestly tried to make education practical.

We might take a look, too, at the extent to which job-related skills are actually learned on the job and ask whether or not this is appropriate. Many business people I have spoken to actually prefer to train employees themselves, and frequently this includes aspects of literacy. Since school training can never fully prepare students for specific tasks of a job—at Sears or city hall or Oldsmobile—the employer might as well set the specifications and do the training himself. (Of course, such a system is dependent upon the schools' graduating students who have solid basic literacy skills in the first place.)

Ivan Illich, one of the more radical of school reformers, claims that thinking of schools as practical institutions distracts us from "a much deeper concern: the manner in which learning is to be viewed":

Will people continue to treat learning as a commodity—a commodity which could be more efficiently produced and consumed by greater numbers of people if new institutional arrangments were established? . . . We must choose between more efficient education of people fit for an increasingly efficient society—and a new society in which education ceases to be the task of some special agency.   [1971]

Illich feels that we must "deschool" society, abolishing the formal, compulsory educational system and allowing education to take place as needed in society. His proposal thus eliminates the schooling/living division by eliminating schools. He argues— frequently persuasively—that the only learning worth having is picked up in society anyway, and he believes that society could function effectively with informal learning networks.

But from a practical point of view the deschooled society seems naïve. Can one realistically provide deschooled experiences for fifty or sixty million school-age youngsters, plus the forty-odd million people who are in their first decade in the job market and need special training, not to mention the remaining one hundred fifty million of us who need some updating of our education? The deschoolers fail to recognize that part of the thrust for efficiency in the schools comes from the need to deal with raw numbers.

Clearly efficiency and preparation can become ends in themselves, obscuring other important aspects of education, in which case, the schools will simply homogenize young people, rather than educate them. Note the tone of this introduction to an English textbook for the schools:

This book can best serve as a body of information adopted by all high school personnel (including administrators, students, secretaries, and teachers). The information should be used as an attempt to go about the business of education most efficiently and constructively, by employing a common directive for what is considered correct or acceptable communicative skills or procedures.

If this quasi-military attitude is to pervade the schools in the name of efficiency and preparation for life, then Illich is right and the schools *should* be done away with altogether.

Of course, one can look toward a third position, that of reforming the schools (and literacy education) so that they effectively meet the needs, interests, and concerns of the human beings in them, rather than the operational convenience of the system itself. If the needs of the learner are kept at the center of instruction—if external forces are not allowed to dictate the curriculum—the schooling/living schism largely disappears. In the previous chapters I have tried to show that English—traditionally a narrowly conceived subject with the indoctrination into Standard English as its goal—can serve as the center for all learning, comfortably cutting across disciplinary lines. It remains in this chapter to show that organic English extends itself naturally into the real world and into the community.

I want to use the world "community" in two different ways. In the broadest sense, "community" will refer to a group of people who are bound together by their use of language as a medium for exploring their lives and their universe—the community of mankind. Every human being participates in the language community for his own ends and purposes. Each person gives *to* the community by sharing ideas, thoughts, and experiences with other people. Each person also takes *from* the community through language that provides information, ideas, aesthetic or affective experiences, and confirmation of his own beliefs. As one grows in experiences and language, one comes to participate more fully in the community of language. "There was a child went forth," Walt Whitman wrote, "and the first object he look'd upon, he became." As I have shown, that process of becoming involves language, as the child uses words to name, describe, and share information about the objects he "becomes."

In the more restricted sense, however, "community" refers to the world immediately outside—be it a community of eight million New Yorkers or a community of one hundred farmers and their families in North Dakota. (It may also include the community of the "global village" projected into our homes by television. [McLuhan, 1968].) The community and its culture—the Greek concept of *paideia*—serve a powerful educational function, at least as powerful as the schools themselves. While keeping the broad sense of community in mind, I will explore in this chapter some possibilites for the English curriculum as a part of *paideia,* in which the community enters into the schooling process, both inside and outside the school walls.

Community Resources for Reading and Writing

Several years ago an organization called the Group for Environmental Education offered an excellent model for community learning: *The Yellow Pages of Learning Resources,* which looks like its namesake, the telephone yellow pages, but is aimed at helping students discover and use the resources available to them in a city. The editor, Richard Saul Wurman, explains:

The city is education—and the architecture of education rarely has much to do with the building of schools. The city is a schoolhouse, and its ground floor is both bulletin board and library. The graffiti of the city are its window displays announcing events; they should reveal the people to themselves, tell what they're doing and why they're doing it. Everything we do—if described, made clear, and made observable—is education: The "Show and Tell," the city itself.   [1972]

The book lists places to visit: airports, gas stations, hardware stores, junk yards, newspaper plants, television stations, and it asks, "What can you learn there?" The students might interview an architect and ask "How did you become an architect?" "How does an architect design?" "What makes buildings stand up?" "What makes some buildings fall down?" "What is the difference between good buildings and bad ones?" Each location can supply an inquiring student with all kinds of information about a craft or trade or area of culture. While I would argue against replacing school altogether with something like the *Yellow Pages of Learning Resources,* it is clear that just about anything a person wants to know can, in fact, be learned in the outside world.

Wurman's emphasis on "city" should not be taken to imply that this is a project limited to large urban areas. He notes, for example, that although a city like Philadelphia has twenty-two banks with 339 branches, Tulare, California (population 13,824), has at least four banks. While New York has hundreds of hospitals, all but the smallest towns have emergency care facilities of some sort, and virtually every community has at least one doctor. What less populated areas lack in some resources (museums, galleries, etc.) they may well make up for in others: feed and grain stores, an all-purpose country hardware store, an honest-to-goodness town meeting.

Most lacking from *Yellow Pages,* it seems to me, is the "tell" part of Wurman's "show and tell." The book makes no mention of the obvious implications for literacy instruction in community-based projects. In the process of exploring local resources, young people will read booklets, signs, and advertisements; they will question, discuss, debate, and explain; they will take notes and keep records; and, if the project is to have significance for other students, they will write or talk about their findings.

To extend the *Yellow Pages* idea, I asked students in a course for teachers to develop a set of reading and writing activities based in the community. We called the project "Write Around Town," and the aim was for students to locate resources in the Lansing, Michigan, area (population, 250,000) and to create language-based learning activities. Here are some of their ideas:

The State Capital. Why in the world is it in Lansing? Who would put it there? Find out why it is here, who put it here, when it was built, and anything else in its history you think is significant. Write up your results in a short historical monograph.

or

Collect some colorful and informative postcards about the Capitol. Make your own magazine. Include an explanation beneath each postcard.

Elderly Instruments [a music store]. Look on all the shelves, racks, and hooks, and in all the cases, etc. and familiarize yourself with the shop. Then choose the most interesting instrument or gadget you've seen and write about it.

or

Write with a slide camera. Even an inexpensive camera can take slides. Follow the repair of a broken instrument from start to finish (this may take more than one visit). Take notes on the different tools, processes, etc. used. Then create a slide-tape presentation for the class.

Greenhouse.
Write a gardening booklet for houseplants for the class, gaining information from the greenhouse keeper about how to water, how to provide light, how to trim, etc.

How do they make perfume from flowers?

Do plants have feelings? Read an article on plant communications and ask the greenhouse keeper about it. Write an imaginary dialog between plants.

Cable TV Offices. As you may know, all cable television companies must keep certain channels available for public access. This means that within limits, you can create any kind of show you want and have it presented. Visit our Channel 11. Take a tour and write down your impressions of the place. Write a script for a play or for a game show and prepare a production. After you have finished writing and performing, make a list of the things you have learned. What would you do differently next time?

Library.
With the help of your teacher or librarian, go on a scavenger hunt around the library, learning how to find interesting or obscure information.

Try to figure out the library's coding system. If you were planning a library, how would you file the books? Work out a design for a coding system and discuss it with the librarian.

Imagine you are locked in the library overnight. You cannot get out until morning. What would you do? What would you read? Write a report of your nocturnal wanderings.

Of course, such activities require a considerable amount of organizing. One clever way of doing this is represented in a set of activity cards prepared by the Alexandria, Virginia, Branch of the American Association of University Women. *A Child's Introduction to Historical Alexandria* (n.d.) is a set of a dozen printed cards, each 8″ × 8″, featuring a map of a portion of the town, an illustration of a building or other historical artifact, and appropriate activities for children:

scavenger hunt among antique furnishings, looking for such oddities as bootscrapers and carriage stones.

exploring an old church.

a word puzzle about the Alexandria railroad, dating back to the Civil War.

While few communities have the historical richness of Alexandria, the activity card concept is a useful way of helping to organize learning experiences in or out of school. Community members, teachers, and even the students themselves can prepare guide cards or activity cards about key features of a community, setting a pattern for reading and writing assignments.

As I have described community-based projects to groups of teachers and parents, I have heard a common objection: "This idea doesn't seem practical. It requires school buses and field trips. We can't have kids running around loose outside of school." Yet most elementary teachers are quite accustomed to the ritual of field trips, and regularly take their students to museums and malls, to farms and old schoolhouses, to firehouses and city hall. For many teachers in the grades, then, all that is needed is the addition of a literacy component, letting the students find a writing/speaking outlet for their observations.

Parents and teachers (and probably local merchants as well) have some legitimate concern about having older students running around unchecked. These fears can be minimized, however, if projects are well planned and well organized. The fact is, young people nowadays are quite mobile anyway, using bike, skateboard, public transportation, and, if old enough, a car, to get around town for lessons, sporting events, and meetings. While the schools have to take legal precautions—usually securing parental permission for off-campus trips—most students can pursue and enjoy community-based excursions without creating strain or inconvenience for adults.

School-Based Projects

It is important to emphasize that community learning need not be (and should not be) a completely out-of-school project. Most of the organizing, talking, planning, showing, and telling will take place inside the school. Further, a surprising amount of real world learning can occur without the students' actually visiting off-campus locations. The students can "let their fingers do the walking" to explore and learn from the world around them through the telephone, newspapers and magazines, letter writing, guest speakers, and so on.

The Telephone. Students can telephone around town to elicit all kinds of information. The conventional yellow pages provide the principal resource here, and they are one of the finest, best organized, most useful learning resources around. You can learn about (or learn where to find out about) everything from Accountants to Zippers. Students can generate questions they want to answer, then survey the yellow pages to find information sources. Teachers can ask "What number would you call to find out about air pollution? home insulation? rare books? services for the blind? youth organizations? magnets? legal aid?" As a supplement to field work, then, students can call a newspaper, a health food store, a library or paperback store, the hobby shop, a pizzeria, or a diary to make real world connections in their learning.

Unfortunately, units on "telephone etiquette" are easily satirized. Many in conventional English textbooks have presented less-than-realistic information to students (recommending, for example, that a young person answer the phone by saying, "The Jones residence, May Jones speaking," rather than "Hullo"). Yet teachers can usefully spend a period or two explaining, and quite possibly having the students roleplay, some basic telephone skills. How do you make an appointment over the phone? What is a secretary likely to ask you? How do you identify yourself so they know you're serious? How can you find out what you want to know quickly so as not to waste somebody's time?

Learning to use the phone effectively in the community has genuine payoff. The "final examination" is based in reality: "Did you find out what you wanted to know?"

Newspapers and Magazines. In *Hooked on Books* (1976), Daniel Fader proposes two useful concepts for teaching literacy using newspapers and magazines: *saturation* and *diffusion*. He suggests that schools (and children) should be *saturated* with the materials of literacy—newspapers and magazines as well as paperbacks— and that the materials should be broadly *diffused* throughout the school so that they are available in all classrooms, English as well as other subjects.

Newspapers are, of course, good for the basic news of the day and, in contrast to the evening television news, which gives only basic coverage of the essential stories, newspapers provide detailed information that includes all sorts of community-related features: "page-two" stories about community events, biographies of local people, obituaries; columns and features; book, movie, and television reviews; debates on key issues; announcements of civic bids, contracts, and board meetings; the arts calendar; science features; quizzes and puzzles; historical essays; letters to the editor; financial and business pages; the sports, weather, and stocks; family living articles; the women's page; and the advertisements, both commercial and classified.

Increasingly, the local papers are being supplemented by area or regional magazines, which are published in middle-sized cities as well as in large ones. Local magazines and newspaper supplements typically include radio and television schedules (including the local cable channels); theater, film, and music calendars; essays on local history and tradition; classified ads; interviews with local personalities; real estate listings; food and shopping guides; and features on area sports. In contrast to the daily papers, these weeklies, monthlies, and bimonthlies emphasize "the stories behind the headlines," material that is less topical and less spectacular, but is described in more detail. Using such stories as a starting point, students can plan field trips or interviews. The occasional magazines are frequently put together by local free-lance writers of some talent, so that the writing and research presented are often a notch above that of the daily paper. The local magazines can also be supplemented by state or regional magazines as well: *Colorado, Arizona Highways, Sunset* (a magazine of "West Coast living"), and *Yankee* (a Down-East magazine), to name a few.

Finally, national circulation magazines offer an obvious connection between one's home town and the global village. *Time, Newsweek,* and *U.S. News and World Report* include, in addition to the news, regular features on medicine, art, law, popular culture, personalities, sports, and so on. In many cases, national stories have implications for home town life; trends and events that are significant enough to be reported at the national level have ramifications locally. Thus the teacher can ask, "What does this have to do with us?" "How is this trend reflected in our town?" The news magazines can be supplemented with a personality and human interest magazine like *People,* which despite its emphasis on the spectacular, provides a useful model for student interviews and article writing. Teachers can draw on specialty magazines like *Sports Illustrated, Consumer Reports,* and *Changing Times* for classroom use as well.

Letter Writing. Despite postage increases and service inadequacies, the first-class stamp is still one of the best communications buys around. In addition to its obvious function in teaching literacy skills, letter writing makes a real world education possible. Letters are, by and large, more likely to bring a satisfactory response from "important" people than phone calls, and as tools for research and action, they are frequently more satisfactory than the phone.

Like the telephone unit, classroom instruction in letter writing has often overemphasized social niceties and the details of letter form. If students actually write to someone outside the school, letter conventions can be taught in a matter of minutes. On the other hand, if letter writing is made a schoolroom exercise, mere practice in social graces through the writing of make-believe thank yous and service requests, no amount of instruction will teach the appropriate forms.

Students can write letters to anybody, anyplace. For starters, the teacher merely needs to check the yellow pages, the local newspaper, and the national magazines for names and topics. In *Getting in Touch with Your Government* (1975), Robert Liston shows some of the letter writing possibilities for civic action, describing governmental offices and suggesting what may appropriately be requested with letters. In addition to giving young people a brief introduction to letter form, he supplies a directory of addresses where students can write for information on such diverse topics as aging, agriculture, atomic energy, banking, civil rights, consumerism, energy, environment, food, forests, housing, jobs, spying, science, seashores, and television.

Free and Inexpensive Materials. At relatively low cost a teacher can—with the help of students, some stamps, and the telephone—fill a classroom with real world learning resources. For example, Ward's and Sears' catalogs are easy enough to obtain for classroom use and supply a great deal of information about goods and prices. By reading between the lines, one can quickly learn techniques, strategies, and strong and weak points of products. (If the top-priced microwave oven is "Guaranteed Against Leakage," what does this say about a lesser-priced oven that isn't? Leakage of what? Why is this bad? Where can we find out more?) Hundreds of other catalogs are available free, catalogs of seeds and bulbs, automotive parts, office supplies, kitchen equipment, herbs and spices, cheeses and fruits. (A useful resource for teachers is Marie DeLaIglesia's *A Catalogue of American Catalogues* [1973], which describes catalogs and how one can obtain them.)

Students can do much of the letter writing for free and inexpensive materials ranging from publicity pamphlets and promotional fliers to inexpensive government publications. *1001 Things You Can Get Free*, published and updated regularly by Bantam Books, supplies names and addresses. The latest edition includes such materials as a CB slang dictionary, a portfolio describing accomplishments of American women, free posters and maps, a first-aid guidebook, books on hunting and fishing, cookbooks, career guides, and sources of health information. Each year *The English Journal* also prints a listing of free and inexpensive materials of special interest to literacy teachers.

Visiting Firemen. Adults generally love invitations to come to school to talk about their specialty—be it career or hobby. They will come free, and they bring the real world into the classroom with them. As an alternative or supplement to field work, teachers and students can arrange to bring in speakers: not just the fireman, but pediatricians and politicians; bakers, boxers, and bankers; car and house salespeople; doctors and nurses; scientists and engineers; actors and athletes.

Simulations. In recent years, educators have done a good deal of work developing simulations and simulation games as a method of instruction. While a good simulation is obviously not identical with the real world, it can re-create many of the elements of the original situation. For *The Creative Word* (1974), I developed "The Dennison Dilemma," a simulation of a small town—Dennison—faced with the decision of whether or not to allow new industrial construction that would bring new jobs but pollute the rural environment. Students roleplay the people involved—selectmen, townspeople, attorneys, the newspaper editor, business representatives—and the discussion raises the facts (and emotions) that surround such real world issues.

In *The Micro-Society School* (1973), George Richmond describes a program where students are immersed in a number of social studies and economics games, interconnected with the use of play money or scrip, to simulate the basic functions of society's lawyers, bankers, judges, police, and citizens. *Interact,* a publishing house specializing in simulation, has schoolroom games on such topics as newscasting, advertising, tracing your roots, inventing codes, predicting the future, planning careers, and writing biography. Lynn Troyka and Gerrold Nodelman's *Taking Action* (1975) describes English-related games that simulate problems in conversation, women's roles, government spending, and population control. Finally, Kenneth Davis and John Hollowell (1977) have developed materials showing how English teachers can create simulations and games to fit almost any curriculum topic from publishing to learning about Shakespeare.

The Media. The electronic media provide an obvious connection between school and community. Using *TV Guide* as a start, a teacher can regularly identify programs centering on issues, problems, and concerns of the class. Local luminaries appearing on area TV can be brought to class as a follow-up. Documentary, instructional, and art films are available through school, community, state, and university libraries on almost any topic an English or other teacher might want to cover. Filmstrips, which used to be a poor substitute for films, have improved dramatically in the past two or three decades and in most cases are both informative and graphically interesting. Media resources include tape and disc recordings, radio, video-cassette or videotape, and cable TV.

To stress the point: Real world materials can be brought into the classroom just as easily as students themselves can foray out into the community for exploration and research. Both kinds of activities are legitimately a part of education.

Learning in the Real World

Obviously the organization of community-based projects will differ from school to school, from elementary to secondary levels, and from subject to subject. Interdisciplinary team teaching allows different options from teaching in a self-contained or single-subject classroom. If teacher aides are available, the teacher can organize more sophisticated projects than if he or she is working alone. Urban schools will organize differently from suburban and rural and, equally obvious, the kinds of resources available to teachers will dictate some limits to the project.

Nevertheless, almost any school subject—English or other—can be developed with a community-based component. Whether one is studying Shakespeare (where interviews with local theater people are a possibility), magnetism (call the power company), home economics (visit a bakery or institutional kitchen or clothing distributor), shop (call on a carpenter), or economics (visit bankers, real estate brokers, the city treasurer), there are local resources to draw upon.

In *Reality Centered Learning* (1975), Hy Ruchlis and Belle Sharefkin, who teach at Fairleigh Dickinson University and Brooklyn College, have outlined community-based projects in detail.

(See the list of the topics they propose.) One can see that all subject matter areas are included, from Civics ("Our Community") to science ("Gravity—Could We Do Without It?") to the humanities ("Understanding Other People," "Music Today and Yesterday"). Each of these topics could be a course in itself, a component or unit within an established course, or, quite possibly, the focus of a whole year study.

Once a topic has been selected the teacher can begin the process of developing a set of guiding problems or key topics. A procedure I have used successfully raises three major questions:

1. *What do we already know about the topic?* (This question provides a route into the topic, an informal assessment of knowledge, ideas, and resources already available to the group.)
2. *What do we want to know or need to find out?* (Here students brainstorm. No idea is ruled out as ridiculous or impractical. Creative ideas are encouraged.)
3. *Of those questions, which are the most important?* Do some of them overlap? Can we combine several related questions into one big one?

The result is usually a list of good solid questions directed toward some knowledge worth having, and they provide the driving power for the rest of the unit.

"How can we best answer our own questions?" becomes the next concern. The teacher and class review the range of resources available—inside and outside the school—the teacher serving as a guide to resources, a knower of books and other materials. My checklist runs this way:

What can we learn about the topic through printed materials?

Books
    Nonfiction materials
    Novels
    Reference books (encyclopedias, almanacs, etc.)

COMMUNITY-BASED PROJECTS

Our Community
Education and the School
Human Resources
Understanding Yourself
Understanding Other People
Understanding Parents
Understanding Brothers and Sisters
Architecture, Good and Bad
Industry, Pros and Cons
Improving the Distribution of Goods
How Local Government Functions
Politics in Your Town
Eliminating Political Corruption
The Prison System
The Death Penalty
Drug Abuse
Investigate an Industry or Business
Labor Unions
Improving Health Care
Fire Prevention
Improving Television
Newspapers, Good or Bad?
Improving the Use of Radio
Land Use and Abuse
Air, a Precious Resource
Rivers, Lakes, and Oceans
Outer Space
How Books (or Newspapers) Are
    Written and Produced
Building a Home
Building a Bridge
What Is Good Art?
How Sculptors Work
Painting a Picture
Music Today and Yesterday
A Finite Earth
Should Industry Keep Growing?
Controlling Population
What Is the Real Purpose of Sex?

How Does Man Resemble
    All Other Animals?
Man and Ape
Women's Liberation
Child Abuse
Rights and Responsibilities
    of Young People
Comparative Religions
What Is Time?
Gravity—Could We Do Without It?
Light—Suppose There Was None
Problems of Old Age
Why Young and Old Disagree
City Planning
Mass Transportation
Improving Recreational Facilities
Cultural Differences
Nature of Conflict
The Human Mind
Mass Media
Justice and the Court System
Americans All
Consumer Law
Insurance Business—Should It Be
    More Strictly Regulated?
Body Language
Better Movies
Big Cars versus Small
Propaganda—How To Analyze It
Poverty, Its Cause and Cure
Causes of Dissent
Change, Today and Tomorrow
Maps
Liberty and Freedom
Managing the Oceans
United Nations, Success or Failure?
World Law
What Is Life?

From Hy Ruchlis and Belle Sharefkin, *Reality Centered Learning* (New York: Citation Press, 1975), 75–76.

Other literature (poetry, drama)
Magazines (list possible periodicals)
Newspapers (local, regional, or national)
Catalogs, yellow pages, government publications, brochures and
pamphlets

What can we learn around town?

People to interview
Places to visit
Phone numbers (check the yellow pages)
Places to write
Possible consultants
Class speakers or presenters

What can we learn through the mass media?

Films
   Feature films
   Documentaries
   Educational films
Television programs
Radio
Other media (filmstrips, tape recordings, etc.)

Such brainstorming and researching may require several days to
a week of class time. What is produced is an extensive list of print,
non-print, and human resources for exploration, both inside and
outside the school walls.

What happens next will be dictated, in large measure, by the
kinds of resources that have been listed. If students are conducting
interviews, they may telephone for appointments, then make visits
after school hours. Some students will head off for the library for
research in books; others may go to the business education rooms
to type a series of letters. A speakers committee may be formed to
invite consultants to visit the class.

Finally, the students condense and synthesize findings to share with rest of the class. Reports may be written and read, presented through visual media, or turned into a panel discussion or drama. As in the "webbing" approach described in Chapter 8, the full spectrum of print and non-print language forms should be seen as possibilities.

2. COMMUNITY-BASED LITERACY PROJECTS

There are no rigid rules for reality-centered projects. "Reality" can be discovered inside the classroom as well as out on the streets, and community resources are so diverse that one is reluctant to set limitations of any sort on their possible use in school-related programs. The program descriptions that follow barely scratch the surface but suggest the diversity and depth of community-based literacy projects.

Understanding Language and Media. Marshall McLuhan, the controversial "media prophet," has, along with Kathryn Hutchon and Eric McLuhan, prepared a useful book for secondary level students, *City as Classroom: Understanding Language and Media* (1977). It involves both community-based learning experiences and an examination of the media of contemporary society.

The authors begin by explaining a concept familiar to readers of McLuhan's books: Figure/Ground Analysis. "Ground," they explain, is the background on which "figures"—the images we perceive—are imprinted. "Ground," McLuhan argues, often becomes so familiar to us that we ignore its effects on us: We can recall the pattern on somebody's necktie but can't tell you the background color of the tie itself (much less the color of the person's shirt or coat). In *City as Classroom,* students are shown that media are part of the ground on which they live. TV, for example, is so pervasive and common that we become unaware of its effects on us. Thus, though a single program may shock, delight, amuse, or revolt us (a single "figure"), we tend to forget that day in and day out television affects our perceptions and values (the "ground").

The authors include newspapers, magazines, books, photographs, television, videotape, and telephone in their study, but then go a step farther to include as "media" such technological and cultural phenomena as the automobile, light bulbs, computers, planes, satellites, and money. While these latter are not communications media in the usual sense, they do have latent "messages" (the way we use and value dollars, for example, tells a good deal about who we are) and they clearly influence our lives, almost minute by minute.

The community-based part of the McLuhan program involves explorations of the media. The authors outline dozens of projects and explorations for each form, sending students out to study effects. For example, for the lightbulb, they ask:

What sort of effect has fluorescent lighting on fabric colors and design and fashion and clothing design? What effect has it on makeup?

For the telephone:

Why can't most people resist answering a ringing phone? Are there groups of people who despise or fear or resent the phone?

On radio and news reporting:

Ask radio news reporters how a radio news story is put together from incoming information, what governs rejection of items not used and the editing of items that are used. Look for any clues of assumptions made about the audience, their interests, attention span or bias. Does the news vary greatly from one station to another?

The computer:

Find out what kinds of agencies keep computerized files on people. For what segment of population does each agency keep information on file? What kinds of information does each keep? What happens when the computer registers erroneous information about someone? Can anyone find out what information *is* on tape about him or her? What must a person do to correct misinformation?

Money:

Should our society return to a barter system, exchanging bicycles for baby carriages or live cattle for groceries?

Most exciting about this approach is its emphasis on teaching new patterns of seeing, new ways of thinking about and using communications media. Through *City as Classroom* the students use community resources, not simply to amass information, but to learn a new way of perceiving themselves and their environment.

Skills in Citizen Action. One of the most detailed community-based projects that I have encountered was developed at the University of Wisconsin by Professor Fred Newman and his staff at the Citizen Participation Project (1977). The model program is proposed as a full year of study, with students taking three English/social studies courses each of two semesters. (The authors acknowledge that some practical scheduling problems exist here, but the problems seem to have been solved in the Madison-area high schools where the program was piloted.) The courses alternate between school and community, with academic courses being taught in the school and internships taking place in town.

During the fall semester the students enroll in three closely related courses:

Political-Legal Process Course. School based, this is a civics or government course, exploring the structure of the political-legal system, human rights and legal processes, and political structures.

Communications Course. Also school based, this course studies English from the point of view of effective communications, beginning with personal communications (writing and reading for oneself), and moving through group and public writing and speaking.

Community Service Internship. Here the students work in the town, two full mornings each week, with an afternoon seminar to discuss issues and problems. Students are placed in volunteer service positions in social agencies, government bodies, public interest groups, and so on, both to learn about the organization and its procedures and to offer genuine services as aides or helpers.

During the second semester the focus of the course moves more directly into community participation through three more courses.

Citizen Action Project. Consuming the major block of the students' time—four mornings per week—the course places students in teams to work on influencing public policy—working for public or civic improvements. The aim is for the students to select an area of their community where change is needed and work to accomplish that change. The community action project is also accompanied by skill clinics to teach specific skills—e.g., canvassing, petitioning—that the students need in their work.

Action in Literature Course. While engaged in trying to change the town in which they live, the students also make connections between their own interests and those reflected in literature. A thematic course, "Action in Literature," has the students examine fiction, poetry, drama, and nonfiction dealing with social and civic change with writers from Gandhi and Thoreau to Robert Penn Warren and James Baldwin.

Public Message. This is the final component of the program, developed late in the second semester. The students synthesize the results of their community action project and create a presentation that may be a formal report; a radio, video, or cable TV program; a play; a film or photo essay. Through the communications project the students try to assess their learning.

To many teachers and parents, this kind of program seems terribly complicated ("We could never do that here") and even dangerous ("We don't want a bunch of kids running around trying to change things"). Yet in many ways, this program offers an ideal model for education. The schools have long claimed that they educate children "to participate fully and intelligently in a democracy." If that is so, why not give the kids a crack at actually doing what the school claims they can do?

However, if internships seem too complex for a school and community, the concept of school-based community action projects still remains a possibility. For instance, in *The Great Learning Book* (1977), Ann Rahnasto Bogojavlensky and Donna R. Grossman propose a unit in "Law Related Education," which allows students to understand the law and to see how they can exercise control through it. The unit includes discussion of safety laws and regulations, gun laws, citizen rights, and shoplifting. Activities range from writing safety booklets for distribution to younger children, to launching a campaign to publicize the laws relating to minibikes, all conducted within the school, but with clear impact on the community.

Schools Without Walls. Philadelphia's Parkway Program is a community-based high school developed in the late 1960s, which has provided the model for numerous city-as-schoolhouse projects across the country. In the Parkway Program (Bremer, 1971) students learn directly through internship projects, developed in cooperation with school tutors and local businesses and institutions. Academic credit is given in appropriate subjects for each experience, so that through careful selection of experiences a student can earn his or her diploma. Although Parkway has a number of political as well as practical problems, it has been widely praised as an alternative to conventional education.

Other cities have experimented with these kinds of alternatives. Arthur Greenberg (1976), assistant director of a New York City city-as-school project, has described some of his school's offerings in English:

—*Journalism:* working on the staff of a community newspaper.

—*Research Assistant:* helping a nonfiction writer research and collate information for a book.

—*Theater Apprenticeship:* everything from sweeping the floor to reading scripts and helping to mount a production.

—*Public Relations:* writing press releases for a light opera company.

—*American Studies:* working on a historical newsletter for a museum.

—*Speech Pathology Assistantship:* tutoring pre-school students who have speech problems.

While few cities have the richness of New York City to offer students, no town, no matter how small, is totally devoid of opportunities. Leon Westbrock (1973) has described a community-based project he launched, single-handedly, as the only English teacher in rural Hoffman, Minnesota. Although facilities were limited, Westbrock worked with three institutions—a nursing home, an activity center for retarded children and adults, and an elementary school—to provide fifty hours of tutoring experience for each junior and senior in the high school. Students were given training in discussion and tutoring skills, introduced to the kinds of people and problems they might encounter at each institution, then sent into the field—with appropriate supervision and evaluation—to work with people of all ages.

English and Careers

Career education has been a hot topic in education in recent years, attracting a considerable number of school and Federal dollars as well as a lot of print. I have written disparagingly about some career education programs earlier in this book, and as part of a chapter on language and community it seems appropriate to amplify those criticisms and to describe in detail the sound career education options that exist, particularly with reference to reading and writing.

I want to initiate my discussion by saying that I am in no way opposed to the schools' preparing children for careers (whether careers in business and industry or professions that carry them into higher education). At the same time, it seems to me wasteful of human resources—both children's and teachers'—to perceive of the schools as exclusively career oriented. The fact is, a great many real life skills can only be learned on the job, and that includes many language skills. The philosophy of education that I have espoused throughout this book is essentially one that values the traditional liberal education: We must educate children— through language—to the level of their capabilities, by providing a broad, general (but by no means impractical) education that will provide them with the ability to respond creatively to situations they may face in later life.

A great many career education programs, in contrast, focus on teaching what's called "the marketable skill," with the aim of providing each student with at least one such skill before he or she graduates. On the surface that goal seems quite reasonable, and politically it is quite astute, which is why such programs are easily mandated. It seems "reasonable" to suppose that after twelve years of schooling at the taxpayers' expense a child should be able to go out and get a job rather than winding up on the welfare rolls or in the unemployment office. But such reasoning buries a number of assumptions about the nature of education and work. Is schooling responsible for the nation's employment picture? Can the schools realistically prepare anyone for the specifics of a job in the distant future? Who determines "marketability"? If schools must train for careers, do employers want to accept the high school diploma in lieu of their own application forms and interviews?

Most important, when the schools try to offer training for a specific job, they start playing a kind of Russian roulette with the job market. For example, in the 1960s colleges discovered teacher shortages in both schools and colleges and geared up to produce large numbers of new teachers. But by the 1970s, when these programs had begun to operate at full strength, the post-World War II baby boom had begun to decline, the nation went into recession, and the demand for college graduates shifted to other areas. As of this writing, the universities are producing thousands and thousands of unemployed and unemployable teachers. In the meantime, shortages in other areas have cropped up. At the moment, veterinarians and business specialists are in great demand, and university programs are expanding to accommodate. While the mistakes of the 1960s may not be repeated, it seems distinctly possible that ten years from now we'll experience a glut of vets and business people on the job market. While this may drive down the price of getting your dog spayed or your tax records prepared, it certainly won't have helped thousands of people find work through the possession of a "marketable skill."

Career preparation involves far more than simply anticipating the vagaries of supply and demand. Even if we could forecast job needs with one-to-one accuracy—one graduate for every vacancy on the market—to focus on supplying the marketable skill seems inadvisable. In the first place, it has only short-range emphasis, preparing students for jobs they will take at age seventeen or twenty-two, rather than considering what they will be doing, needing, and wanting at, say, age forty or fifty. Second, it carries the danger of forcing career choices prematurely, so that young people barely into adolescence must turn their attention to the nine-to-five routines of adulthood.

I now want to outline a career education program that seems to me to avoid the pitfalls of a marketable skills approach, while still helping students see that their education makes connections with the real world. Most important, I want to show the centrality of *the word*—of language study—to any kind of career exploration. For whether one is entering carpentry, counseling, teaching, or aerospace technology, language is central to the process of learning about jobs and often crucial to performing successfully on the job.

Work as a Medium. Work pervades our society and our culture, and our lives and the lives of our children literally revolve around work. (It's no accident that so many terms in education draw on the language of work: *assignment, task, deadlines, assessment.*) Yet as McLuhan would observe, *work* has become a part of the "ground" of our lives, the background against which other "figures" appear. Just as most people are unaware of how television has affected their perceptions, a great many of us are unconscious of how jobs and careers influence how we think and act day by day.

To begin a career program, then, students can investigate work as if it were a *medium,* like TV, the newspaper, or the lightbulb. Students should ask questions, not just about the requirements for specific careers, but about the effects of work and careers on the way people think and act and feel. Students might explore some of the following:

—What would it be like if everybody didn't have to go to work every day? How would life change?

—Interview people about how their job influences their life. Does their work intrude on their life? Supplement it? Occupy a central part in it?

—How would life change if we went to a four- or three-day work week?

— What does a person's career have to do with his or her self-image? What careers seem "glamorous"? Which seem routine? How might a person in either feel about himself or herself?

—Do people hold jobs chiefly to earn money or for some other reason(s)?

—What is the relation between education and getting a job? Do you need an education to get a job? What jobs? What do people in education say about this? What do people on the job say? Can you explain any differences?

—Investigate credentials, certificates, and diplomas. What do these pieces of paper have to do with jobs?

—What feelings do people have toward the unemployed?

—Look at the way work is portrayed on television. What jobs do people have? Which jobs are portrayed most frequently? What kinds of actors are selected to represent different jobs?

—Do some historical work on apprenticeships. How did the apprenticeship system work? Do you think it was a good or bad way of training people? Could it work today?

—What is "the work ethic"? Does it exist today?

—Investigate the future of work in this country. How are work patterns likely to change in the coming fifty years (your lifetime)?

As students explore such questions, reading can provide an important resource. Almost every major writer in this century has touched on the topics of work, careers, the work ethic, and so on. Studs Terkel's *Working* (1974) presents a series of interviews with Chicagoans that touch on a great many of the questions I have listed above. The book is readable and realistic and can be used as a resource with high school students. William O'Rourke has anthologized a number of short fictional pieces in *On the Job* (1977), including selections by Wilfred Sheed, Bernard Malamud, Ken Kesey, Nelson Algren, Joyce Carol Oates, and John Updike. Science fiction provides a gold mine for discussion, as writers regularly present visions of careers in the future, either evolutions of existing jobs or new occupations generated by the needs of the twenty-first century and intergalactic travel. Even children's literature has evolved a career component, and contemporary children's books make a point of portraying work realistically, including working mothers and women with executive and professional careers.

It is crucial to stress that when literature is brought into a discussion of work and jobs, teachers should not distort either literature or careers. It seems fruitless to search for examples of occupations in literature or to use such nuggets as an opportunity to introduce career preparation materials: "Under the spreading chestnut-tree/ The village smithy stands, . . ." "Now class, who can tell us what training is required to become a blacksmith?"

Rather, careers, jobs, and work should be discussed only as they shape the plot, influence the characters, or reflect human problems and values. For instance, in John Updike's "A&P," a short story frequently taught in school and college English classes, a cashier at the A&P quits his job when the store manager rudely ejects some girls who enter the store wearing bathing suits. The story should not be treated as somehow centered on the theme of work or as something on the merits and deficiencies of a career as a cashier. Nevertheless, the motifs of regimentation, routine, and humiliation enter into the story, both in the narrator's view of his work and in the manager's dehumanized treatment of the girls, and such topics merit discussion as a natural part of the story. Furthermore, most of the high school and college discussions of the story I have observed or led have boiled down to the question, "Should the cashier have quit?" The answers frequently reflect the student's unconscious view—his or her "ground"-ing—in the work ethic. Whether the students respond positively or negatively to that discussion question tells a good deal about their priorities: work-and-the-paycheck versus moral decisions. Without being judgmental or distorting literary appreciation, a teacher can help students perceive how these values affect their response to literature and, in turn, how work values penetrate their lives.

Making Decisions. Several years ago as editor of *The English Journal* I published an essay entitled "Choosing: How To, Not What." The author of the article, Eva Moore (1975), was a retired English teacher, then seventy-eight years old. She told me, "I keep myself busy writing activity strategies for the elderly at a nursing home, so they won't let their minds go to waste." Ms. Moore's article describes a high school course in "Choosing," and as I read the article and have thought about its ideas since, that course seems to me one of the most important a student could ever take.

Young people are always being told to make decisions, Ms. Moore suggests, but they are given very little instruction in how to make choices. Thus when they enter the real world they are frequently lost, without teacher or parent to tell them either what to choose—as a career, as a lifestyle—or whom to choose—as a spouse, as a boss, as a friend. In her scenario for the course, Eva Moore begins:

You have been taught that teachers ask questions and students must answer. That's acceptable practice in some areas, but not in a class called *Choosing.*

The thrust of the course was for the students to raise questions, think about and discuss answers, and explore ways of finding answers to their own questions. The scenario continues:

What about questions? What about answers? Do you have questions for which you must have correct answers?
Is the right answer the same one for each of you?
If you need different answers, do I know each of those different answers? Do I know to whom each belongs?
What kinds of questions are there?
About facts?

About opinions?
About feelings?
About beliefs?

Who has these questions?
You, one student?
Every student the same question?
The teacher? ME? Do I have questions you can answer to help me?
Every teacher the same questions?
Everybody?
Every you / me identical, no me / SELF, no you / SELF, just a bunch of anne non mouses?

Who has the answers?
Shall we get ourselves a computer?
Where does a computer get answers?
Who will program it?
Will the program be identical to you? To me?

The course then had the students assess themselves as human beings and as learners. How do I learn best? How do I go about making choices now? The students discussed decision-making: How does one use information and/or intuition to make a choice? Where do one's values and expectations enter in? What kind of help can you get in making a choice? How can you determine whether a decision was a good one?

Finally, the students used the class as a laboratory and made a decision on a problem they proposed themselves or on one of a series of models proposed by the teacher. It seems to me that this experimental phase would also be a good place to provide off-campus experiences, with students exploring the making of choices in society, participating in the decision-making process, and observing results.

Eva Moore did not make direct reference to career planning in her course, and in most respects it is appropriate that she did not. The purpose of the course was to teach the process of choosing with the expectation that students themselves would encounter career choices, family choices, and moral decisions on which to practice their skill. However, two books edited by Joyce Slayton Mitchell, *Free To Choose: Decision Making for Young Men* and *Other Choices for Becoming a Woman* (1977), make a connection with career planning in addition to addressing themselves to the broader topic of decision-making. In *Free To Choose*, for example, Mitchell includes essays on making sexual choices, choosing friends and spouses, deciding about drugs and alcohol, discovering one's sexual identity, and making spiritual choices, before moving on to athletic, educational, and career choices. Both books could be used productively in Moore's course on choosing.

Courses in Career Planning. For my money, offering students the experiences described in the previous two sections—exploring work as a ground of experience and learning about the process of choosing—would offer satisfactory preparation for the world of work for a majority of young people. It seems appropriate, too, that schools use community-based projects. The methods and techniques of the *Yellow Pages* approach seem ideal for allowing young people to immerse themselves in the world of work and understand how it functions. (So, might it be added, are programs like Westbrock's tutorial program and the Wisconsin internship project.) Thus instead of dealing with pre-packaged curriculum materials, students might write their own career education book. Young people with a specific interest in, say, public service work, a skilled trade, the law, medicine, teaching, business, or social work would seek out professionals in the community and ask questions like the following:

—What do you do all day?

—How much training did you receive? Where did you get it? Where should a young person interested in the career consider going for training?

—How much do people in your line of work make? How does promotion work? Who determines pay raises?

—What are the drawbacks to this line of work that you didn't know about when you entered it? Were there advantages or positive aspects that you didn't anticipate?

—What's the job market like these days in your field? Could you move to a new state and find a job easily?

In exploring educational opportunities, the students might make a study of the colleges and vocational schools and learn about such matters as:

—Cost

—Schedule (Does the school teach at night? Do you have to go full time?)

—Placement and counseling services offered

—Curriculum (What courses are required? Which are elective?)

Students can frequently arrange to have college or training school representatives come to class to speak. Alternatively, the students can visit the institution itself to interview admissions officers, view the campus, review facilities, and talk to students.

Finally, any career course needs to concern itself with the literacy forms of the job world. We've all heard enough about high school graduates who cannot fill out an application blank to know *that* basic skill should be covered. Students should also receive precise instruction on preparing vitae and résumés, opening a file at a placement service, securing letters of recommendation, writing job application letters, applying to colleges or vocational schools, taking civil service and college aptitude tests, reading classified "help wanted" ads, and seeking out other sources of employment information. Most of these skills and forms can be taught to upper-level high school students as they apply for summer jobs, for college, or for an actual career. Those items that can't be taught in actual practice can often be simulated (e.g., a role-play of a job interview) or described by outside speakers and consultants. Nor should teaching these forms preoccupy teachers for a long period of time. Job-related literacy forms can be taught efficiently through a short-term mini-course or elective, or a series of workshops offered jointly by the counseling, business, and English departments.

Most important, these job-specific skills of literacy can be mastered successfully only if the students have a thorough grounding in reading and writing extending back through the elementary years. The problem with a young person who bungles a job application or writes poorly on a résumé is not his or her lack of knowledge of forms, but lack of a broader kind of literacy. Teaching the filling out of forms to students who have a solid background in reading, writing, listening, and speaking is relatively easy. We can assume, further, that such people will succeed with the on-the-job literacy demands they encounter, whether reading assembly line instructions or writing insurance forms. For the student who hasn't written or read much, who has spent his or her time in workbooks or drills—or even in a specialized business English class—instruction in application writing may be largely a waste of time.

Reading and Writing Within the Community

It has long been an aim of English programs to make students "life-long" readers and users of good English; yet curiously, language use is largely ignored and left to chance (or merely complained about) in a great many communities. What people read and write may or may not bear any relationship to their school learning, and nobody seems to care about finding out. Clearly, literacy outside the walls of the schoolhouse is a community concern, not exclusively that of a board of education. Yet if the schools' concern for developing students to function in a literate society is genuine, they must enlarge their focus. The school and community must ensure that interest in reading and writing does not end with receipt of a high school diploma, that understanding the processes of literacy is not restricted to inside the school.

Newsletters and Magazines. In Bellport, New York, Emily

Stong improved school/parent relationships and promoted literacy by turning the school newspaper into a community journal. She observed that most school papers are relatively expensive and thoroughly inefficient, put out by a small clique of journalism students. The paper frequently carries last week's news plus a little bit of school gossip and serves little real purpose. Stong launched *The Dinghy,* an alternative newspaper that had as its stated purpose "to print (or request the rewriting for publication of) every article submitted to it." While some members of the community felt this editorial policy was too liberal, it served its purposes of attracting previously unpublished writers, including both students and some of Bellport's "closet writers." The editorial board, members of an informal Writers Club, evaluated all manuscripts submitted. If a paper did not seem acceptable (if, for example, it included language that the Club felt would be offensive to members of the community), it would be sent back to the author with instructions for revision. Guest writers for *The Dinghy* included the editor of the *Long Island Advance,* a local novelist, the principal and various faculty members, and a number of community members. Mimeographed copies of the magazine were given to contributors, the librarian, English teachers, and any member of the school or community who cared to request one. The magazine came out more frequently than the school newspaper and it wound up costing less money.

Outsiders In: Parents as Teachers. Volumes have been written on the use of parents as paid or unpaid paraprofessionals in the schools, so I will limit myself to observing that drawing on parents in this way strengthens relationships between school and community and provides an extraordinary boost to the reading/writing program. Whether or not they have much formal training, parents can tutor in reading and writing, edit young people's papers, assist the staff of the newspaper or yearbook, and generally provide the kind of relief that allows the teacher to do "all those things I've wanted to do, but haven't had the time."

Community-based learning projects naturally involve parents as teachers in the fields of their expertise. The father or mother who is an attorney comes to school to speak or is interviewed about his/her profession; the dry cleaner and mayor become involved in the education of their own (and other people's) children; hobbyists, craftsmen, and artisans are given a chance to show their skills; and the community elders have an opportunity to share their knowledge with the younger generation.

It is also useful for the schools to involve parents in book and materials selection procedures. The number of censorship cases in the courts in the past decades indicates that parents want more of a say in the books their children will read. However, this should not mean giving community members absolute veto power over the books used in school. A review group can provide a positive service by examining the new material that is made available to teachers each year and helping the schools make selections. Instead of censoring books, parents must actively search for materials they would like to see taught. A review group could also concern itself with the whole question of the management of materials: How can we guarantee the rights of students to read without impinging on the rights of some community members to have their children not read what they consider objectionable material?

Learning Exchanges. Although I have argued against the completely deschooled society on practical grounds, alternative learning experiences are currently very popular with adults and young people and provide a useful supplement to the schools. In the San Francisco Bay Area, for example, a newspaper describing non-institutionalized courses and educational experiences is circulated to over 100,000 people, and it lists experiences ranging from creative and expository writing to the art of constructing castles in the sand. Kansas City's Learning Exchange, staffed largely by community volunteers, offers a range of courses in the arts, education, humanities, and community living. Alternative schools, most financed privately, have sprung up all over the country to offer informal education for school-age children. Arts, crafts, and writers' collaboratives offer instruction to those willing to learn, and YMCAs and YWCAs have gotten into the act and now teach everything from Yoga to Chinese Cooking. Nor have public institutions been excluded from this kind of deschooled learning. For generations libraries have offered their own educational programs—films, speakers and lecturers, instructional programs, and so on. Several years ago federal proposals were developed to teach adult illiterates to read, and the site for these "reading academies" was the public library, an approach that brought the learner to the source of materials. Given the fact that libraries are also sources of writing reference materials, it seems to me they would be well advised to set up informal writing centers as well, places where community members of all ages could go for assistance with writing projects.

The schools themselves are beginning to expand non-traditional education offered during late afternoons and evenings. It seems predictable that as they do more of this kind of teaching, they will begin to realize the value of alternative programs as part of the conventional school curriculum. Thus evening schools may themselves come to offer an alternative model for schooling.

Life-Long Learning Programs. The competition created by deschooled learning exchanges has also been good for the public institutions and their life-long learning programs. For instance, adult education courses were for many years limited to basic literacy and naturalization courses. In recent years, however, an array of courses for all interests has evolved. Similarly, in many areas universities have developed "free" or Saturday colleges that offer inexpensive courses in subjects not covered by the usual curriculum at places and times that make them accessible to people who cannot afford to be full-time students. University English departments have begun to move off campus in the past few years, developing reading and writing courses for non-traditional students: inmates at prisons, the elderly, community groups, and so on.

Life-long learning programs have never come close to measuring up to their full potential. As the work week continues to grow shorter, as more and more young people cont nue to graduate from secondary school and college, and as the mass media continue to make diverse experiences available inexpensively to more and more people, it seems likely that the demand for both formal and informal life-long learning opportunities will increase. The teaching and using of literacy skills ought to play a central part in this expansion.

3. CAREERS IN WORDSMITHING

I would be remiss if I closed this book without pointing out that society is highly dependent on wordsmiths—professional users of language—for its day-to-day operation. The quality of language produced by the wordsmiths has a strong influence on our lives, affecting everything from newspapers to politics.

English is not presently a popular major in college. "What can you do with it besides teach?" is the usual query from students who come to my office. First off, I have to note that teaching English is a pretty satisfying, if often frustrating career. At the moment, though, there are too many English teachers and too few jobs (despite the fact that English classes are badly overcrowded). Nevertheless, some of the most interesting, vibrant people I know are among the half million or so engaged in teaching reading and writing to young people and adults.

Language use extends far beyond the community of those who teach it, however. For example, though they would prefer to be called "defenders of the public trust," attorneys and politicians are, in fact, wordsmiths; they wheel and deal in English, translating human concerns into legal language and interpreting human actions in terms of words.

Though print is said to be dead, the volume of books, magazines, and newsletters being published in this country suggests something to the contrary. The production of print creates the need for a range of professional language users: editors, columnists, reporters, rewriters, copyeditors, proofreaders, and headline writers. Librarians are wordsmiths too, and in modern libraries do far more than just file, catalog, and retrieve books. The advertising industry is language based to a high degree and supplies work for people who write and evaluate questionnaries, prepare and test copy, and write the ads. Although one has to question seriously the quality of much of what the ad people sell, there is no denying that some of the most creative language we see today comes from advertising agencies.

Poets are wordsmiths who come in two main varieties: underpaid and starving. Yet a good many people in this country manage to make a living as professional creative writers. A glance at *Writer's Market* shows the myriad possibilities for picking up a buck writing stories, articles, fillers, jokes, riddles, and even a poem or two, and the circulation of a magazine like *The Writer* shows that there are thousands and thousands of writers trying to pick up those bucks, many of them successfully. Among the most successful are those who can write about scientific and technical matters, preparing everything from lab reports to instructions on how to assemble a bicycle or lawn spreader.

The communications industry is one of wordsmithing: Whether one is working in bits, bytes, and FORTRAN at the computer center or figuring out how to bounce thousands of messages off a satellite simultaneously, the end of the process is translating messages into English so that somebody can think and act on them. Even Ma Bell, who seems intent on killing off print by having us spend our money on long distance phone calls will, for the time being, need to employ people who can read and write as well as speak and listen.

The list of wordsmiths goes on and on: disc jockeys, weather forecasters, business executives, public relations people, paralegal professionals, secretaries. . . . For a few of these, a specialist's degree in English or communications will be required. For all, a school system and community committed to quality literacy instruction seem vital.

Most important, however, is that language is what binds all of us together in the human community. We are all inexorably committed to careers as wordsmiths.

Bibliography

Abruscato, Joe, and Jack Hassard. *Loving and Beyond: Science Teaching for the Humanistic Classroom.* Pacific Palisades, California: Goodyear Publishing, 1976.

A Child's Introduction to Historical Alexandria. Alexandria, Virginia: American Association of University Women, n.d.

Agee, Jane M. "The Realities of College Composition Courses." *The English Journal* 66 (November 1977): 58–60.

Angoff, William. "Why the SAT Scores Are Going Down." *The English Journal* 64(March 1975): 10–11.

Arbuthnot, May Hill. *Children and Books.* Glenview, Illinois: Scott, Foresman, 1972.

Barth, Carl. "Kinds of Language/Knowledge Required by College Entrance Examinations." *The English Journal* 54(December 1965): 824–829.

Beach, Leondus. "Old Testament Literature." *The English Journal* 64(January 1975): 72.

Beach, Richard. "Self-Evaluation in an Activity-Oriented Classroom." *The English Journal* 64(March 1975): 59–63.

Beck, Robert, ed. *Uses, Abuses, Misuses of Standardized Tests in English.* Urbana, Illinois: National Council of Teachers of English, 1973.

Behrens, Laurence. "Writing, Reading, and the Rest of the Faculty: A Survey." *The English Journal* 67(September 1978): 54–60.

Berger, Patrick, and Lane Page. "From Laputa to Bioethics." *The English Journal* 65(October 1976): 52–54.

Blodgett, J. H. "Claims of English Grammar in Common Schools." *Journal of the Proceedings of the National Education Association* (1870): 160–164.

Bogojavlensky, Ann Rahnasto, and Donna R. Grossman. *The Great Learning Book*. Menlo Park, California: Addison-Wesley, 1977.

Bremer, John, and Michael Von Moschzisker. *The School Without Walls*. New York: Holt, Rinehart, and Winston, 1972.

Brill, Stephen. "The Secrecy Behind the College Boards." *New York* (October 7, 1974): 67–83.

Britton, James Nimmo. *The Development of Writing Abilities (11–18)*. London: Macmillan Education, 1975.

Bruner, Jerome. *The Process of Education*. New York: Vintage, 1960.

Carlsen, G. Robert. "Literature IS." *The English Journal* 63(February 1974): 23–27.

Chronicle of Higher Education, The. "All's Not Well Aboard the 'Indomitable' " (October 3, 1977): 40.

Cianciolo, Patricia, ed. *Adventuring with Books*. Urbana, Illinois: National Council of Teachers of English, 1977.

Cleaver, Eldridge. *Soul on Ice*. New York: McGraw-Hill, 1968.

Coggins, Kim, and Ron Emaus. "Analysis and Synthesis in Education." Unpublished paper, Michigan State University, 1976.

College Entrance Examination Board. *On Further Examination: Report of the Advisory Panel on the Scholastic Aptitude Test Score Decline*. New York: College Entrance Examination Board, 1977.

Comers, Mary C. "Myths and Modern Man." *The English Journal* 64(January 1975): 70.

Conant, James Bryant. *The American High School Today*. New York: McGraw-Hill, 1959.

Conference on College Composition and Communication. "Students' Right to Their Own Language." *College Composition and Communication* 25(Fall 1974).

Cooper, Charles. "Measuring Growth in Writing." *The English Journal* 64(March 1975): 111–119.

Cox, Burton. "The High School English Teacher, the College Freshman Composition Instructor, and Walt Whitman." *The English Journal* 62(December 1973): 1245–1247.

Creber, J. W. Patrick. *Sense and Sensitivity*. London: University of London Press, 1965.

Cushman, William. "A Letter to Parents." *The English Journal* 66(October 1977): 45–48.

Daigon, Arthur. *Violence U.S.A.* New York: Bantam, 1975.

Daniels, Harvey. "Is There a Decline in Literacy?" *The English Journal* 65(September 1976): 17, 19–20.

Davis, Kenneth, and John Hollowell, eds. *Inventing and Playing Games in the English Classroom*. Urbana, Illinois: National Council of Teachers of English, 1977.

DeLaIglesia, Marie. *A Catalogue of American Catalogues*. New York: Random House, 1973.

Diederich, Paul. *Measuring Growth in English*. Urbana, Illinois: National Council of Teachers of English, 1974.

Dixon, John. *Growth Through English*. London: National Association for the Teaching of English, 1967, 1975.

Donelson, Kenneth, ed. *Books for You*. Urbana, Illinois: National Council of Teachers of English, 1976.

———. "Censorship in the 1970's." *The English Journal* 63(February 1974): 47–51.

Dyer, Daniel. "When Kids Are Free To Write." *The English Journal* 65(May 1976): 34–41.

Dyer, Henry. "Testing Little Children: Some Old Problems in New Settings." *Childhood Education* (April 1974).

Elbow, Peter. *Writing Without Teachers*. New York: Oxford University Press, 1974.

Erikson, Erik. *The Child and Society*. New York: Basic Books, 1963.

Eyewitness. Princeton, New Jersey: Visual Education Corporation, 1975.

Fader, Daniel. *Hooked on Books*. New York: Berkley Medallion, 1976.

Fantini, Mario. *The People and Their Schools: Community Participation*. Bloomington, Indiana: Phi Delta Kappa, 1975.

Franza, August. "ETF 2000." *The English Journal* 67(September 1978): 16–17.

Friedenberg, Edgar. *The Vanishing Adolescent*. New York: Dell, 1962.

Friend, Beverly. "Strange Bedfellows: Linguistics and Science Fiction." *The English Journal* 62(October 1973): 998–1003.

Fromm, Erich. *The Revolution of Hope: Toward the Humanistic Uses of Technology*. New York: Harper & Row, 1968.

Gattegno, Caleb. *Towards a Visual Culture*. New York: Discus/Avon, 1969.

Gay, Peter, ed. *John Locke on Education*. New York: Teachers College Bureau Publications, 1964: 154.

Gelb, I. J. *A Study of Writing*. Chicago: University of Chicago Press, 1965.

Geller, Conrad. "Guarding the Innocents: English Textbooks into the Breach." *The English Journal* 63(December 1974): 76–78.

Gere, Anne R. "writing and WRITING." *The English Journal* 66(November 1977): 60–64.

Gillis, Candida. "The English Classroom 1977." *The English Journal* 66(September 1977): 20–26.

Goodrich, Samuel Griswold. *The Tales of Peter Parley, in America.* Boston: Published by the author, 1827.

Greenberg, Arthur. "City as School: An Approach to External Interdisciplinary Education." *The English Journal* 65(October 1976): 60–62.

Hawes, Gene. *Educational Testing for the Millions: What Tests Really Mean for Your Child.* New York: McGraw-Hill, 1974.

Hayakawa, S. I. *Language and Thought in Action.* New York: Harcourt, Brace, Jovanovich, 1972.

Haynes, Elizabeth. "Using Research in Preparing To Teach Writing." *The English Journal* 67(January 1978): 82–88.

Hillerich, Robert L. "Toward an Assessable Definition of Literacy." *The English Journal* 65(February 1976): 50–55.

Hoffman, Banesh. *The Tyranny of Testing.* New York: Collier, 1964.

Hook, J. N. "My Love Song." *The English Journal* 66(October 1977): 14–17.

———. *The Story of American English.* New York: Harcourt, Brace, Jovanovich, 1972.

Horowitz, Edward. *Words Come in Families.* New York: Hart, 1977.

Howell, Suzanne. "The Research Paper Redux." *The English Journal* 66(December 1977): 52–55.

Illich, Ivan. "DeSchooling: A Working Paper for Discussion," in *De-Schooling, De-Conditioning.* Menlo Park, California: Portola Institute, 1971.

Insel, Deborah. "Foxfire in the City." *The English Journal* 64(September 1975): 36–38.

Jacobs, Suzanne. "Letter to the Editor." *The English Journal* 64(October 1975): 16–18.

Judy, Stephen (Senior Author), Patrick L. Courts, Geoffrey Summerfield, and Richard Peck. *The Creative Word I–VI.* New York: Random House, 1973, 1974.

Judy, Stephen. "A Likely Story." *The English Journal* 65(December 1977a): 7–8.

———. "The Semantics of Reading." *The English Journal* 63(November 1974): 7–8.

———. "Teacher 1999." *The English Journal* 66(October 1977b): 5–6.

————. "The Teaching of Composition in American Secondary Schools, 1850–1893." Northwestern University, unpublished doctoral dissertation, 1967.

Judy, Susan J. "The Spirit of '76 Revisited." *The Inkwell* (January 1977): 1–8.

Katzner, Kenneth. *The Languages of the World.* New York: Funk and Wagnalls, 1975.

Kirschenbaum, Howard, Rodney W. Napier, and Sidney Simon. *Wad-Ja-Get? The Grading Game in American Education.* New York: Hart, 1971.

Knapton, James. Quoted in *Newsweek* (December 8, 1975).

Konigsburg, Elaine L. "A Book Is a Private Thing." *Saturday Review* (November 6, 1970): 30–33.

Kozol, Jonathan. "The Politics of Syntax." *The English Journal* 64(December 1975): 22–27.

LaBrant, Lou. "The Profession in Perspective." *The English Journal* 66(February 1977): 6–7.

Lacan, Jacques. *The Language of the Self.* Baltimore: Johns Hopkins University Press, 1965.

Lampert, Kathleen, and Edna Saunders. "Readers and Nonreaders: What's the Difference?" *The English Journal* 65 (September 1976): 34–38.

Leavitt, Hart Day, and David Sohn. *Stop, Look, and Write.* New York: Bantam Books, 1964.

Lester, Mark. *Constructing an English Grammar.* New York: Random House, 1973.

Liston, Robert. *Getting in Touch with Your Government.* New York: Julian Messner, 1975.

Mackey, James. "Discussing Moral Dilemmas in the Classroom." *The English Journal* 66(December 1975): 28–30.

Manniche, Lisle. *How Djadja-Em-Ankh Saved the Day.* New York: T. Y. Crowell, 1976.

Marsh, Philip. *How To Teach English.* New York: Bookman Associates, 1956.

Martin, William, and Dan Verner. "To Cope with the Current." *The English Journal* 64(January 1975): 85–86.

McClelland, Marjorie. "The Nineteenth Century Meets the Media." *The English Journal* 63(October 1974): 85–86.

McDavid, Raven. *Americans Speaking.* Urbana, Illinois: National Council of Teachers of English, 1967.

McLuhan, Marshall, Kathryn Hutchon, and Eric McLuhan. *City as Classroom: Understanding Language and Media*. Agincourt, Ontario: Book Society of Canada, Ltd., 1977.

McLuhan, Marshall. *The Medium Is the Massage*. New York: Bantam, 1967.

————. *War and Peace in the Global Village*. New York: Bantam, 1968.

Meadows, Leon Renfroe. *The Teaching of English Composition in Teachers Colleges in the United States*. New York: Teachers College, Columbia University, 1928.

Mitchell, Joyce Slaton. *Free To Choose: Decision Making for Young Men and Other Choices for Becoming a Woman*. New York: Dell, 1977.

Moore, Eva A. "Choosing: How To, Not What." *The English Journal* 64(November 1975): 40–45.

Moran, Mary Jo. "Nobel Prize Winning Literature." *The English Journal* 66(September 1977): 59.

National Interest and the Teaching of English, The. Urbana, Illinois: National Council of Teachers of English, 1961.

Newman, Edwin. *A Civil Tongue*. Indianapolis: Bobbs, Merrill, 1976.

————. *Strictly Speaking*. Indianapolis: Bobbs, Merrill, 1974.

Newman, Fred, Thomas A. Bertocci, and Ruthanne M. Landsness. *Skills in Citizen Action*. Madison, Wisconsin: Citizen Participation Curriculum Project, 1977.

Nystrand, Martin. "The Politics of Rank Ordering." *The English Journal* 66(March 1975): 42–45.

Oakley, Don. Column appearing in the *Jackson (Michigan) Citizen Patriot* (February 5, 1975): 7.

Ohmann, Richard. *English in America*. New York: Oxford University Press, 1975.

Ornstein, Robert. *The Psychology of Consciousness*. New York: Penguin, 1972.

O'Rourke, William, ed. *On the Job*. New York: Vintage, 1977.

Page, Ernest. "Black Literature and Changing Values: Does It Do the Job?" *The English Journal* 66(March 1977): 29–34.

Passell, Peter. *How To*. New York: Ballantine, 1976.

Perkins, Flossie L. *Book and Non-Book Media*. Urbana, Illinois: National Council of Teachers of English, 1972.

Perrone, Vito. *The Abuses of Standardized Testing*. Bloomington, Indiana: Phi Delta Kappa, 1977a.

————. "Documentation: A Process for Classroom/Program Evaluation and Personal/Professional Learning." *INSIGHTS into Open Education* 9(April 1977b).

Piaget, Jean, and Barber Inhelder. *The Psychology of the Child.* New York: Basic Books, 1969.

Postman, Neil, and Charles Weingartner. *The School Book.* New York: Dell/Delacorte, 1973.

Quackenbos, George Pyn. *First Lessons in Composition.* New York: D. Appleton, 1841.

Rakes, Thomas, and Lana McWilliams. "Two Alternatives to the Standardized Test." *The English Journal* 67(October 1978): 48–50.

Reynolds, Jerry. "Alienation." *The English Journal* 64(January 1975): 56–57.

Reynolds, William. *The Nature of Language.* New York: Random House, 1973.

————. *Dialects in America.* New York: Random House, 1973.

Richmond, George. *The Micro-Society School.* New York: Harper & Row, 1973.

Rogers, Joseph. "Black, White, Language, and Decalang." *The English Journal* 64(April 1975): 30–34.

Rosen, Deborah. "American Nonfiction: Dreams and Nightmares." *The English Journal* 64(January 1975): 66.

Rosenblatt, Louise. *Literature as Exploration.* New York: Noble and Noble, 1968.

Ruchlis, Hy, and Belle Sharefkin. *Reality Centered Learning.* New York: Citation Press, 1975.

Schmidt, Jane. Letter to her daughter, Susan J. Judy, October 1977.

Scholastic American Literature Program, The. New York: Scholastic Magazines, 1977.

Shaughnessy, Mina. *Errors and Expectations.* New York: Oxford University Press, 1977.

Shaw, Phyllis. "Human Renewal Through Nature." *The English Journal* 65(April 1976): 64–65.

Shuy, Roger. *Discovering American Dialects.* Urbana, Illinois: National Council of Teachers of English, 1967.

Silberman, Charles. *Crisis in the Classroom.* New York: Random House, 1970.

Smith, Frank. *Understanding Reading.* New York: Holt, Rinehart and Winston, 1971.

Snider, Sarah. "Developing Non-Essay Tests To Measure Affective Response to Poetry." *The English Journal* 67(October 1978): 38–40.

Springer, Mark. "Science in the English Classroom." *The English Journal,* 65(October 1976): 35–36.

Squire, James, ed. *Response to Literature.* Urbana, Illinois: National Council of Teachers of English, 1968.

Squire, James, and Roger Applebee. *High School English Instruction Today.* New York: Appleton-Century-Crofts, 1968.

"Standardized Tests and Their Alternatives." *The English Journal* 67(October 1978).

Stilinovich, Charmaine. "Problems of the '70s." *The English Journal* 64(January 1975): 75.

Stokes, Ruth. "This World of English." *The English Journal* 65(February 1975): 20.

Stong, Emily. "Launching the Informal School Newspaper." *The English Journal* 66(May 1977): 37–40.

Suhor, Charles. *Mass Testing in Composition: Is It Worth Doing Badly?* New Orleans: New Orleans Public Schools, n.d.

Summerfield, Geoffrey. *Topics in Engish.* London: Batsford, 1965.

———. *Creativity in English.* Urbana, Illinois: National Council of Teachers of English, 1968.

Tashlik, Phyllis. "Science Fiction: An Anthropological Approach." *The Engish Journal* 64(January 1975): 78.

Terkel, Studs. *Working.* New York: Pantheon, 1974.

Thompson, Peggy. *Museum People.* Englewood Cliffs, New Jersey: Prentice-Hall, 1977.

Tracing Your Roots. Skokie, Illinois: Illustrated Publications, 1977.

Troyka, Lynn, and Gerrold Nodelman. *Taking Action.* Englewood Cliffs, New Jersey: Prentice-Hall, 1975.

Van Allen, Roach, and Dorris M. Lee. *Learning To Read Through Experience.* New York: Meredith, 1963.

Veley, Charles. *Catching Up.* New York: M. Evans, 1978.

Wagner, Maria, and Jeanette Ainsworth. *Basic Concepts in the Humanities.* Ann Arbor, Michigan: University Microfilms, 1977.

Walker, Jerry L. *Your Reading.* Urbana, Illinois: National Council of Teachers of English, 1975.

Ward, C. H. *What Is English?* Chicago: Scott, Foresman, 1917.

Weisinger, Mort. *1001 Things You Can Get Free.* New York: Bantam, 1977.

Weitzman, David. *Underfoot: An Everyday Guide to Exploring the American Past.* New York: Scribners, 1976.

Westbrock, Leon. "INPUT: A Communications Experience." *The English Journal* 62(October 1973): 1004–1007.

Whitehead, Alfred North. *The Aims of Education*. New York: Macmillan, 1929.

"Why Johnny Can't Write." *Newsweek* (December 8, 1976).

Wilkinson, Sylvia, and Ed Campbell, eds. *Change: A Handbook for the Teaching of Social Studies and English*. Durham, North Carolina: LINC Press, 1971.

Wilsford, James. "The Experience/Context Inventory." Unpublished paper, n.d.

Wood, Pamela, ed. *You and Aunt Arie: A Guide to Cultural Journalism Based on Foxfire and Its Descendants*. Washington, D.C.: Institutional Development and Economic Affairs Service, Inc., 1975.

Workman, Brooke. *Teaching the Decades: A Humanities Approach to American Civilization*. Urbana, Illinois: National Council of Teachers of English, 1975.

Wurman, Richard Saul, ed. *The Yellow Pages of Learning Resources*. Arlington, Virginia: National Association of Elementary School Principals, 1972.

Yesner, Seymour. "Let's Not Return to Basic Skills." *The English Journal* 62(September 1973): 892–895.

Index

Accountability, 93-95
Achievement, assessment of, 152. *See also* Tests
Administration, school: projects for, 112-120; support for programs, 102-104
Adolescent literature, 192, 193, 197, 199. *See also* Literature
Arbuthnot, May Hill, 130
Argument, 66
Articulation, 85-88, 118
Assessment of student needs, 110-114. *See also* Tests
Audience, 132, 205

"Back-to-basics," xii
Basic skills, 54-75; taxonomic model of, 55-57
Beach, Leondus, 216
Bias, cultural, 145
Binet, Alfred, 149
Blodgett, J. H., 7
Brill, Steven, 27-29
Bruner, Jerome, 47
Budgets, school, 116-117

Career education, 19, 308-10, 320-329, 343-345
Carlsen, G. Robert, 179-180
Censorship, 8 9
Change humanities program, 257-259
Children's literature, 121, 184, 240-243; Newbery Medal books, 186-187. *See also* Literature; Reading
Chronological literary study, 253-254
Cianciolo, Patricia, 130
Class size, 119, 123. *See also* Administration
Cleaver, Eldridge, 64
Cloze testing, 160
Collaborative learning, 127
College English, 39-40, 73-74, 95-96, 226-227
College Entrance Examination Board, 13, 25-33. *See also* Scholastic Aptitude Test
College preparation, 25-33, 95-96, 211-212, 305-307
Comers, Mary C., 218
Community: involvement, 104-106; projects for, 120-123; needs assess-

Community (*continued*)
  ment of, 113; visitors from,
  319-320; volunteers, 340-341
Community-based literacy projects,
  315-321
Community resources, reading and
  writing, 311-315
Composition. *See* Writing, and Oral
  English
Conference on College Composition
  and Communication, 36
Conferences, 161
Conversation, 120
Cooper, Charles, 157
Cox, Burton, 96-97
Creber, J. W. Patrick, 194
Crisis, literacy, xii; solutions to, 77-78.
  See also Literacy
Criterion-referenced tests, 153-154
Criticism, aesthetic, 230-231
Cultural history, 213
Culture, popular, 264-266. *See also*
  Humanities
Curriculum: elementary, 181-190; En-
  glish, 176-222; evaluation of,
  114-115; junior high/middle school,
  190-203; senior high, 203-220
Cushman, William, 120-122

Daigon, Arthur, 207
Daniels, Harvey, 35
Dartmouth seminar, 49
DeMott, Benjamin, 233-234
Dewey, John, 69, 149
Dialect study, 295
Diederich, Paul B., 156
Dimensional education, 17
Dixon, John, 177
Donelson, Kenneth, 9, 130
Drama, creative, 185-190
Dyer, Daniel, 89-90

Editors, students as, 127
Elbow, Peter, 85, 161
Elective courses, 26, 51, 104
Eliot, Charles W., 34, 36

English. *See* Curriculum, Language,
  Literacy, Literature, Reading, Writing
Evaluation, 138-165; philosophy of,
  149-151. *See also* Tests

Fader, Daniel, 84, 119
Failure, 76-77
Fantini, Mario, 78
Field trips, 315
Foxfire, 236-237
Free and inexpensive materials, 319
Friedenberg, Edgar, 191

Gattegno, Caleb, 270
Geller, Conrad, 7
Genre approach, literary, 254-255
Geographic-ethnocentric approach,
  literary, 254
Gillis, Candida, 51-52
Goodrich, Samuel Griswold, 6
Grading, 163-164
Grammar: as science, 296-297;
  "baby," 66; "new," 49-50; on SAT
  examination, 50. *See also* Language;
  Dialect
Grantsmanship, 118

Hazelton, Robert, 13
Herndon, James, 49
Hillerich, Robert L., 3, 16
Historical-cultural approach, literary,
  215-220
History, writing in, 98. *See also*
  Humanities
Holistic evaluation, 156
Holt, John, 49
Home instruction, 6, 183
Hook, J. N., 44, 264
Howell, Suzanne, 211-212
Humanities, 228-270; approaches to,
  251-256; backyard, 234; reading re-
  sources for, 240-251

Illich, Ivan, 309-310
Illiteracy: adult, 3; of non-standard
  speakers, 11

Insel, Deborah, 236-237
Interdisciplinary studies, xv, 67-68, 98-101, 129, 173-175; projects for subject teachers, 130-134
Internships, 327

Jackdaws, historical, 261-263
Jacobs, Suzanne, 97
Journalists: and the literacy crisis, 106; involvement in school affairs, 118

Knapton, James, 34
Konigsburg, Elaine, 3
Kozol, Jonathan, 12, 49

LaBrant, Lou, 42
Lampert, Kathleen, 90-91
Language: and community, 308-345; and perception, 58-67; and reality, 59; and thinking, 60-63; historical study of, 263-264; study as science, 293-298; uses of, 63-67
Learning: and knowing, 210-211, centers, 80, 128; exchanges, 341-342; life-long, 342
Leavitt, Hart Day, 194
Lee, Dorris, 182
Leonard, George, 49
Letter writing, 318-319
Lexicography, 297-298
Librarians, 124-125
Life-long learning, 342
Literacy: and financial reward, 6, 11; and journalists, 106-107; as learn-by-doing skill, 82-85; centers, 128; community-based projects, 325; definition of, 13-17; education, xvii; historical functions of, 5-8; image of, 10; in humanities, 228-270; inter-disciplinary, 99-101; of children, 15; of yesteryear, 41-46; projects for improving instruction, 111-137; science, 271
Literature: and science, 299-305; and status quo, 109; instructional methods, 127; multiethnic, 217,

246-249; secondary school, 208, 243-246
Locke, John, 7, 11
Lodge, Helen, 150
Logic, 66

Magazines, 131, 316-318
Marsh, Philip, 34, 37
Massachusetts School Laws, 6
Materials: instructional, 83; free, 319; saturation, 124
Maxwell, Rhoda, 275
McClelland, Marjorie, 237-238
McLuhan, Marshall, 268, 325, 332
Meadows, Leon Renfroe, 41-42
Media and English, 266-270
Minimum competencies, 148
Minority concerns, 108-109
Moore, Eva, 335-336
Moran, Mary Jo, 217

National Council of Teachers of English, 18, 103, 119
National Defense Education Act, 48-49
National Science Foundation, 47
Needs assessment, 113
New England Primer, 5
"New" English, 50-53
Newman, Edwin, 35-37
Non-readers, skilled, 91
Nystrand, Martin, 108

Ohmann, Richard, 12
On Further Examination, 30-32
Oral English, 127, 133, 185-190
Organic English, 178
Ornstein, Robert, 61

Paperback books, 49, 119
Parents: concerns of, 113; expectations of, 308; involvement of, xv, 119; projects for, 120-122
Performance mastery, 153-154
Perkins, Flossie, 130
Perrone, Vito, 149, 151

Pilot projects, 117
Plan A/Plan B thinking, 79-82
Postman, Neil, 267
Priorities, setting, 76-109
Project English, 48
Publication of student work, 128
Public criticism, xi

Quackenbos, George Pyn, 33

Reading: about science, 271-301; circles, 184; community resources for, 311-315; elementary years, 183-185; evaluating, 158; failures, 76-77; "free," 84-85; in subject classes, 131; oral English and, 120; skills, 90-91
Reference libraries, home, 121
Reform, educational, 78
Released time, 117
"Relevance," 50
Research, educational, 89-91
Research papers, 211-213
Reynolds, Jerry, 206
Right-To-Read, 3
Rogers, Joseph, 18
Romantic critics, 49
Rosen, Deborah, 219
Rosenblatt, Louise, 213
Ruchlis, Hy, 321-325

Saunders, Edna, 90-91
Schmidt, Jane, 44
Scholastic Aptitude Test, 25-33, 46, 50, 104, 109
School boards, projects for, 112-120
Schools without walls, 329-330
Science: and humanism, 304; humanistic teaching, 285-291; in English classes, 274-279; literacy in, 271-307; reading in, 99
Self-evaluation, 161; teacher, 164-165
Sequence, 85-88
Service clubs, 118
Sharefkin, Belle, 321-324
Shaughnessy, Mina, 108

Simulations, 320
Skills, basic, 83, 95, 201-205. See also Literacy
"Skyhooking," 146
Snow, C. P., 274
Sohn, David, 194
Sputnik, 45-47
Standard English, 11. See also Dialect
Stilinovich, Charmaine, 209
"Students' Right to Their Own Language," 36
Summerfield, Geoffrey, 194, 238, 239

Tashlik, Phyllis, 218
Telephone, use of, 316
Television: and English teaching, 266-270; guides to, 269; monitoring, 122-123
Tests, 138-165; alternatives to standardized, 151-164; formal, 142; mania for, 139-140; objective, 142; standardized, 91, 142; tyranny of, 145; weaknesses of standardized, 144-148
Thematic approach, literary, 255
Theme grading, 133
Thinking, 60-63
Thompson, Peggy, 238
Thorndike, E. L., 149
Time, released, 92-93

UNESCO, 3, 14

Van Allen, R., 182
Veley, Charles, 228-230
Verner, Dan, 209
Vocabulary, specialized, 134

Walker, Jerry, 130
Ward, C. H., 34, 37
"Webbing," 286-288
Weingartner, Charles, 267
Weitzman, David, 234-235
Whitehead, Alfred North, 182
Woods Hole Conference, 47-48
Word games, 120

Wordsmithing, careers in, 343-345
Writers, student, accomplishments of, 119
Writing: as literature, students', 128; as personal narrative, 132; assignments, 131; community resources for, 311-315; evaluation of, 155-158; guide to content in, 133; in elementary years, 188-190; in science, 271-300; quality of, 157; skills in subject classes, 131; technical, 135; without teachers, 85

Yesner, Seymour, 54

DATE DUE

12. 15. '80	
8. 3. '81	
12. 15. '81	
6. 15. '82	
8. 6. '86	
JUN 15 '00	

BRODART, INC.   Cat. No. 23-221